For Sally
The road continues . . .

GUERRILLA MARKETING
FOR
CONSULTANTS

Breakthrough Tactics for Winning Profitable Clients

JAY CONRAD LEVINSON
MICHAEL W. McLAUGHLIN

WILEY

JOHN WILEY & SONS, INC.

Published by John Wiley & Sons, Inc., Hoboken, New Jersey.
Published simultaneously in Canada.

For general information on our other products and services please contact our
Customer Care Department within the United States at (800) 762-2974, outside the
United States at (317) 572-3993 or fax (317) 572-4002.

Wiley also publishes its books in a variety of electronic formats. Some content that
appears in print may not be available in electronic books. For more information
about Wiley products, visit our web site at www.wiley.com.

Library of Congress Cataloging-in-Publication Data:

Levinson, Jay Conrad.
   Guerrilla marketing for consultants : breakthrough tactics for winning profitable
clients / Jay Conrad Levinson and Michael W. McLaughlin.
      p. cm.
   Includes bibliographical references and index.
   ISBN 0-471-61873-X (pbk.)
   1. Marketing. 2. Consultants—Marketing. 3. Professions—Marketing.
4. Business consultants. I. McLaughlin, Michael W., 1955– II. Title.
HF5415.L4762 2004
001′.068′8—dc22

                                                            2004042253

Printed in the United States of America.

10   9   8   7

Contents

PART III   GUERRILLA SELLING FOR CONSULTANTS

PART IV   PULLING IT ALL TOGETHER

Acknowledgments

There's pure joy in thanking those who helped bring this book to life. None of this would have been possible if my good friend, colleague and confidante, Marty Rosenthal, hadn't taken a chance and hired me as a consultant.

Over the past 20 years, my partner at Deloitte, Mike Deverell, taught me the art and craft of consulting and showed me how integrity, professionalism, and value draw clients to a consulting practice.

I've been fortunate to work alongside some of the finest consultants in the profession. A very special thanks to Tom Dekar, John Demetra, Peter Gertler, Erik Gilberg, Greg Seal, Phil Strause, and Jack Witlin. Hundreds of others at Deloitte also shaped my thinking about this book. I wish I could thank each of you personally for your generosity and collegiality, but you know who you are.

Most of all I learned from clients. They always let you know when things are right and when they're not.

From our first conversation, my co-author, Jay Levinson, provided the glue that holds this book together. From the roughest proposal outline to the completed manuscript, Jay steered the project with his experience and keen intellect. No problem was too big or small for Jay's attention. All I had to do was ask and Jay was there to lend a hand.

It was a rare treat to work with my agents, Michael Larsen and Elizabeth Pomada. They knew exactly when to apply the right pressure to keep the project moving, and they never gave up on the idea. Without their guidance, this book would still be a pile of notes.

The team at John Wiley & Sons made the editing and production of the book seem like magic. My editor, Mike Hamilton, was there to answer every question, solve any problem, and keep the book on the right track. Deborah Schindlar, my Wiley production editor who worked with Pam Blackmon and her team at Publications Development Company; Kimberly Vaughn; and Michelle Becker brought the book from rough manuscript to the bookshelves, and I owe each of you a debt of gratitude.

Mark Steisel, my friend and colleague, contributed his blood, sweat, and tears to this book. Mark has a feel for the language that most of us simply dream about. His perseverance, editorial touch, and inspiration helped bring this book to a whole new level.

Every author has a secret weapon—that one person who is there to do whatever is needed, no matter what. My generous sister-in-law, Mary Dillon, is my secret weapon. Thank you, Mary, for tending to just about everything when writing and editing took over my life.

To my wife, Sally, you stuck by me when the going got the toughest. You gave selflessly of your days, nights, and weekends editing and reediting every last chapter of this book. I have no words to describe what your devotion has meant to me. You are in my mind and heart at all times. This book is for you.

M.W.M.

The Guerrilla Marketing brand has grown in 20 years from a single book to a library of books available around the world. One of the main reasons for that success is authors such as Michael W. McLaughlin who bring the spirit, the wisdom, and the practicality of Guerrilla Marketing to vibrant life.

I want to acknowledge Mike's painstaking work and superb writing. It is not easy to write a Guerrilla Marketing book. But he has done it with grace and aplomb.

I also single out for gratitude some of the same people that Mike has identified–Mark Steisel, writer and editor extraordinaire, and Mike Larsen and Elizabeth Pomada, the shepherds of the brand–who have been my literary agents since the first book–and will be my agents for many more books.

Finally, I thank Jeannie Huffman, president of Guerrilla Marketing International, who has built the brand, as people like Michael and I have crafted the words.

J.C.L.

Introduction

Are you a consultant? That title applies to professionals from actuarial advisors to Web site designers, including management consultants, accountants, architects, investment counselors, lawyers, public relations consultants, engineers, human resources experts, executive coaches, professional speakers, technology consultants, internal consultants, and others.

All consultants are different and each specialty requires unique skills. One of those skills, though it may not say so on your business card, is marketing. If you're not a top-notch marketer, expect an uphill road all the way. And don't expect that road to lead to the bank.

Professional service providers need powerful marketing now more than ever. You may be a brilliant advisor or strategist, but in our highly competitive world you must convince clients that your services are head and shoulders above the competition if you want to stay in business.

This book was written from the perspective of a management consultant—coauthor, Michael McLaughlin. But the message of guerrilla marketing is equally relevant for all professional service providers.

Whatever consulting you do, guerrilla marketing can separate your practice from the pack. That's not to say that classical marketing principles have no validity. But they are not a potent enough response to the rapidly changing demands of today's clients.

Guerrilla marketing strategy and tactics will take you to the next level, where profits flow abundantly. Guerrillas use their time, energy, creativity, and knowledge to maximize the return on their marketing dollars. This book isn't about good marketing. It's about great marketing and long-term success—an investment in your future.

Think of *Guerrilla Marketing for Consultants* as an owner's manual for your career and your practice. In these pages, there is a wealth of information on why, where, when, and how to push your consulting practice to new performance levels.

The guidelines in this book are prescriptive but flexible. Work through them on a step-by-step basis to create a guerrilla marketing program that fits your objectives, markets, budget, and skills. You can find strategies and tools for handling every aspect of marketing a consulting practice—from building market visibility to creating winning proposals and pricing your services.

We also include unbeatable guerrilla strategies for selling your services and creating profitable client relationships once you've been hired. Those relationships are keys to building a sustainable and profitable business.

If you want to review recent practices in just one area of marketing, you can simply flip to that chapter. Whichever way you use this book, you have access to the latest intelligence for creating a profitable guerrilla consulting practice.

If you are a consulting client or are thinking about becoming one, this book offers you many insights on how consultants work with clients. You might want to focus on the chapters about projects, proposals, and pricing. These and the other chapters can help you identify the traits you should look for in a consultant.

We look forward to seeing you in the trenches—and at the bank.

Part

I

Marketing for Consultants the Guerrilla Way

Chapter 1

Why Consultants Need Guerrilla Marketing

New business will be won only to the extent that the client believes that the professional is interested, cares, and is trying to help.

—David H. Maister[1]

For decades, consulting seemed like a dream job. The promise of challenging, satisfying work and great compensation attracted legions of smart, talented people to the profession. And consulting grew into a global industry that is forecasted to be a \$159-billion-a-year market by 2005.[2]

Businesses—inundated by successive waves of new technologies, market shifts, and bold ideas—clamored for independent experts who could help them implement complex strategies to keep up with changes and embark on new ventures. The ranks of consultants swelled, and consulting firms racked up record-setting profits on high fees. Consulting became a serious business with a focus on making big money.

A more recent sign of the times, however, is apparent in the title of a seminar offered by the Institute of Management Consultants: "Management Consulting: Dream Job or Worst Nightmare?" Why might consulting be a nightmare?

Maybe it's because of several developments that have turned the industry on its ear. They include:

➤ Sluggish growth rates for many consulting firms, declining fees, the unpredictable economy, and the cyclical nature of consulting

➤ A market saturated with experts and fierce competition, which has led to aggressive selling wars over even the smallest projects

➤ Widespread corporate scandals, consulting firm mergers, practice dissolutions, and trends like outsourcing that have clients scratching their heads about who does what and which consultants are trustworthy

➤ Projects that have failed to live up to consultants' promises, leaving clients wary of making further investments

➤ New firms that entered the market out of nowhere in search of a fast buck and quickly vaporized

These changes have tarnished the images of all consultants, whether they are individual practitioners or members of larger firms. Consultants are facing nothing less than a crisis in clients' confidence.

WHAT IS A CONSULTANT?

A consultant offers professional advice or services for a fee.

■ CAN CLIENTS HEAR YOU NOW?

Consultants haven't altered their methods for marketing their services in response to these events. In fact, their marketing hasn't changed much in decades except to get slicker and flashier (and more expensive). Although consultants are struggling to get their messages across to clients, they can't break through the babble that is the hallmark of modern marketing.

The time is right for consultants to adopt guerrilla marketing techniques. The battle in consulting is no longer just about vying for projects; it is about competing for relationships with those who award those projects. This book focuses on how to win *profitable* work from a new, more discerning breed of consulting clients.

Guerrilla marketing can overcome the obstacles that many consultants face: clients' growing cynicism, today's new buying environment, and the feast-or-famine syndrome.

■ THE NATIVES ARE RESTLESS

Perhaps the most serious challenge for consultants is to reverse clients' growing dissatisfaction with project results. The fact that only 35 percent of clients are currently satisfied with their consultants is not exactly a ringing endorsement.[3]

The business analysis firm, Ross McManus, has been warning consultants that even long-term client relationships are at risk. According to Ross McManus principal, Steven Banis, "It doesn't matter what function—information technology, human resources, legal, accounting, or consulting—across the board relationships are being reexamined. In areas where there is frustration, providers are being booted out at an incredible pace."[4]

William Clay Ford Jr., chief executive of Ford Motor Company, said about consultants: "If I never see one again, it will be too soon."[5] His comment, which can make even seasoned consultants wince, is all the more ominous because for decades his company has had no shortage of consultants working on projects.

Cynicism about consultants isn't new. No doubt, you have heard the old joke that a consultant will steal your watch to tell you what time it is. But clients' skepticism about consultants has soared to new heights as they question whether the results consultants provide are worth the fees they charge. And having a marquee brand name no longer confers the *Good Housekeeping* seal of approval.

■ ROOTS OF SKEPTICISM

Dissatisfaction with consultants' work is not the only explanation for skepticism about the profession. Other legitimate concerns are that the consulting industry is barely organized and is not regulated internally or by any government agency.

Consulting has no real barriers to entry. It is easier to become a consultant than it is to get a fishing license. Anyone with a business card can say, "I'm a consultant," hang out a shingle, solicit, and, most frightening of all, advise clients. As Tom Peters observed, ". . . we are going to become a nation of consultants. Perhaps we already have."[6]

Peters isn't too far off when you realize that such unlikely companies as United Parcel Service, Dell, Hitachi, and General Electric—to name just a few—have made successful inroads into consulting services. No doubt, other companies will add further competition to an oversupplied and skeptical market.

In these times of heightened sensitivity about ethics, the lack of formal standards governing consultants, absence of regulation, and intensity of competition make it easy to understand the growing cynicism about the value of consultants' offerings. At the same time, clients' expectations of consultants have evolved to a higher plane.

■ THE EMERGENCE OF THE GUERRILLA CLIENT

Decades of learning from consultants and other experts plus the impact of technology-fueled approaches to business have made clients more sophisticated. Consulting has entered the era of guerrilla *clients*—buyers who have a wealth of information at their fingertips and use it. Guerrilla clients have many options to choose from and pose tough questions about the value that consultants can add to their businesses. The balance of power in the relationship has shifted to clients.

Guerrilla clients not only tend to be less satisfied with consultants, they are less loyal and more results-oriented. They are hard to impress, demand more for less, and are outraged by the prices that some consultants charge. And they don't believe consultants' marketing claims. You can imagine them displaying the bumper sticker: "So Many Consultants, So Few Results."

■ THE NEW BUYING ENVIRONMENT

In *The Anatomy of Buzz*, Emanuel Rosen[7] refers to the "invisible networks" that connect us all. According to Rosen, people evaluate and buy goods and services on the basis of comments by friends and family members, hallway conversations with colleagues, e-mail, and Internet research and discussion groups. These nonstop exchanges are all part of the buzz that helps people cut through the chaos of marketing to find what they need.

Rosen points out, "In order to compete, companies must understand that they are selling not to individual customers but rather to *networks* of customers." Guerrilla marketing recognizes this new buying environment and the power of guerrilla clients. It takes into account that guerrilla clients find out about consultants' services in many ways that have nothing to do with the consultants' sales pitches.

Since clients are more apt to act on the opinions of people they trust, consultants must build their marketing programs around champions who will create positive buzz throughout the invisible networks that are filled with potential clients.

■ BRANDING IS IN A COMA

Consultants and other service providers have done a lousy job of branding themselves, or fixing what their firms represent, in their clients' minds. In fact, the concept of branding for consultants is in a virtual coma. As Ellen Lewis of the *Financial Times* put it, "If the professional services sector sold its wares on a supermarket shelf, the aisles would be stacked with white logos on dark backgrounds carrying the same buzzwords—excellence, teamwork, and unique culture. It is hard to think of an industry whose members or products would be more difficult to tell apart."[8]

According to an old saying, "You can't get fired for hiring IBM." Well, those days are long gone. Today, clients make the best choices, not the best-known choices. The name on your business card may get you in the door, but today's clients are seeking talent, not firm names. The competition for new work is not between firms, but between people and their ideas. Your marketing must convey more than buzzwords; it must tell the full story of the talents and potential benefits you can offer clients.

■ WHAT'S THE BIG IDEA?

Some analysts claim that we are on the downside of the business innovation cycle, and that the lack of new big ideas has led to a decline in the demand for consulting services. That conclusion is as insightful as the 1943 statement attributed to Thomas Watson, founder of IBM: that the world market for computers would consist of five machines.[9]

Without question, big ideas induce clients to seek outside help. Recent big ideas—outsourcing, reengineering, and the Web-based business model—have definitely kept brand-name consultants busy making tons of money. Big ideas have prompted the largest consulting firms to field armies of consultants outfitted with the latest strategies and technologies. When the big guys throw their considerable resources into the fray, competition is difficult for all firms.

Whatever the size of your practice, the presence or absence of a big idea is irrelevant. Clients *always* need expert assistance. Guerrilla marketing focuses your communication to the market on *all* ideas that can help clients achieve their goals.

■ FEAST OR FAMINE

Consultants can run into long successful or losing streaks that have nothing to do with either economic or business innovation cycles. They ride the roller coaster between feast and famine.

GUERRILLA INTELLIGENCE: FEAST OR FAMINE		
	Feast	*Famine*
Sales leads	Rolling in	Trickling in
Sales backlog	Full	Running on fumes
Revenue	Record breaking	Stagnating
Profits	Exceed expectations	What profits?
Pricing	Consultant-driven	Highly negotiable
Mindset	Life is good	Sense of urgency
Forecast	Sunny	Stormy

During feasts and business booms, consultants are often so busy serving clients that they can spare no time for anything else. Marketing is at the bottom of their priority list.

When consultants don't actively market their services, they unwittingly sow the seeds of famine. If a consultant's market visibility ebbs, the result is a dwindling sales pipeline and eventual famine. Guerrilla marketing provides the cure for this destructive syndrome and enables consultants to sustain the feast and forestall the famine.

■ WHAT YOU WILL GET

For consultants who understand the challenges of this emerging, new business environment, this can be a golden moment. The right guerrilla weapons can level the playing field, and *any* firm can win.

Guerrilla marketing is a strategy that can help all consultants to:

➤ Learn how and why clients buy services.

➤ Overcome and capitalize on clients' skepticism.

➤ Compete for client relationships, not just projects.

➤ Demonstrate what clients want—results.

➤ Use the stockpile of their ideas—their intellectual assets—to their advantage.

➤ Wield the right mix of marketing tactics to build and sustain a profitable consulting practice.

Consultants who understand and take full advantage of guerrilla marketing tactics will prosper. Guerrilla marketing will show you the way.

Chapter 2

What Is Guerrilla Marketing for Consultants?

Marketing is everything.

—Regis McKenna[1]

Although marketing has many definitions, for guerrillas, marketing is a full-time business that includes every aspect of a consulting practice. It begins the moment you decide to become a consultant and never stops. Marketing involves more than just trying to sell your services; it affects how you comport yourself, run your practice, bid on projects, perform for clients, and build relationships.

Guerrilla marketing extends beyond selling and completing projects—it applies to *everything you do.* Your firm's name, its services, methods of delivering services, pricing plan, the location of your office, and how you promote your practice are all part of guerrilla marketing. And there is much more, including the clients with whom you choose to work, how you answer the telephone, even how you design your invoices and envelopes. The object of guerrilla marketing is to build and maintain *profitable relationships,* not merely to get clients.

■ YOU ARE THE PRODUCT

As a consultant, you face a vastly different challenge than those who sell cereal or toothpaste. *You* are the product and, unlike a bottle of mouthwash, your services are expensive, intangible, and sold *before* they are produced. Your success hinges on the relationships you forge and the quality of your work. You must focus all your efforts on those factors: It's your guerrilla mission. Everyone you deal with—especially your clients—must be convinced that you will always deliver what you have promised.

■ VALUE, VALUE, VALUE

Consulting begins and ends with results. To succeed, you must offer and deliver results and solutions. You must deliver undisputed value to your clients and everyone else in your network. Value is the foundation on which you must build your marketing.

If your services can't meet those standards, put down this book now and focus on building your consulting skills, not on marketing.

■ TRADITIONAL VERSUS GUERRILLA MARKETING

Many consultants have taken to the airwaves to promote their practices. Large firms use mass media advertising, event sponsorships, and public relations to grab attention. The resulting brand wars not

What Is Guerrilla Marketing for Consultants?

Traditional Marketing	Guerrilla Marketing
Central to the business	*Is* the business
Fuzzy message	Focused message
Consultant-focused	Insight-based
Invest money	Build intellectual assets
Build brand identity	Build client relationships
Enhance revenue	Enhance profit
Create media perception	Reveal reality
Tell and sell	Listen and serve
One size fits all	One size fits none
Take market share	Create markets

only are expensive, but also emphasize the sharp differences between traditional marketing programs and guerrilla marketing.

■ SIX PRINCIPLES OF GUERRILLA MARKETING FOR CONSULTANTS

Open any marketing textbook and you are likely to read about the classic *Four Ps* marketing model, which advocates using a mix of product, place, price, and promotion to create customer demand. For decades, marketers have used the Four Ps to decide where they should sell products, at what price, and whether to include buyer incentives. Today, the Four Ps are no longer enough to penetrate the fog of information about products and services. The guerrilla extends marketing to six more principles.

➤ Principle 1: Insight-Based Marketing Wins

Al Ries and Jack Trout, in their classic book, *Positioning,* remind us, "Today's marketplace is no longer responsive to the strategies that worked in the past. There are just too many products, too many companies, and too much marketing noise."[2]

Modern marketers are busy plastering every available inch of our world with their messages. Bathroom stalls, grocery store floors, and even bunches of bananas are now advertising spaces. Consumers are weary of the onslaught and tune it out. The rising popularity of digital video recorders that let you zap out television commercials proves the point.

GUERRILLA INTELLIGENCE: ZERO TOLERANCE FOR FLUFF

Clients and prospects have zero tolerance for marketing fluff, but a deep thirst for ideas that can help them. Selling services is not just about price, qualifications, or your firm's long string of success stories. First and foremost, it is about the insights and ideas you bring to clients. If you can't provide great ideas, you might as well stay home.

Clients also ignore jargon-rich and content-free messages. They have become desensitized to such messages and skeptical about whether they reflect reality.

Your insights into an industry, a discipline, or a specific company should be the fuel for your guerrilla marketing plan. Your qualifications may get you that first client meeting, but the ideas you propose will be your strongest selling points.

Consultants are often hesitant to disclose their best insights in their marketing materials. However, insights are the guerrilla's ultimate weapon. They cut through the marketing morass. Frame your marketing to help clients resolve urgent, substantive issues. Give them original, insightful, and valuable ideas at every step of the marketing process.

Don't be afraid that you will give too much away before you are hired. Howard Aiken, co-inventor of one of the world's first computers, advises, "Don't worry about people stealing an idea. If it's original, you'll have to ram it down their throats."[3]

➤ **Principle 2: Guerrilla Marketing Is Cohesive and Coordinated**

Guerrillas employ a wide assortment of marketing tactics to send cohesive messages to targeted clients. They use their Web sites, newsletters or zines, speeches, research and survey reports, presentation materials, proposals, endorsements, testimonials, references, and even their letterhead and business cards. Unless your marketing strategy is well integrated and all elements are coordinated with each other and your overall plan, they won't get the job done.

Each of your marketing approaches must support, reinforce, and cross-promote the others. Your goal is to imprint multiple, positive impressions on clients in your target markets. The right mix of marketing tactics working in unison will create an overall market impact that is more potent than the sum of its parts.

Reference your articles and Web site in your proposals and your research in direct mail and speeches. Design your business card and Yellow Pages ad to promote special features of your practice. If your firm specializes in improving warehouse workers' productivity, highlight that fact; or if strengthening employee attitudes is your forte, showcase it in all your market communications.

Clients equate success and competence with sustained presence, so blanket your targeted industry. For a cumulative effect, hit your target markets simultaneously on many fronts. When clients repeatedly see your articles, read about your speeches, and see the results of your research, they will accept you as an expert and fight to hire you.

➤ Principle 3: Consulting Is a Contact Sport

Relationships are the lifeblood of a consulting practice. Most consultants spend considerable time in contact with clients but fail to build enduring client relationships. Forging long-term relationships can take months or even years. Guerrillas invest in building those relationships as the core of their marketing strategy.

GUERRILLA CONSULTING RELATIONSHIPS ARE BASED ON . . .

➤ Mutual respect and trust
➤ Deep knowledge of the client's business
➤ Straight talk, honesty, and objective advice
➤ Multiple interactions over time
➤ Personal chemistry
➤ Value for client and consultant

Strong relationships are essential to successful marketing; they provide the path of least resistance to profits. When you invest in your existing client relationships, your marketing efforts will yield higher dividends and generate larger and more frequent projects with your current clients and their networks.

 Try to produce 60 percent of your new business from current clients or referrals from current clients. They will provide you with more business with less effort at a lower cost.

A superb performance record and strong relationships will have a multiplier effect on your marketing efforts. They will position you at the head of the pack for new consulting projects. You will be invited to work on projects before your competitors even hear about them, and you will receive recommendations for other highly prized assignments.

Be selective about relationships. Seek to build long-term relationships instead of those that last for one or two projects. Expect some clients to keep you at arm's length and to maintain a strict

> ### GUERRILLA INTELLIGENCE: RAISING THE BAR ON EXPECTATIONS
>
> A strong client relationship can be a two-edged sword. The benefits can be enormous, but clients may demand more from you as their expectations grow along with the relationship. It is a paradox of consulting that it can be harder to sell to existing clients than to new ones.

supplier-customer relationship that focuses solely on getting more for less. Those relationships are seldom worth your effort.

Also build supportive nonclient relationships. A public relations consultant may need to join forces with a freelance copywriter to properly serve a client; a technology consultant may need a computer programmer to sort out thorny technical issues.

To meet client needs, rely on a cadre of trusted associates who can fill in project gaps. Nonclient relationships with colleagues, suppliers, past clients, and even your competitors can provide a competitive advantage. Treat them with the same care as clients . . . plus, they may become clients or refer business to you.

➤ Principle 4: High Tech Is for High Touch

Rely on technology. It can provide untapped opportunities to bring new dimensions to your business. Use low-cost software to produce targeted communications for clients, instead of tired old boilerplate that clients routinely pitch in the trash. Stay on top of virtually every detail of your industry, clients, and competitors for just pennies a day. Package and repackage your speeches, research, books, and articles. Publish and sell them through Internet channels to earn money while you sleep.

Create personal connections with clients and prospects. With a few keystrokes, reach out to your prospects, clients, and network with up-to-the-minute information and ideas that encourage dialogues. Use e-mail and your Web site to give clients and prospects a resource that will help them solve problems and establish you as an expert. Technology should *supplement*, not replace, personal contact with your clients and prospects.

Guerrilla clients expect every consultant to be technologically advanced. Clients don't want yesterday, they want tomorrow; and technology is the gateway to tomorrow. Tip the competitive scales in your favor by integrating powerful, low-cost technology into every aspect of your practice, from gathering business intelligence to marketing, billing, and revenue generation. Use technology to manage and simplify your practice, strengthen client relationships, reduce reliance on high-priced specialists, and promote your practice, guerrilla style.

➤ Principle 5: Focus on Profits, Not Fees

It is not true that any revenue is good revenue. The guerrilla measure of success is not how much money you make, but how much you keep. A long-term, high-fee project that isn't profitable can lock you into a ruinous financial downspin.

Keep a handle on all operating costs and make pricing decisions that will yield high profits down the road. Walk away from projects that can't meet your profitability goals, no matter how large the fee.

➤ Principle 6: One Size Fits None

For decades, Hong Kong's Jimmy Chen's Custom Tailors have delighted customers with finely tailored, custom clothing, despite overwhelming competition from lower priced options. In Jimmy Chen's shop, one size fits none. Each customer order begins with the basics, but after a series of careful fittings, every garment is shaped to fit the customer's precise dimensions and to meet demands for high-quality materials and workmanship.

Tailor your marketing as if you were crafting a custom suit. Start with the basics—a vision for the business, your value proposition, and the markets you will pursue—and then shape the details. Meet the precise needs of your clients and the market. Strike a balance between building on your existing business and attracting new clients. Adjust this balance as your practice matures.

Create a marketing plan. It will force you to examine each project in detail and confront the tough issues—who are your clients, what do they need, and what can you do for them? As Harry Beckwith notes in *What Clients Love,* "Planning teaches you and your colleagues about your business . . . writing a plan educates you in a way that nothing else can."[4]

Your marketing plan doesn't have to be a book-length volume brimming with colorful charts and graphs. Your plan should be comprehensive, but simple enough to be clear to your colleagues, clients, and suppliers.

Begin with a few well-crafted sentences. Once you sift through your options and make critical marketing decisions, identify and launch the guerrilla marketing weapons that will move your practice in the desired direction. After you get started, you can broaden your plan or embellish it with analyses, charts, and appendixes.

■ FOLLOWING YOUR PLAN

Marketing can be a painfully slow process that moves in sudden bursts, instead of in a predictable fashion. The speed of your progress can be surprising and tempt you to pull back on your marketing efforts. On other occasions, what appears to be stagnation may make you want to abandon your plan and begin again.

In either case, take the long view and stick with your plan. It will take time for the market to recognize and trust you as an expert. Sudden changes to your strategy or market identity can create confusion and set back your marketing gains:

➤ *Adjust your plan, but first give it time to take hold with your clients and prospects.* How long? In some cases, results are evident in the first few months. In others, it can take longer. Make patience and consistency your allies.

➤ *Market yourself creatively.* Following the pack is a surefire path to oblivion, so blaze new trails. Keep in mind that your goal is to win clients, *not* marketing or advertising awards.

➤ *Invest your hard-earned cash, time, and energy in marketing.* For the guerrilla, time is not money—it is more valuable than money. To maximize the return on your investments, take the "brains-over-brawn" approach to conserve your resources.

➤ *Be flexible.* Adaptability is the guerrilla's strength. Carefully monitor the results of your marketing tactics, realizing that some will hit the mark and others will fall flat. Double up on the winners and drop the losers.

➤ *Capitalize on your passion.* Helping clients is the core of the consulting business. Your passion for serving clients must drive you to jump out of bed each morning and make you burn the midnight oil. Passion inspires others and makes them want to support your efforts and sing your praises. Without passion for the profession and genuine enthusiasm for solving client problems, the demands of the business will quickly overwhelm your best-laid plans for success.

■ WHAT GUERRILLA MARKETING ISN'T

Although guerrilla marketing is low cost, it certainly isn't free. Be prepared to invest time and money. You may need professional help for elements like Web site design, computer programming, copywriting, graphic design, or even marketing; but your goal should be to get the biggest bang for your marketing buck, every time. Your expenditures for guerrilla marketing will usually be far less than the expenses you would incur with traditional marketing.

Guerrilla marketing requires more than planning, strategizing, or navel-gazing. It demands action. Sure, you must create a marketing plan that serves you, but you also must develop a bias for action in the process. Plan, test, act, and measure. And since everything is always changing, continually fine-tune your plan until it is just right.

Whatever the size of your practice and whether you are a novice consultant or a seasoned veteran, you can easily use the tools in this book to master guerrilla marketing. The biggest challenge you face is deciding which combination of tools is right for you. That decision only takes research and thought on your part. Then apply your own brand of creativity to bring your services to the market and knock the socks off your clients and your future clients.

Chapter 3

Thirteen Guerrilla Marketing Secrets

Professional service marketing is certainly among the "safest" I've ever seen. Because it appears to take no risks, it's actually quite risky.

— SETH GODIN[1]

Every profession has its secrets: Chefs have carefully guarded recipes, lawyers have surprise witnesses, and carpenters know all the angles. Guerrillas also have insider information.

Okay, maybe the details guerrilla marketers know are not exactly *secrets,* but they might as well be for all the attention they get. While some of the following thirteen guerrilla secrets may strike you as intuitive, too many consultants consistently overlook them. These rules lay the essential groundwork for the guerrilla approach to marketing.

■ SECRET 1: SELL YOURSELF FIRST

Before you agree to put yourself on an operating table, a surgeon must first earn your trust. You'll find out as much as possible about that surgeon through your network of friends, family, coworkers, other doctors, and patients. It makes sense to research the surgeon's credentials and experience. Even when those qualifications are impeccable, if the surgeon doesn't inspire your confidence, you'll probably keep searching for someone who does.

The role of a consultant is not unlike that of a surgeon. In buying your services, clients may feel they are putting the fate of their businesses, their finances, and their careers in your hands. So your first job is to earn their confidence.

You may have reams of relevant case studies, glowing testimonials, and a blue-chip business card. But they won't make an iota of difference if the client doesn't believe that you will deliver what you promise. If the client doesn't trust you, your firm will probably be eliminated from the running.

Personal selling is not a grab bag of manipulative tricks to get clients to like you, but rather a strategy of engaging the client in a substantive discussion of the issues impacting the client's business. For guerrillas, personal selling is not selling at all, in the traditional sense. Instead, it is a give-and-take with the client characterized by:

➤ intense listening;

➤ insightful questioning; and

➤ presentation of creative ideas.

If the client perceives that you understand the macro issues and nuances of the discussion, you will advance to the next step. If not, the client will politely show you the door.

Of course, have the stacks of case studies and testimonials tucked away in your briefcase, just in case the client asks for them. They provide excellent backup. The key to selling yourself is to focus first on clients and their issues, not on yourself or your firm.

■ SECRET 2: DON'T TORCH THE TOUCH POINTS

Customer service gurus refer to the points of contact between a business and its customers as *touch points*. Every instance when clients or prospects come into contact with you or your firm is a touch point. It is amazing how many consultants understand this concept but take touch points like the telephone and voice mail for granted.

Although it does happen, clients rarely pluck your name and telephone number from the Yellow Pages. Chances are they were referred to you, have checked out your Web site, read an article or two about you, and called their industry contacts. Because of your marketing efforts, the client has a positive impression of your firm. You can easily torch that impression.

It may not seem like a big deal, but think about how you feel when you call a business and a digitized voice says your call is important, but everyone is too busy to talk. That is not the way to show clients they matter to you. Likewise, the generic recording, "Leave me a message and I'll call you back as soon as I can," may work fine for callers to your home, but clients deserve more.

If possible, have a live person answer your telephone. A friendly voice and helpful manner can nudge relationships in the right direction. It doesn't hurt to remember the client's name and use it during the conversation.

Most clients understand when you can't respond immediately. But they might be annoyed to hear that you are in a meeting, went skiing, or are at home. Unless the details are relevant, skip them, take the message, and indicate when the caller can expect a response.

Voice mail is a fact of life, and we all have to use it. Personalize your voice mail by recording a daily message. For example, "Hi, this is Ron. It's Tuesday, November Second. Sorry, I missed your call. I will be checking messages regularly throughout the day, so please leave me one and I will get back to you today. Thanks." Then, make good on that promise.

Your telephone and voice mail system are marketing tools. Recognize that and make the most of a client's first—and every—contact with you.

■ SECRET 3: SOLVE THE REAL PROBLEM

No doubt you have heard the old saying that if all you have is a hammer, everything looks like a nail. The challenge for consultants is to figure out what really needs hammering.

In his 1966 *Harvard Business Review* article, "How to Buy/Sell Professional Services," Warren J. Wittreich says, ". . . often a client who wishes to purchase a professional service senses that he has a problem, but is uncertain as to what the *specific* nature of his problem really is. *The responsibility of the service firm is to identify that problem and define it in meaningful terms.*"[2]

A client may see a puzzle but not know how the pieces fit together. Maybe the client is focused on the wrong problem, or doesn't have a problem at all. Whatever the client's perspective, challenge the client's thinking—and your own—to be sure you are solving the right problem before you try to sell. Too many consulting projects solve symptoms without curing the underlying ailment.

Although guerrilla clients are somewhat cynical about jumping on the latest and greatest technology or management fad, they may be tempted to buy solutions just to avoid being left behind by the

competition. And consultants, especially those who have close relationships with vendors, are often too eager to push their products on
clients.

Your responsibility is to sell only those solutions that are in the
client's long-term best interests. In the end, this approach will also
prove to be in your best interests.

■ SECRET 4: OFFER A GUARANTEE

Most consultants get convulsive at the thought of offering clients
any kind of guarantee. Consultants are notoriously conservative because they fear that uncontrollable elements such as client executive
turnover, a client's surprise merger with another company, or even
bad weather might derail their best-laid plans for a project. The possibility of financial ruin causes even the most confident consultants
to avoid guarantees.

The guerrilla understands this dynamic and uses it to competitive
advantage by offering an up-front guarantee of client satisfaction.
When all other things are equal, a guarantee will send consulting work
your way. A guarantee also motivates consultants and clients to nail
down objectives and responsibilities at the outset of a project so that
everyone understands what must occur for the client to be satisfied
and the consultant to be paid.

A guarantee should be a two-way street. If a consultant is willing
to waive fees or provide other considerations if the client is dissatisfied, the client should be willing to increase the fee if the consultant's
work exceeds expectations. For a guarantee to work optimally, both
client and consultant must have a stake in the game.

Precedents exist for consulting guarantees. In the 1990s, one firm,
eager to be the first to tackle client perceptions of runaway consulting

GUERRILLA TACTIC: GUARANTEED TO WORK

Consider this: Among the top criteria that clients use to choose
service providers is their guarantee to deliver as promised. In
consulting, there is an *implied* guarantee that certain results
will be attained. On many projects, clients hold back part of the
consultant's fee until the project is completed successfully. So
in effect, clients create a guarantee that they will get what they
pay for.

fees, guaranteed to complete projects on a fixed schedule and for a fixed fee. The firm subsequently became the favored consultant for many projects, improved its competitive position overnight, and forced others to address the issues of risk and results.

Let's face it—no one can control all the variables in a project, so consulting is a risky business, with or without on-the-record promises. An up-front guarantee cuts through empty marketing claims and acknowledges your willingness to share some of the risk. This willingness makes you the client's partner; it turns the project into a true collaboration with joint risk.

A guarantee can put you at the top of the client's list for consulting projects and, in reality, doesn't significantly increase your financial risk. And, as a bonus, you are entitled to ask for additional fees if the results exceed expectations.

■ SECRET 5: FIRE 20 PERCENT OF YOUR CLIENTS

In the early 1900s, Vilfredo Pareto, an Italian economist, concluded that 20 percent of the people controlled 80 percent of the wealth. Since then, his now-famous 80:20 rule has been applied to everything from advertising and time management to identifying product defects.

In consulting, one application of Pareto's Principle is that 20 percent of your clients will generate 80 percent of your headaches. It stands to reason that you'll boost the vibrancy of your practice by pruning that disruptive 20 percent of your clients every 18 months or so. Few things damage the long-term health of a consulting practice more than client saboteurs—and there are more than a few out there.

In a "consultant-hostile" environment, higher consultant turnover may occur as team members quit to escape dealing with a difficult client. Your profitability can plummet as you integrate new team members into the project, and you'll spend endless hours reworking material the client thought was excellent earlier in the day.

Sometimes, the client-consultant relationship just doesn't work. Guerrillas are always on alert to spot troublesome clients and let them go.

It may sound crazy to fire your clients, but it is one of the best strategic actions you can take. Clients define the culture of your practice, and serving tiresome clients erodes that culture and poisons the environment. Problem clients create more work and needless stress. They kill your profits and your productivity, and that negativity can seep into your personal life.

**GUERRILLA INTELLIGENCE: SHOULD YOU FIRE A CLIENT?
TELLTALE SIGNS INCLUDE**

➤ It takes days or weeks to get on your client's calendar.

➤ Your client wants to approve or attend all your meetings with decision makers.

➤ You have stopped developing new skills.

➤ Invoices are nitpicked to death or payments are consistently late.

➤ The client fails to review critical documents in a timely manner.

➤ Your profit margin is eroding with no end in sight.

➤ Your work no longer seems to have a substantive impact on the client's business.

It takes courage to walk away from a paying client, no matter what the circumstances. But don't worry; if you excel at what you do, more profitable clients will replace that lost business.

■ SECRET 6: BE A GOOD GUEST

We have all had houseguests from hell. Perhaps they overstayed their welcome, were loud, ate the last of the cookies, broke your favorite chair, or were just ungrateful. You probably couldn't wait for them to leave.

Consultants are frequently houseguests of their clients. They usually need workspace, administrative assistance, access to the client's building and, of course, gallons of coffee. Like any guest, they can be a joy to have around or they can be like the mother-in-law who commandeered the bathroom and refused to go home.

One client recalled that a consultant approached her in the parking lot early one morning and asked, "How can you stand to come to work every day in a company as screwed up as this?" The oblivious consultant had no idea he was addressing the company's CEO. Such tactless comments will wipe out any goodwill you have earned with the client, so watch what you say.

You will forge stronger client relationships by being a gracious guest than by exceeding client expectations on a project. Clients will

GUERRILLA INTELLIGENCE: TEN TRAITS OF A MODEL CLIENT GUEST

1. Mesh smoothly and quickly with the client's staff.
2. When arguments erupt, bring the discussion back to civility.
3. Avoid springing bad news on the client about project delays or budget overruns.
4. When a project succeeds, make the client's staff look good, not the consultant's.
5. Treat every meeting with the client as if it were the first meeting.
6. Always be accessible when the client needs you, even if it is inconvenient for you.
7. Always thank clients—for the use of their facilities, their co-operation, and especially for their business.
8. When at a client's site, focus exclusively on that client's work. Few things aggravate clients more than consultants who conduct other client business while in their "house."
9. Don't appear *too* eager to get that next assignment from a client.
10. Don't overstay your welcome. Do a great job and go home.

dump arrogant consultants, no matter how well they perform. They will stick with firms that do the job *and* are easy to live with. Being a good guest requires more than just washing out your own coffee cup, but that's not a bad start.

■ SECRET 7: DELIVER STUNNING RESULTS— YOUR MOST POTENT MARKETING WEAPON

When you buy a dishwasher, you want your purchase to reflect an informed decision. Once again, you tap your network for information. You consult knowledgeable friends, relatives, and colleagues; read promotional material; look at some Web sites; and talk to salespeople. Armed with the facts, you pick the dishwasher you like best.

Once that dishwasher is home and hooked up, you have the right to expect perfect, maintenance-free performance. If it doesn't live up to your expectations, you won't say good things about your experience. And, you probably won't buy the same model again. People are much more likely to tell others about bad purchasing experiences than good ones, so everyone in your network will likely hear about it if the dishwasher leaks and ruins your oak floor.

A common criticism of consultants is that they oversell their capabilities and underdeliver results. Your marketing program may get you an audience and your analytical and selling skills may land the project. But delivering consistently stunning results is the only way to keep clients coming back for more and praising you to others.

To build a successful consulting practice, you must deliver the goods with competence, speed, and minimal disruption to your client's operation. You must master every aspect of the consulting process, including how to plan a project, manage communications within a client's organization, and influence clients to accept your recommendations.

The premium fees that have evolved in professional services have produced sky-high expectations. Clients hire consultants to solve problems they can't solve for themselves and to come up with ideas that hadn't occurred to them. And they want their money's worth.

Clients scrutinize everything you do, from communicating effectively with staff at all levels of their organizations to defining, executing, and wrapping up projects. They observe how you work under the stress of deadlines, how you recover from stumbles and whether you admit mistakes. With every move you make, the client is watching you.

If your work is substandard, clients will bash you at every opportunity, blame you for their failures, and never forget. By contrast, when your performance is excellent, it speaks louder than any other marketing tool, and your clients will provide you with glowing references. As industrialist Henry J. Kaiser said, "When your work speaks for itself, don't interrupt."

Performance—the results you deliver—is a recurrent theme in the following pages. Doing merely acceptable work is not good enough for guerrillas.

■ SECRET 8: CLIENTS BUY—THEY ARE NOT "SOLD"

Despite softened sales tactics, shopping for a new car is still a challenge. The legendary hard sell still prevails. Today's salespeople may not say it aloud, but you can sense them thinking, "What will it take for me to put you in this vehicle today?" So you go into a dealership prepared for battle and determined to resist being sold until you are absolutely ready to buy.

GUERRILLA INTELLIGENCE: HOW CLIENTS FIND YOU

When looking for consultants, clients rely on seven strategies in the following order:

1. Referrals from colleagues and other in their networks
2. Past experience
3. Internal research staff recommendations
4. Advice from industry analysts
5. Web-based research
6. Business and trade press reports
7. Trade shows and conferences

Like most car buyers, guerrilla clients resent hard-sell tactics. In fact, three out of four buyers of services now hire consultants as a result of their own research instead of from consultants' solicitations.[3]

Clients no longer hire consultants solely because of a firm's brand name, advertisements, or direct solicitations, such as cold calls and direct mail. Instead, they turn to their networks of colleagues and the Internet. And they usually know quite a bit about you before they contact you—particularly about your qualifications to help them.[4]

Clients use initial discussions to see how well you listen and grasp their situation, not to learn how big your practice is or how many clients you have served in their industry. Exploratory client interactions are test-drives. Don't waste your time trying to figure out how to sell to clients, but be prepared to show how you can help them. Since many clients think consultants are trying to sell to them all the time, disarm and surprise them. Don't sell, but show them the benefits you have to offer.

GUERRILLA TIP: SHOW THEM THE GOODS

Clients gravitate to consultants who effectively demonstrate their capabilities and show the value they can add to the client's business. They ignore consultants who merely assert their qualifications with ambiguous marketing statements, glossy brochures, or Web sites. The assertion-based approach cannot compete with a value-based sales process.

■ SECRET 9: TOSS YOUR BROCHURES OUT THE WINDOW

Thomas A. Stewart, author of *Intellectual Capital: The New Wealth of Organizations,* calls information and knowledge the "thermonuclear competitive weapons of our time."[5] Stewart found that for many organizations, intangible assets such as workers' knowledge and experience, patents, and customer information are far more important to success than tangible assets such as buildings and machinery.

Consulting is the ultimate information and knowledge enterprise. Consultancies are rich with proprietary research, methodologies, cumulative experience, brainpower, and databases. They are well stocked with detailed case studies, presentation materials, and proposals. These intellectual assets, collective knowledge, and wisdom are the consultant's primary tools for creating results.

The question is—do your marketing materials (for example, your brochures) communicate the power that your intellectual assets can give clients? If not, you might as well toss them out the window.

For guerrillas, the boilerplate approach to brochures, Web sites, and service descriptions is dead. Instead, guerrillas tap into the repository of the firm's intellectual assets to produce highly tailored materials that are responsive to the unique needs of each client and provide the basis for a substantive dialogue on the relevant issues.

Communicating the precise benefits of your intellectual assets in the sales process gives clients what they want. They want thought leaders—not run-of-the-mill consultants—to take on their toughest challenges. To answer that call, guerrillas show clients the collective wisdom of their consulting practices.

■ SECRET 10: PUT CLIENTS SECOND

It is axiomatic that the consultant puts the client's needs first, right? Consultants' promotional material, Web sites, and mission statements certainly proclaim that clients are the highest priority. But the guerrilla way to achieve consistently profitable results is to put *consultants* first and clients second.

Whether your practice has two consultants or two hundred, their talents and skills are more critical to your long-term success than your roster of clients. It is, after all, great consultants who drive the profitability of your practice.

Consultants must be responsive to their clients' needs, even to the point of working long, crazy hours. Realistically, though, good consultants are tougher to replace than clients.

If you lose a client, it may produce an immediate financial impact. If you lose a great consultant, you lose a lot more than money. You lose a portion of your ability to sell and deliver projects, you lose your investment in training, and you lose the client relationships that the consultant built. And don't forget the high cost of recruiting and breaking in a new consultant.

What is worse, a departing consultant can create a cascade effect that causes others to leave the firm, compounding your losses. Or your ex-colleague can become your competitor, and poach your secrets, clients, and staff.

Turnover is an inevitable part of the consulting business. Minimize the brain drain and take the sting out of a very demanding business by providing a collegial and supportive work environment, offering challenging opportunities and paying consultants what they are worth. Make sure consultants know that they come first in the practice and they, in turn, will make sure clients are *their* first priority.

■ SECRET 11: CLIENT LOYALTY IS AN OXYMORON

The minute they begin working with a client, some consultants set their sights on selling that client additional projects. Apparently they believe that the next sale will be a snap because they have an inside track. Nothing could be further from the truth.

No matter how good you are, you can't count on client loyalty. When a group of clients was recently asked to rate loyalty to their existing consultants, 50 percent said they were indifferent; they would switch to a new consultant without hesitation.[6]

Regardless of the strength of the relationship, clients look for increasingly great work by incumbent consultants. In effect, your own flawless delivery raises the bar for your next proposal. The guerrilla pulls out all the stops when proposing new work to an existing client by using every scrap of intelligence and every relationship in the client's organization to blow away the competition.

As an incumbent, any proposal you submit for new work must prove that the depth of your previous experience increases your value to the client. Otherwise, you can easily lose any competitive advantage.

Clients can be quick to drop an incumbent consultancy in favor of one that looks new and exciting. Never become complacent because clients certainly won't be.

■ SECRET 12: FLOAT TO THE TOP

The guerrilla aims to establish advisory relationships with executives who have management responsibility for the performance of a client's business: the CEO, CFO, COO, or CIO. Interaction with those at the top sheds light on their needs and gives you a chance to offer your help and to channel it in accordance with the client's main objectives or initiatives.

Your relationships with client executives serve you in other ways. They are great sources of information about the potential projects in the organization's pipeline. And they can introduce you to other decision makers inside and outside the company.

Because a client's top executives are often the ultimate decision makers in purchases of consulting services, a strong rapport can shorten the proposal process so you can get to work. Once a project is underway, the backing of a high-level ally can make a huge difference in gaining the cooperation you need from others to stay on schedule.

How do you get to the top people in your client's organization? From day one, start to create a matrix—an influence map—that lays out the routes for essential introductions. In small companies, the progression is usually straightforward; but in large companies, influence doesn't necessarily follow an obvious path. You are a guerrilla. Use your powers of observation and think through the ramifications of what you see and hear. Ask where and to whom it could lead.

Floating to the top clarifies the big picture in your own mind, which helps you serve the client better. And after a successful project, you will be comfortable asking the chief to make referrals or act as a reference. Either way, these relationships are a powerful tool for securing new business for your practice.

■ SECRET 13: MARKETING HAS NO ON/OFF SWITCH

Many consultants have little patience for marketing; they prefer to focus on executing projects. Marketing may appear to be a Herculean task that saps too much time and energy from the "real" work of a consulting business and generates meager return for the effort.

GUERRILLA TACTIC: PERPETUAL MOTION MARKETING

Do *something* every day to market your consulting practice, whether it's making contact with a former client, working on your latest blog, or identifying new speaking opportunities. Constancy is the only reliable power source for your marketing efforts.

It is easier to devote time to the in-your-face demands of your practice such as client work, recruiting, mentoring, and financial planning. To some extent, marketing also goes against the instincts of consultants, who tend to be reactive and opportunistic about pursuing sales leads.

Guerrillas understand that we are in an era of 24/7 marketing. Clients will not take notice of your practice unless you *continuously* promote it. Your business will eventually stall if you think, "We'll focus on marketing after we finish this project."

Marketing must be a daily activity with the same high priority as performing your work for clients. There is no on/off switch in a guerrilla's marketing program.

There is no magic formula for fame and fortune. A consultant must wear many hats—advisor, expert, salesperson, problem solver, coach, referee, banker, publisher, and author. As you juggle the demands of clients, bosses, and your life, toss one more hat into the air—marketer. Your steady focus on marketing, even in the face of client and project distractions, will secure your spot at the top of the heap.

Chapter 4

Anatomy of a Marketing Plan

The aim of marketing is to make selling superfluous.

—PETER DRUCKER[1]

■ WHY YOU NEED A MARKETING PLAN

In his classic book *Ogilvy on Advertising,* David Ogilvy, founder of one the world's largest advertising agencies, reproduced an ad that speaks volumes about the challenge of marketing consulting services. The full-page ad shows a scowling, bow-tied executive with his arms folded across his chest, seated stiffly in his uncomfortable-looking wooden office chair, apparently addressing a salesperson. The ad copy displayed next to the executive reads:

> *I don't know who you are.*
> *I don't know your company.*
> *I don't know your company's product.*
> *I don't know what your company stands for.*
> *I don't know your company's customers.*
> *I don't know your company's record.*
> *I don't know your company's reputation.*
> *Now—what was it you wanted to sell me?*[2]

That is a dead-on description of the uphill battle consultants face in marketing their services, but it is not the full story. Clients are so

32

buried in the constant avalanche of marketing hype that they pitch most of it into the trash without even a glance. And, they are usually indifferent to your business proposition unless it offers them *exactly* what they need at *that* moment. So the odds of your marketing messages getting through to your targets are probably less than the odds of hitting it big at a Las Vegas roulette wheel.

To attract the right clients precisely when they need your help, you must have a well-planned marketing strategy. Some consultants run their practices with no marketing plans at all. That is a mistake. Your marketing plan is more important than your business plan; it can mean the difference between building a successful practice and finding yourself in the unemployment line.

A comprehensive marketing plan is mandatory for you to thrive in consulting, which is an unpredictable, cyclical business. The consulting industry has a 75-year history of peaks and valleys. When times are good, clients hire consultants in record numbers. But when fortunes dip, discretionary spending on consultants often gets the ax.

Even in the best of times, consultants are faced with cutthroat competition and can lose longtime clients to mergers, takeovers, leadership changes, and corporate whims. To counter these uncertainties, guerrillas continuously maintain a creative, proactive, and systematic approach to marketing. And that begins with a solid marketing plan.

■ WHAT IS A MARKETING PLAN?

You can find various definitions of a marketing plan in any resource you check. For guerrillas, the marketing plan and the business plan serve the same purpose: to attract and keep profitable clients. The marketing plan articulates *how* you will get and hold on to those profitable clients.

Of course, the act of planning is based on the flawed assumption that you can see the future with clarity. In military circles, war planners bemoan that the best-laid plans rarely survive first contact with the enemy. Guerrillas embark on the planning process expecting that the path will take twists and turns along the way, but they also realize that they will never reach their goals without a guide.

■ WITH NO DESTINATION, ANY ROAD WILL DO

Duke Ellington, the celebrated composer and holder of the Presidential Medal of Freedom, once remarked, "A goal is a dream that has an

SIX QUESTIONS TO JUMP-START YOUR MARKETING PLAN

Begin to think about your marketing plan by answering these questions about your practice:

1. What kind of consulting do you provide (i.e., strategy, financial, operations, technology, or health care)?
2. Why are your services needed?
3. What is the competitive situation in the market(s) you want to pursue?
4. Why should clients pick you instead of a competitor?
5. What substantial benefits do you bring to your clients?
6. Who cares whether you are in business?

As you address these questions, reflect on your personal and professional goals, the markets you'll serve, the industry contributions you'll make, and how you'll distinguish yourself from the crowd. Only then can you create a custom marketing plan for your practice.

ending." To create your marketing plan, first identify the dream for your practice and then work backward to plot your route. The result should be a series of steps that you can take to make your dream a reality. Each step will be an intermediate goal and will precisely describe what you must do to reach that level.

Business literature stresses the need for goal-oriented behavior to the point that many consultants have become desensitized to the idea. Before you start laying out your marketing route, set the foundation with a few powerful goals that drive your decisions.

The power of your marketing goals and your ability to achieve them depends on their simplicity. A few well-honed goals will take your practice further than an encyclopedic list of aims and objectives. You may choose to create goals in areas such as new business development with existing clients, market visibility, and professional development. As time goes by, you should revisit these goals to validate, challenge, and revise them. But you will have a starting point and that puts you ahead of most consultants.

■ CHOOSING YOUR GOALS

Consider the following ten marketing goals:

1. The specific clients you hope to attract
2. Ideal projects you'd like to complete
3. The steps you should take to become a better consultant
4. Your charitable contribution or pro bono goals, such as volunteering to serve on a committee for a community service organization
5. Your industry contribution goals, such as writing a topical article for an industry newsletter, speaking at industry conferences, or helping to organize a seminar in your field
6. The number of new relationships you want to forge
7. Improvement of your market visibility by developing a new publicity campaign, updating your Web presence, or undertaking a survey or poll on a topic of interest to your clients
8. Your financial goals, such as revenue, profit, and growth
9. Your life/balance goals, such as scheduling nonnegotiable vacations, setting a monthly limit on client service hours, or starting a new hobby
10. New service areas you'd like to develop, which might mean expanding the scope of a service you currently offer, adding capabilities to your practice by hiring new people, or building new services

Powerful marketing goals are inspiring. What's even more important is to confront the question: How will these goals help serve clients more effectively and profitably?

■ WHO ARE THEY GOING TO CALL?

It is a myth that consultants can be all things to all clients based on their wits, experience, and consulting process. Clients are not buying that anymore. Guerrillas know that you must be the leader in an area of expertise that is in demand. An example of this principle is firefighter-extraordinaire, Red Adair. For more than three decades, Adair battled the worst wildcat fires on remote offshore oil rigs and oil fields. In 1991, when hundreds of oil-well fires burned out of control in Kuwait and threatened the global environment, the U.S. government knew exactly whom to call.

GUERRILLA TIP: YOU CAN'T DO IT ALL

You can't be an expert at everything, so don't try to be all things to all clients. Focus on doing a few things and do them exceptionally well.

To deal with that crisis, the government didn't call just any firefighters; it called the undisputed authority on handling such emergencies, Red Adair. Although his firm probably wasn't the only one with the ability to control the menacing blazes, it was considered the best of the best. Adair and his crew might not have been called for every emergency, but you can bet they were paid well for the assignments they received. Like Red Adair, consultants who have recognized competence and strong results in a specific area can achieve consistent paydays.

■ STANDING OUT IN A CROWD

In side-by-side comparisons, most consultants look pretty much the same to clients because consultants tend to mimic each other's marketing identities. Differentiating your practice from the competition, even slightly, can bring you more clients, higher fees, and lower cost of sales. Too often, consultants attempt to distinguish their practices in ways that have little or no influence on the reasons clients hire consultants. As a result, clients have come to view consulting services as a commodity like winter wheat or pork bellies. They have also put the commodity label on legal, medical, and financial services.

In his classic 1986 book, *The Marketing Imagination*, Theodore Levitt reminds us, "There is no such thing as a commodity. All goods and services can be differentiated and usually are."[3] No matter what service you provide, you must convince clients that you have more to offer than the norm or they will view you as a mere commodity.

If your services are considered to be a commodity, you will face severe price competition—if you even get called. Although no two consultancies are identical, the staggering numbers of consultants out there and their marketing efforts have created the perception that most consulting firms are indistinguishable from each other.

It doesn't help that many consultants cast a wide marketing net to snare any and all potential clients. In some cases, their marketing pitches reach a level of abstraction that makes it virtually impossible for clients to understand what the consultants actually do.

A typical Web site states, "Our service offerings are designed to help our clients generate revenue, reduce costs and access the information necessary to operate their businesses on a timely basis." Sounds good, but how are they going to do that? Check out 15 other consultant Web sites, and you'll find lots more of the same. Not only do the sites look alike, they all make equally ambiguous, noncompelling claims.

Fuzzy marketing communications are guaranteed to result in fewer sales, lower fees, and anemic profit margins. Consultants who compel attention can easily eliminate competition from me-too firms. Prospective clients often call me-too consultants simply to create the illusion of competition. The me-too firms then squander their precious resources chasing sales opportunities they never had a chance of winning.

Guerrillas seize on the consulting industry's lack of marketing differentiation to produce precise, cogent statements of their specialized expertise—that's what makes the telephone ring. For example, one firm states, "We help nonprofit organizations strengthen donor loyalty, enhance board dedication, and expand community commitment."

A clear statement of your firm's uniqueness simplifies the marketing challenge by informing prospective clients exactly who you are. It separates you from the pack. It also saves you the time, energy, and expense of educating prospects who may not understand, or need, the services you provide.

■ EIGHT DIFFERENTIATORS THAT DON'T WORK

You can start by avoiding the following eight mistakes. Using any of these trite, overused, ineffective pitches will show clients that you are not creative and are living in the past. Clients don't have the time or patience to dig deep to identify what differentiates you from other consultants; don't expect them to do so. Jettison these surefire losers when you explain why your practice stands above the crowd:

1. *Quality service.* Every client expects consultants to provide "quality" service. Every competitor will make this claim, thereby neutralizing its impact.

2. *Best price.* Most clients do not hire the cheapest consultants to handle their toughest problems. A study on the impact of varying pricing methods showed that almost 50 percent of the professional service firms trying this strategy reaped no measurable increase in sales.[4] Clients rarely choose the lowest-price candidate or the one with the most pricing options. Some clients, such as those in the public sector, are exceptions: Lowest price may always be their primary criterion.

3. *Methods, tools, and approaches.* If you hire a carpenter, you expect that tradesperson to show up with all the tools needed to complete the job quickly and efficiently. Clients expect the same from consultants. A study on effective differentiation strategies of professional service firms showed that 40 percent of firms that boasted new techniques and tools to deliver services ended up with dismal marketing results.[5]

   Trying to sell services based solely on your consulting prowess is foolish. Competitors with newer and ever more complex tools will pop up every time you take that approach. Clients expect every serious competitor to have the proper tools.

4. *Service responsiveness.* It is a waste of your breath to promise clients quick responses to questions or on-time and on-budget project performance. Clients who pay high consulting fees expect quick service, and they will pressure you to provide it. Unless you can move quickly, they'll find firms that can meet their demands.

5. *Credentials.* Many firms stress the academic pedigree of their team to show why they are special. However, most clients couldn't care less where your team was educated; they want to know what your team has done that relates to their project.

6. *Importance of the client.* Some consultants stress how important clients are to the firm's business and promise them special attention. Clients will shrug off this offer as hype unless they have a special status with your firm that confers benefits to them not extended to others.

7. *Testimonials and references.* Don't provide clients with testimonials. Instead, show them your complete client list and invite them to call whomever they wish. Clients will contact the firms they know and put more stock in the opinions of their trusted network members than in praise from unknown clients.

8. *FUD.* Consultants often try to convince clients that there is an urgent need for a specific service by instilling fear, uncertainty,

and doubt (FUD) in their minds. Clients routir
this ploy and will stop listening if you try it.

◼ NINE DIFFERENTIATORS THAT DO WORK

Distinguish yourself by focusing on how you will provide benefits
and insight for clients. Zero in on clients' needs and give them solutions, not slogans:

1. *Category authority.* Nothing trumps the power of undisputed
competence. The market embraces experts far more quickly
and rewards them with higher fees than jack-of-all-trades consultants. Most people don't call a general contractor to fix a
plumbing leak—they call a specialist, a plumber. Similarly, a
client who wants to develop a plan for employee retention is
more apt to look for help from a consultant with relevant expertise than from a generalist consultant.

2. *Simplicity.* Some consultants get so enamored with the ele-
gance of their solutions that they fail to make sure that
clients understand the offering and feel good about buying it.
If you are proposing a complex service, show it to the client
in small pieces, instead of in one overwhelming chunk. Support each part of your proposal with white papers, in-person
meetings, and case studies. Recognize that it may take clients
time to comprehend the brilliance of your ideas. Be patient,
expect multiple interactions, and educate clients at their
speed, not yours.

3. *A real guarantee.* As suggested earlier, offer your clients a tangible guarantee such as that turnover will decrease by 10 percent or that production capacity will increase by 7 percent. A
few words of caution: If you offer a guarantee, make it simple
and easy for all parties to understand. A guarantee that looks
like a piece of congressional legislation loses its punch.

4. *Giving something away.* In the early stages of relationships,
clients continually size up their experience with you. Move
relationships forward and demonstrate the power of your
practice by offering a complementary seminar, a telephone
briefing, or a research report that could benefit the client.

A wine industry consultant periodically holds an open
house for wine company executives, where they discuss pressing issues. The consultant does not charge for this service, and

clients and nonclients can attend. Studies have found that consultants' one-on-one interactions with clients are the most effective way to reduce clients' perception of risk; flashy marketing materials are considerably less effective.[6]

5. *Honesty*. Clients are ultrasensitive to overblown claims about results. They sense fact from fiction in marketing communications, so report only honest results and tell clients what they can realistically expect if they work with you. Reality wins and hype loses in the era of guerrilla clients.

6. *Highly recognized, third-party testimonials.* Clients are more likely to react favorably to testimonials from respected, well-known authorities in their fields. If your firm has an active, productive alliance with a university, think tank, or other well-known institution, an endorsement from that organization adds credibility to your marketing message and provides an additional measure of security for clients.

7. *Being first (at something).* To emerge from the pack, stress one benefit that you are the first or only one to offer. You may need to search through past projects, but after some digging you'll find it. For example, your firm may have been the first to increase a client's profits by reducing sales.

8. *Innovation*. Consulting firms tend to hawk similar services. A few firms innovate boldly and bring new ideas that change their clients' competitive positions. You will also find fast-follower firms that develop practices around a set of client services only after demand has been established. Being regarded as an innovative firm will inspire forward-thinking clients to call you. You'll be the first one in and will set the agenda for your competitors.

9. *Defying conventional wisdom*. A herd mentality dominates the consulting business. When a new service is hot, firms rush to clients with marketing materials and aggressive sales campaigns. This has happened repeatedly with the Y2K scare, reengineering, e-business, and outsourcing. When the tide of a new service seems to be rising, most consulting firms say, "jump in the water." Others, however, take a reasoned, but contrary view of megatrends before entering the fray.

Focus on bringing original, independent, and insightful thinking to clients on trends and developments, not the latest babble. In the long run, you will gain clients with your balanced and independent approach.

■ WHAT ARE YOUR STRENGTHS?

To discover the areas where you can stand out in the crowd, you must identify your strengths. What are you really good at helping clients achieve? What can you help them increase, reduce, improve, or create? Maybe you can help clients create new products or services, improve the quality of the information they use to make decisions, or reduce employee turnover.

When thinking about these questions, you might find it useful to look at the list of possible drivers of consulting value in Chapter 17 (see Table 17.1). Reflecting on your strengths will help you differentiate yourself from the competition. It will also help you clarify the specific clients you want to target in your marketing.

■ HITTING YOUR TARGETS   Horiz/vert

Carefully choose the market(s) you wish to serve and those you will ignore. Then relentlessly pursue the market(s) you select. Some consultants try to be all things to all clients and end up squandering their marketing resources because they lack market focus. The guerrilla aims, not at a mass market, but at targeted markets that use consulting services.

It is easy to target too broadly. Some consultants serve the small business market, but find it impossible to provide compelling offerings to so broad a group of clients. If you target small businesses, narrow the field to a few segments and build your presence with those segments.

Other consultants choose to serve an industry like health care and then narrow their focus, say, to life science companies. You can also target specific companies within an industry.

Some firms specialize in addressing particular functions or problems that are not industry specific, such as employee diversity. They choose target organizations based on functional knowledge of human resources instead of relying solely on industry knowledge.

■ HOW TO COMPLETE A MARKETING PLAN

For more than 50 years, Mr. Potato Head, the world's first "action" figure, has been sparking the imagination of children. His mock-potato torso and pile of accessories give a child's creativity free rein to invent distinct characters from an assortment of eyes, ears, limbs, and outfits.

For guerrillas, Mr. Potato Head epitomizes the creating of a customized marketing plan: Sort through a variety of options to create a unique blueprint that will attract profitable clients to your practice at the least possible cost. Keep in mind that a primary objective in working with clients is to make their complex problems or issues simple to understand and solve. The same logic applies to the creation of the guerrilla's marketing plan—you want to simplify a complex task.

To focus your thinking on the plan's most critical elements, first write a one-page marketing plan. Show the plan to others for their feedback, and expand the plan once you have refined your main ideas for reaching your markets.

Guerrillas build their plans around seven sentences:

1. Sentence one explains the purpose of your marketing.
2. Sentence two explains how you achieve that purpose by describing the substantive benefits you provide to clients.
3. Sentence three describes your target market(s).
4. Sentence four describes your niche.
5. Sentence five outlines the marketing weapons you will use.
6. Sentence six reveals the identity of your business.
7. Sentence seven provides your marketing budget.

The following three sample marketing plans illustrate how to incorporate these seven points in your plan.

➤ Sample Marketing Plan 1: Spinnaker Consulting

The purpose of Spinnaker Consulting's marketing program is to make Spinnaker the leader in selling high-profit services to the world's major boat manufacturers and boating suppliers. This will be accomplished by positioning Spinnaker as the industry expert in helping clients accelerate manufacturing operations, improve sales processes, and boost product profitability.

Our target market is the chief operating officers, sales executives, and manufacturing executives of the 50 largest boat manufacturers and their suppliers. The firm's niche is to provide practical, action-oriented advice that guarantees clients will achieve improvement in profitability that exceeds Spinnaker's professional fee.

We plan to use the following marketing tools:

➤ A Web site that promotes Spinnaker and provides resources for our clients

➤ A free monthly electronic newsletter (zine) on topics of interest to clients and prospects

➤ Presentations by our consultants at targeted trade shows

➤ Direct mailings to follow up on contacts made at the trade shows

➤ Publication of articles four times a year in industry trade journals

➤ Sponsorship of one regatta each year, for which we will seek free publicity

➤ Semiannual seminars on profit improvement strategies for boat manufacturers

➤ Promotion of seminars on our Web site, in our zine, and with paid advertising in industry publications

The Spinnaker team will be seen as creative, collaborative, highly competent, results-oriented, and easy to work with. The marketing budget for the practice will be 20 percent of fees.

➤ Sample Marketing Plan 2: FairPay Consultants

The purpose of FairPay Consultants' marketing program is to establish FairPay as the premier firm in designing and implementing equitable executive compensation programs for clients in the Financial Services and High Technology industries. We will do that by positioning FairPay as the market leader in developing compensation programs that are market based, equitable, and highly tailored to the needs of the individual client.

FairPay will target human resources executives, compensation specialists, and board members in the Financial Services and High Technology industries. The firm's niche is to use data-driven analysis and the expert judgment of its consultants to create equitable executive compensation programs that save up to 15 percent of the client's total compensation.

We plan to use a variety of marketing tools to reach our targets:

➤ Yellow Pages ads in major metropolitan areas

➤ An annual 80-page guide to executive compensation

➤ A paid subscription to a review of the latest trends in executive compensation, published three times each year

➤ A free, quarterly zine covering the latest government regulations on executive compensation

➤ Speeches at annual conferences of human resources, financial services, and high-tech industry associations

➤ E-mails delivered after every speech informing our contacts that summaries and slides from the speeches are available on our Web site

➤ Publication of annual articles in *HR* and *CEO* magazines

➤ Use of the firm's Web site as a repository for information on executive compensation

➤ Development of a continuous search engine optimization program that will attract targeted clients to our Web site

➤ Two pro bono projects for charitable or civic groups each year

FairPay will have a reputation for using fact-based analyses with strong business judgment to prepare recommendations for client consideration. The marketing budget will be 15 percent of fees.

➤ Sample Marketing Plan 3: TechNot Consulting

The purpose of the TechNot Consulting marketing plan is to make the firm the leader in helping clients capture the return on investment (ROI) for their existing technology investments. We will do this by positioning TechNot as a technology-savvy, but not technology-dependent, firm that focuses exclusively on helping clients get a higher return on their information technology investments.

TechNot will target executives in the health care provider and insurance markets who have responsibility for the budget and performance of their organizations' information systems. The firm's niche will be to guarantee technology-operating improvements, such as lower cost of operating computers and better-trained employees, without spending additional money on hardware or software.

We plan to use the following marketing tools:

➤ Distributing to targeted clients the results of a satisfaction survey of technology performance and effectiveness

➤ Conducting a direct mail campaign to 20 top health care CEOs after our speech at the annual conference of health care CEOs

➤ Developing a Web site diagnostic tool that will allow prospective clients to rate the effectiveness of their existing information technology

➤ Hosting a series of teleseminars entitled "Before You Spend More on Your Systems"

➤ Publishing articles in the three major health care and insurance journals each year

➤ Producing a monthly zine on how to get the most from your information technology investments.

Our consultants will be known for educating clients on how to achieve swift, excellent results; helping them do that; and then getting out of their way. Volunteers from our firm will give back to the community by participating in a local hospital's technology training program. The marketing budget will be 12 percent of fees.

The marketing plans for these three consulting firms are short and to the point. They state the purpose of each business, how the purpose will be achieved, the target markets, and the tactics each will use. The plans differentiate the practices by focusing on their competencies; one adds a guarantee. The plans highlight the precise niches the firms will serve and describe the firms' cultures so clients will know the kind of people they will be working with, from the start to finish of projects. Most important, these brief plans show how the firms will make multiple impressions on clients and the market to generate sales leads.

GUERRILLA INTELLIGENCE: DIVVY UP YOUR MARKETING RESOURCES

The preceding examples illustrate the basics of designing a customized marketing plan. Now add one more layer to the plan—how you will allocate your marketing budget and other resources (time, energy, and effort) to target three groups of clients:

1. *Current clients.* This is the smallest of the three groups but, as mentioned, existing clients should generate the largest percentage of your profits. Plan to devote 60 percent of your marketing efforts to these clients.

2. *Prospective clients.* Your goal is to convert prospective clients into clients—if they fit your client profile and have problems that you can solve. Commit 30 percent of your marketing resources to win work from this group.

3. *The broader market.* This includes everybody in the business world not represented in the first two groups. Invest 10 percent of your marketing resources in the broad market. Devoting resources to this group is less efficient, but it has the potential to generate important contacts and leads.

■ IT'S ALL RELATIVE

The 60/30/10 percentages are rules of thumb, not gospel. The one size fits none principle of guerrilla marketing applies. Every consulting practice is different and must customize its marketing approach. And how you combine tactics and decide to allocate your resources among the three groups of clients will change from time to time. The preceding marketing plans are intended to spark your creative ideas and keep them rolling until you arrive at your destination.

Chapter 5

The Guerrilla's Marketing Road Map

When you try to be all things to all people, you end up being nothing.

—Al Ries[1]

Every October, more than 1,500 competitors go to Kona, Hawaii, where they face off in the Ironman Triathlon. The contest features a 2.4-mile ocean swim, a grueling 112-mile bike ride, and a punishing 26.2-mile run. Mark Allen, who was dubbed the "World's Fittest Man" by *Outside* magazine, has won the Ironman an amazing six times, the last at age 37.

Allen credits his extraordinary success to the rigorous, step-by-step training plan he follows. To develop that plan, he inventoried his talents and charted a course to perfect his skills for peak performance. He also identified his weaknesses and built them into strengths. He coordinated his training activities into a coherent program and entered practice triathlons to hone his skills.

Consultants should approach marketing in the same way that Mark Allen does training. To attract new business, consultants must continually, not just occasionally, market their services. To market themselves successfully, consultants must also plan, coordinate, and practice.

The core of a consultant's marketing campaign is the one-page marketing plan discussed in Chapter 4. Your one-page plan is the vision for your practice that identifies your target clients, your value to the market, and your marketing strategies. Now it's time to lay out the route you will follow to turn your vision into reality. We call it your Guerrilla Marketing Road Map. The Road Map takes your one-page marketing plan and adds two dimensions to make it real: sequence and timing.

■ WHERE THE RUBBER MEETS THE ROAD

Have you ever been convinced that you knew where you were going only to belatedly discover that you really had no clue? When you're lost, looking at a map—assuming you have one—can quickly get you back on route. Your Marketing Road Map shows you how to keep your consulting practice on the route to profitability.

Without the Road Map, marketing your consulting services can be erratic, unpredictable, and hard to manage. When client and project demands overwhelm you, marketing will fall to the bottom of the list. It's simply a matter of priorities.

Preparing your Road Map is a strategic, tactical, and creative venture. It begins with your ideas on how to present your practice to the market and attract clients, and sets a schedule for each marketing activity.

The creation of your Road Map can't be haphazard; it requires precision. You must commit to specific marketing activities and to the times you plan to use them. The more tightly you build your plan, the stronger your marketing campaign will be. You must plan each entry well before executing it. You also must coordinate it with all other activities that it may affect or influence. As you prepare the Road Map, include these four steps:

1. Identify the resources that you'll need to design and implement each marketing activity. If your Road Map calls for a bimonthly zine and three industry speeches, account for the time, effort, and costs of those activities.

2. Forecast how the various marketing tactics you plan to use will create profit for your practice. What value, for example, do you estimate your practice will get if you attend a trade show and sponsor a booth? Estimate the number of inquiries, leads, and even projects that might result. Your forecast will be imprecise, but it will give you a rough idea of your plan's relative impact.

3. Determine the message you want to convey with your marketing tactics. Think backward from a sale of your services. What

might clients be looking for as they search for you? Where will they look, and what will they hope to find? Craft your message around what clients are looking for, not what you provide.

4. Develop a mechanism for measuring the effectiveness of each element of the Road Map. Consultants who fail to measure marketing effectiveness frequently waste money and effort.

Although your Road Map sets time frames, it is more than a schedule. It is also a vital creative exercise that will stretch your thinking and force you to examine the full implications of your marketing strategy. Explore all possibilities, brainstorm, and let your imagination run wild. Don't hold back. Be adventurous and unrealistic.

Then come back to earth, but bring with you some of the ideas you conjured up and find new and interesting ways to express them in your marketing materials. Most consultants' marketing is about as interesting as watching paint dry, so you should have little difficulty breaking the mold and catching the attention of those you'd like to work with.

■ A WINNING ROAD MAP

The ultimate litmus test for your Road Map is that you can execute it at low cost while earning high profits for your practice. That is the primary objective here. A magic formula for a profitable map doesn't exist, but winners share seven characteristics. Your Marketing Road Map:

1. *Helps you sell.* Its primary purpose is to help you acquire profitable, career-enhancing projects. You will enhance your visibility, and thus your brand, as you execute your Road Map, but its purpose is to generate leads, not to create the next great consulting brand in the market.

2. *Keeps you engaged.* Unless you market continuously and concertedly, leads can vanish, forcing you to scramble when your ongoing projects run dry. When your Road Map is an integral part of your practice, you'll always know the status and schedule of your marketing efforts. A map pushes you to market proactively and makes your marketing needs much more difficult to ignore.

3. *Uses the power of focus.* Great Road Maps aim squarely at targeted clients. Potential clients must be exposed to your

marketing message multiple times before they even know your business exists, let alone call you for help. Guerrillas target potential clients with enough frequency and compelling content to grab their attention and get on their radar screens. If your message is on point, you will get through.

4. *Creates confidence.* Your Road Map isn't like a moon shot that launches once every six months. Use an assortment of marketing weapons in a continuous pattern to help prospects develop confidence in your business. Clients who frequently see your firm in a positive light will believe your firm is legitimate and can help them. Familiarity that is done well will not breed contempt—it will breed project opportunities.

5. *Keeps your marketing tactics in sync.* Deliver the full power of your message to the market through multiple tactics working in concert. Guerrillas simultaneously aim an array of weapons at their targets, and each weapon reinforces their core messages. Cross-promote relentlessly to bring as many impressions of your firm to your target markets as possible.

6. *Builds your brand.* Your primary objective is to use your marketing activities to generate project leads, but building your reputation in the market will also draw clients to your practice. Build your reputation brick by brick with outstanding client work and effective marketing. Your consistent identity in the market, compelling message, and assortment of marketing weapons will elevate your brand recognition several notches.

7. *Clarifies visual identity.* Create a strong and consistent visual identity and project it across every facet of your practice. It should express your style and declare that you are innovative, well organized, and professional. Develop a single identifier that is unique and distinctive, but is appropriate for the clients you hope to attract. Place that identifier on everything related to your practice so it will be quickly recognizable and remind others of you. For a minimum investment, even a small firm or individual practitioner can create a strong professional identity.

■ THE DEATH OF THE LOGO?

In 1976, Oxford University biologist Richard Dawkins coined the term meme (rhymes with cream), which he defined as a basic unit of cultural transmission that passes from one mind to another and instantly communicates an entire idea.[2] For example, the skull-and-crossbones symbol on a bottle label is a meme that conveys the idea "dangerous to life, proceed with extreme caution."

Other well-known memes are the hitchhiker's thumb, the white flag indicating surrender, the Red Cross, and the nuclear mushroom cloud. Memes, with their power to communicate a complete thought in a flash, have the potential to revolutionize marketing.

Memes are more effective than logos because they do more than just identify an entity. One of the most recognized logos in the world, the Nike swoosh, identifies the company for consumers. Other logos, such as Coca-Cola and Microsoft, do the same. But logos don't tell consumers what those companies actually do.

By contrast, a well-conceived meme can cut through the marketing clutter and instantly inform clients what your practice does. Creating a meme is less difficult than it may sound. The key is to boil down the essence of what you do for clients.

Review the specific benefits you offer clients, especially those benefits you provide that are unique. Then, think about how you can express your benefits visually or in a few words.

One consultant, who serves as an executive coach, uses a meme showing an individual wearing a baseball cap and the ubiquitous microphone headset worn by professional football coaches. One look at this meme, and you know the consultant is a coach.

Create a list of your target clients' characteristics and their needs, such as growing the business, reducing costs, or improving productivity. Create a wide range of visual images and determine which one or combination best communicates the message you want to convey. Then translate those needs into visual images that communicate a complete idea.

The concept of memes is new to marketing, and many shrug it off just as they did online marketing before it exploded onto the scene. But just wait. Guerrilla marketers already understand the power of memes, and you'll see more and more of them.

■ FINDING ON-RAMPS

The first rule for choosing the right marketing tactics is that there is more than one choice. The right message and sequence for launching marketing weapons will vary from practice to practice. Your constraints are your creativity and, of course, your budget.

Here's one piece of advice, though. As you decide how to construct your marketing Road Map, ignore what other consulting firms are doing. Start fresh. Otherwise, you'll find yourself squeezed into the "we have to be conservative" marketing strategies that are the norm for professional service firms.

Large firms that have more than one type of consulting practice will probably need a different Road Map for each practice. The specific tactics and timing may not be the same for your health care practice and your technology practice.

The content of your Road Map depends on the clients and industries you target as well as your budget, expertise, talents, and the stage of your career or firm. If you're just starting your career, you may not have many clients. So focus on external marketing activities like writing articles and giving speeches. Conversely, when you have many existing clients, focus more of your marketing investment on them than on attracting new clients.

Some marketing tactics may be especially suitable for your use. If you are a great writer, take advantage of that talent. On the other hand, if speaking in front of an audience ties your tongue into knots, leave that off the Road Map for now. Get some coaching on how to improve that skill. Once you are more comfortable with public speaking, you can add it to your Road Map.

Like Mark Allen, pinpoint your weaknesses and build them into strengths. Look for professional training or consider collaborating with other experts to help you when you need it.

Consider outsourcing certain marketing endeavors such as developing, writing, and producing newsletters and Web sites. Trade services or collaborate with other consultants. For example, if you're a human resources expert and a consultant in another firm is an authority on the motion picture industry, join forces to author an article on how to motivate stressed-out creative people.

Assess your marketing options and use Table 5.1 to help choose the right marketing weapons for your practice. The table shows the relative level of effort, market impact, and cost of the most commonly used marketing weapons.

■ ROAD MAP UNDER CONSTRUCTION

The following two examples demonstrate how to construct a marketing Road Map. Both cases use the fictional firms that were discussed in Chapter 4; they illustrate how a firm can approach the market in a winning and differentiated manner.

Table 5.1 Assessing Your Marketing Weapons

Marketing Weapon	Level of Effort	Market Impact	$ Cost
Printed Brochures	Medium	Low	Medium-High
Case Studies	Low	Medium	Low
Surveys	Medium-High	High	Medium-High
Special Reports	Medium	High	Medium
Web Sites	Medium	High	Medium
Zines/Newsletters	Medium	High	Low
Speeches	Medium	High	Low
Sponsored Events/Trade Shows	Medium-High	Medium-High	Medium-High
Directory Listings	Low	Medium	Low
Articles	Low-Medium	High	Low
Direct Mail	Medium	Low-Medium	Medium-High
Books	High	High	High
Pro Bono Work	Low-Medium	High	Low
Publicity	Medium	High	Low-Medium
Relationships	High	High	Low

■ SPINNAKER CONSULTING

The Spinnaker Consulting firm serves the world's leading boat manufacturers and suppliers by helping clients accelerate their manufacturing operations, improve sales, and boost their profits.

Spinnaker's marketing agenda gives the firm substantial market
exposure at low cost. It targets Spinnaker's existing and prospective
clients throughout the year. Based on its basic marketing plan, Spinnaker might establish the Road Map shown in Table 5.2.

Spinnaker's plan is aggressive, but economical. The largest cash
investments are the Profit Improvement Seminars and the regatta
sponsorship.

■ FAIRPAY CONSULTANTS

FairPay Consultants uses many of the same techniques as Spinnaker
Consulting, but adds a paid subscription publication and pro bono
work to the marketing mix (see Table 5.3). FairPay's zine isn't published as frequently, but is still important in maintaining close contact with clients and prospects.

The Road Map is a summary and it doesn't list all the intermediate tasks you must accomplish. You'll have to break the work down in

Table 5.2	Marketing Road Map for Spinnaker Consulting
Month	Marketing Activity
January	Conduct Profit Improvement Seminar Publish monthly zine
February	Publish trade journal article Publish monthly zine
March	Attend and speak at industry trade show Conduct direct mail follow-up for trade show contacts Publish monthly zine
April	Publish trade journal article Publish monthly zine
May	Advertise Profit Improvement Seminar Promote seminar on Web site Issue press release Send invitations to Profit Improvement Seminar Publish monthly zine
June	Conduct Profit Improvement Seminar Publish trade journal article Conduct seminar follow-up activities Publish monthly zine
July	Promote sponsorship of annual regatta Invite clients to networking event Publish monthly zine
August	Attend and promote practice at sponsored regatta Publish monthly zine
September	Host client networking event Publish monthly zine
October	Publish trade journal article Publish monthly zine
November	Send invitations to Profit Improvement Seminar
December	Advertise Profit Improvement Seminar Publish monthly zine

sequence. If you want a speaking gig in a certain month, you'll have to arrange it well in advance. Plan your zine content around upcoming events and your reports on past events. Use your Road Map to systematically assign resources and people to practice development activities.

Table 5.3   FairPay Consultants Marketing Road Map

Month	Marketing Activity
January	Publish Annual Guide to Executive Compensation Issue press release to announce publication of guide Update Yellow Pages and other directory listings
February	Send direct mail inviting clients to attend upcoming HR Conference Publish quarterly zine Promote upcoming HR Conference on Web site and in zine Issue press release on conference details
March	Publish Review of Compensation Trends (paid subscription) Publish industry article
April	Speak at HR Conference Follow up on conference attendee inquiries
May	Conduct pro bono project 1 Publish quarterly zine Send direct mail inviting clients to attend upcoming High-Tech Conference Promote upcoming High-Tech Conference on Web site and in zine Issue press release on conference details
June	Publish Review of Compensation Trends (paid subscription)
July	Speak at High-Tech Conference Follow up on conference attendee inquiries
August	Conduct pro bono project 2 Publish quarterly zine Send direct mail inviting clients to attend Financial Services Conference Promote upcoming Financial Services Conference on Web site and in zine Issue press release on conference details
September	Publish Review of Compensation Trends (paid subscription)
October	Speak at Financial Services Conference Follow up on conference attendee inquiries
November	Promote upcoming Annual Guide to Executive Compensation Publish quarterly zine
December	Send direct mail promoting Annual Guide to Executive Compensation Publish industry article

Another feature of marketing that is not explicitly spelled out in the Road Map is one of the guerrilla's weapons of choice—the telephone. Just as with other marketing tactics, the telephone is an integral part of your marketing program.

■ YOU MAKE THE CALL

Everyone knows that the telephone figures prominently in many aspects of marketing. But it is worth a slight detour to talk about the most effective uses of this tool.

Placing cold calls—unsolicited telephone calls to unknown people to try to drum up business—is uncomfortable for most of us. Consultants don't like to make cold calls, the person on the receiving end doesn't want to get them, and the response rate is low.

Yet some professionals swear by the technique. One tax accountant reports a good response rate for cold calls made to businesses close to tax time. You may find cold calls effective in limited situations. If you have sent a direct mailing to clients you don't know about an upcoming seminar, you might follow up with a call to find out if the recipient plans to attend. For the most part, though, cold calls are a waste of time.

By contrast, "warm" calls based on referrals or to follow up on contacts made at conferences, speeches, or other events are an easy, effective, and low-cost way to keep your firm's name fresh in prospects' minds. Also, you should regularly call those in your professional network and in your firm's client base to follow up on articles you have sent, discuss your most recent report, or invite them to events.

To avoid bugging clients and contacts, call infrequently, but have a consistent plan to keep in touch. Rehearse calls in advance and keep them short and to the point. Keep a log of your calls and document the issues you discuss. Don't try to sell on the telephone; use your calls to stay on the radar of clients, prospects, and colleagues.

■ REVISING YOUR ROAD MAP

Be willing to change your Road Map when necessary. If you intended to conduct three seminars but the first two bombed, cancel the remaining seminar or make adjustments to turn it around. Conversely, when something works, do more of the same. For example, if your

Web site generates significant subscribers to your zine and several leads, continue that program.

When tactics work, they build momentum. Your targeted clients begin to know you. If you fail to market continuously you risk losing that impetus and your visibility. You also risk losing everything you've invested in marketing—time, money, and energy—and will have to make those investments all over again. So, stick with the program.

Constantly measure the effectiveness of your marketing efforts. If you run a workshop, measure how many prospects subsequently contact you and the quality of those contacts. When you send direct mail, note how many responses you actually receive. Also measure the number of subscribers to your zine, hits on your Web site, and telephone inquiries.

Measurements should focus first on whether your efforts produced leads, not on whether they generated sales. The object is to measure leads. Prospects aren't going to hire you because they read your article, but it may convince them to contact you. From those contacts, you can go forward and try to land a project.

Frequently, you won't need measuring devices to know whether your efforts have paid off. If the consultants in your firm are consistently on the beach—that is, with no project work—you need to re-assess. If they are busy with profitable work, you are on the right road.

Every two months, review *specific* marketing elements: your Web site, articles you write, the speeches you present, and seminars you run. Material quickly gets stale and out of date. Keep your marketing current because prospects will bypass the same old stuff and think less of you for using it.

If you continually update your marketing content, prospects will notice. At first they may visit your site or read your zine just for the information but, in time, they may contact you to help with their business.

Every six months, formally review your *entire* marketing Road Map. Examine it thoroughly and discard and replace whatever hasn't worked. Check whether you're actually completing the items listed in your plan because some items always fall through the cracks.

■ PUT YOUR MARKETING ON THE MAP

Sometimes simplest is best. The Marketing Road Map is a simple, yet powerful, idea that drives your marketing activities right where they belong—to the center of your practice. You'll have a reliable guide to translate your vision for your practice into a profitable reality.

You'll no longer see marketing as a sidelight or something to insert between client projects. Your marketing program will be predictable, consistent, and continuous, which will keep your telephone ringing in good times and bad.

Part

II

Guerrilla Marketing at Work

Chapter 6

Beyond Web Sites

Create a Client–Centered Web Presence

Toiling away in a lab in Geneva, Switzerland, Tim Berners-Lee brought his creation, the World Wide Web, to life on Christmas Day 1990. At the time, some people appreciated his ingenuity, but most could not envision the practical applications. So, Berners-Lee used his creation to speed up access to the lab's telephone directory. Some of his colleagues resisted even that use, arguing that what they had was just fine.

For many consultants, the Web is still an untapped resource, when it should be a central part of their strategies to differentiate themselves from their competitors. Most consultants realize that they must have Web sites, but have created poorly designed sites that often do more harm than good.

■ SO WHAT'S WRONG?

When customers enter a new store, they notice little things that they ignore in their favorite shopping spots. They quickly size up the store's layout, the quality of the merchandise, the attentiveness of the sales staff, and the overall feel of the place. They form a quick impression and decide whether to shop or move on.

Web site visitors, especially those new to your site, are no different from other shoppers. They make decisions about the credibility, value, and professionalism of your site, often before the home page finishes loading. If the site appears unprofessional, slow, or out-of-date, your visitors are likely to move on, leaving you with lost opportunities.

In our era of self-service, consumers routinely make vacation plans, buy presents, and form impressions of consultants solely on the basis of contacts they make on the Web and through e-mail. So, they demand that sites be easy to navigate and understand. Although the standard of quality for Web sites seems to increase monthly, many consultants fail to keep up. They simply convert recent brochures to their sites and hope they'll generate leads.

■ WHY YOU NEED A GREAT WEB SITE

When a potential client can access the archives of the Smithsonian Institute, the Library of Congress, and the complete works of Leonardo Da Vinci using a mouse and a browser, they are unlikely to be satisfied if their review of a consultant's Web site turns up nothing but marketing babble. Potential clients expect consultants' sites to look and feel professional, with insightful content that helps them understand whether you and your firm can help them.

Patterns for buying consulting services are quickly changing, and there's no going back. A study by the Information Technology Services Marketing Association (ITSMA) found that 77 percent of decision makers now find service providers, including consultants, using the Web, even after they receive referrals.[1]

Clients use the information on the Web to make preliminary assessments of consultants' talents and to gauge how well they would fit with their organizations. Nearly 75 percent of buyers find consultants through their own research, not through contacts initiated by consultants.

Without a great Web site, you will not be considered a serious player, and the most desirable potential clients won't invite you to the game. As technological breakthroughs emerge, it will become even more important for consultants to establish an outstanding presence on the Web.

And that's not all. As the Web penetrates organizations further, consultants will need to use it for many routine business matters such as delivering proposals, processing billing and collections, and creating client-specific microsites for projects, to name just a few.

Most consultants' Web sites suffer from one or more of the following seven deadly afflictions:

1. *Templates and artists.* Web sites are often designed either by local programmers using inexpensive cookie-cutter templates or by graphic artists who create eye-pleasing, but sluggish sites. Both tend to drive visitors to your competitors. When you look for help with your site, balance the need for an effective, high-performing site with a design that conveys your professional image.

2. *Gratuitous images.* Some Web site owners paste stock images of unknown people on their home pages and other parts of their sites. You may see a group of individuals gathered around a conference table staring at a computer screen that another person is operating. This meaningless scene conveys no message. Every image on every page of your site should have a purpose.

3. *Us/our syndrome.* Many sites are filled with navigation buttons, or tabs, bearing titles such as "Our Services," "About Us," "Our Clients," "Our Qualifications," and "Our Clients." Clients want more about their issues and less about your triumphs. Vincent Flanders, author of *Web Pages That Suck,* says the biggest mistake consultants make is "to talk about how wonderful, smart and brilliant they are."[a] The fatal flaw for thousands of such sites is that they are consultant focused, not *client focused.*

4. *Splash pages.* Web sites that incorporate the latest flashy technology—explosive graphics, streaming video intros, and

---

[a] Vincent Flanders' quote is from the interview, "This Month's Featured Master-Mind: Vincent Flanders on Web Pages That Suck," *Management Consulting News* (September 3, 2002). Available from www.managementconsultingnews.com /newsletter_sept_02_final.htm.

Flanders reminds consultants that "people come to your site for one reason: to solve a problem. They don't care if you're wonderful and they probably don't care about much of anything other than "Can you solve my problem now? You've got to convince your visitors that you can solve their problems, so the information you provide should be about that, not about you."

(Continued)

shock ware—may initially be fun, but they quickly grow old. These annoying, graphic-intensive pages are slow to load, waste your visitors' time, and imply that you'll waste even more of their time once they get past the splash page. If you're trying to attract potential clients, cool it on the overly cool.

5. *Errors.* No matter how small, errors send visitors scurrying away with a bad impression of your practice. One visitor to a consulting firm's site commented, "I thought the firm was reputable but I spotted two spelling mistakes right on the home page. How professional is that?" Even the smallest typos can mean a lost opportunity.

6. *Confusing navigation.* If visitors can't easily navigate around your site or can't instantly figure out where they are, they'll quickly exit. Steve Krug, author of *Don't Make Me Think,* a book on Web site usability, says that you "should not do things that force people to think unnecessarily when they're using your site."[b] You want visitors to focus on reading the content, not on trying to navigate your site.

7. *Poor writing:* With the advent of the Web, anyone can be a publisher. But not everyone is a great writer. One consulting firm's site proclaims that its mission "is to connect you with information and resources to achieve your maximum potential." That is so vague that it's not worth saying. Creating prose for the Web is not exactly like writing a memo to your staff. Web site prose must be crisp and easy to read, and must motivate visitors to look at all pages on your site.

---

[b] Steve Krug's quote is from the interview, "Meet the MasterMinds: Common Sense Web Design with Steve Krug," *Management Consulting News* (September 3, 2002). Available from www.managementconsultingnews.com/newsletter_sept_02_final.htm.

Krug goes on to say that the first law of Web site usability is "Don't make me think. I've used it for years with my clients, and it really means exactly what it says: Don't do things that force people to think unnecessarily when they're using your site. I find that most people are quite willing and able to think when it's necessary, but making them do it when there's nothing in it for them (other than compensating for your failure to sort things out properly) tends to be annoying—and worse, confusing."

The information-intensive consulting industry is perfect for Web marketing. Seize on its capabilities to make your site credible, valuable, and easy to use. Tap into the Web's low-cost power to draw leads to your practice and to build your presence in the market.

As the marketing hub of your practice, your Web site is equal parts consulting office, demonstration lab, library, and publicity machine. Its content, appearance, and ease of use show your competence and professionalism.

Your site paints a powerful portrait of your visual identity by reflecting your style, taste, and presentation. It serves as your showroom in cyberspace, a display case for exhibiting your wares. The site provides a platform from which to tell your story, describe your mission, list your clients, and distribute information. It also gives you visibility both within and outside your industry.

Firms can create a repository on their Web sites for their intellectual assets—articles, papers, proposals, studies, surveys, and reports—which prospective clients can examine. These materials help visitors understand how the consultants think and how they tackle problems.

■ TEN CHARACTERISTICS OF A KILLER WEB SITE

1. *Show legitimacy as a business.* You will build credibility with visitors by including such basic information on your site as the physical address of your business and photographs of your offices, or by listing membership in professional and industry associations.

2. *Update content frequently.* Some sites fail to regularly change the content of their site, leaving outdated information about time-sensitive items such as conferences and other special events. Web visitors assign more credibility to sites that are current, or at least demonstrate that they have been recently reviewed.

3. *Encourage action.* On each page of your site, find a way for visitors to interact with you, whether by signing up for a newsletter, requesting a special report, linking to another page on your site, or sending you an e-mail. Your site should engage visitors, not just let them "click and go."

4. *Exchange value for time.* Web site visitors, particularly those looking for consultants, will gladly exchange their time for value and insight. Provide relevant, valuable, and usable content, and prospective clients may put you on their short list. In addition to content such as white papers, some consultants'

sites provide interactive diagnostic tools that help clients measure the impact of issues they're facing.

5. *Provide rapid response.* If you receive an e-mail inquiry from a visitor, follow up immediately, no matter how busy you are. That e-mail inquiry about your services will not improve with age; don't let it get moldy in your e-mailbox.

6. *Keep it simple.* Create your site for clients, not for the artist within you. Make its design simple, intuitive to use, and easy to read. Provide lots of white space on pages because visitors tend to skim pages and seldom read every detail. And stick to a simple, eye-pleasing color palette. Your site layout should be logical. Navigation buttons and features such as newsletter sign-up boxes should be in the same place on all pages. Make it easy to download material by providing explicit instructions and confirming for visitors that they have successfully received the material they downloaded.

7. *Speed doesn't kill.* Make sure each page and link loads quickly, no matter what type of browser or machine a visitor uses. Don't assume that all visitors are using high-speed connections when they access your site. Visitors will leave your site in a heartbeat if your pages load too slowly.

8. *Test it.* Before you launch a new or revised site, ask clients and colleagues to thoroughly test every element. Ask them, Is the site easy to use? Does it provide useful information? Would you go back to it?

9. *Maintain ongoing site quality.* Some consultants create a site just because "we need a site," but then let it languish. Your site should not be an afterthought, but an integral part of your external marketing program. Assign accountability for its long-term strategy and tactical uses to someone in the practice so your firm can take full advantage of the Web's potential.

10. *Go easy on data collection.* On some consultants' sites, visitors must provide pages of information before they can receive a simple white paper. Keep it simple. Ask only for their e-mail addresses, and send them the information they requested. If they find value in your material, they'll call you.

An effective site must contain more than a firm's name, contact information, sales pitch, and eye candy. The best graphics and other splashy features can't make up for meager content. The site must convey how you think, how you operate, and what your perspective is on issues of concern to clients. Provide visitors with the details they seek.

■ THE DEVIL IS IN THE DETAILS

When visitors form an initial impression of your Web site, they will either stay on the site to find out more or move on based on their answers to four simple questions:

1. What does your firm actually do?
2. Do you prove that your firm is able to handle the client's issues?
3. What makes your firm uniquely qualified to solve the client's problems?
4. Have you clearly described the benefits and results that clients can expect?

If you answer these questions to the satisfaction of prospective clients, you'll likely get e-mail or a telephone call. Web site designs vary and each must be structured to reflect your own unique talents and mission. However, all consultants' sites should allow prospective clients to quickly answer those four essential questions.

Remember that your site will serve a diverse audience that may include current and prospective clients, media representatives, researchers, students, other consultants, or aspiring consultants. Try to make the experience easy and valuable for every viewer.

GUERRILLAS AT WORK: SITE CONSTRUCTION

Most consultants focus on developing the content of their Web sites and let computer programmers handle the technical details. Guerrillas stay involved and in control of the construction process to make sure they end up with client-focused sites that include the following sections:

➤ Home
➤ Solutions and results
➤ Case studies and testimonials
➤ How you work with clients
➤ Your story
➤ Alliances and affiliations
➤ Media center
➤ Resource library
➤ Terms of use and privacy policy

■ THERE'S NO PLACE LIKE HOME

Your home page is the most frequently visited page on your site. Your home page is the front door to your practice. It directs visitors to other parts of the site and presents the overall format and design.

As the first page that visitors access, your home page must have visual appeal. It also must be clean and uncluttered. Never incorporate graphic elements that are painfully slow, excessively long, or don't always work. Links to other parts of the site must be clear and easy to follow.

Forget about using sappy welcoming statements on your home page and get straight to the mission at hand. In clear, compelling language, demonstrate to visitors that the content on your site will help them. Emphasize how you can make a dramatic difference in their businesses.

Include your contact information on the home page and on every page of your site. Each page should also contain a link for visitors to sign up to receive your electronic newsletter, or zine, if you publish

GUERRILLA INTELLIGENCE: WHAT'S A BLOG?

A *blog* (short for "Web log") is a Web-based journal. Blogs can be news columns or personal communications; they can focus on one subject or a range of topics. A blog can be part of your Web site or a stand-alone feature. Blogs are not sent to readers. Rather, interested readers find them. Blogs are updated frequently—sometimes daily—with commentary, links, or photographs. Unlike Web site design, creating and updating blogs is easy because most blog software requires no technical background.

Use a blog to keep an updated, personalized message on the home page of your site, or to provide information on the latest developments in your industry. You might want to use a blog to announce a new service, rant about a controversial issue, or solicit client feedback.

You can scan a directory of blogs at www.google.com, www.yahoo.com, and other search engines. Just enter the search term "blog directories" in your browser. Some widely used blogging software tools are Blogger (www.blogger.com), TypePad, and Moveable Type (www.typepad.com). Some blogging products are free and others are offered for a fee.

one. Most important, keep your home page short and simple, while encouraging visitors to review other parts of the site.

■ SOLUTIONS AND RESULTS

Most consultants' Web sites drone on about their "world class" services, "best practices," and "methodologies." Clients don't buy services; they buy solutions. Guerrillas dump the consultant-speak and focus on providing solutions. Clients may not be interested in the latest high-tech inventory management system, but they do want to hear how you can help them manage inventory better.

So talk about the solutions you offer, giving real-life examples of the results you helped clients achieve. For example, "We helped Allied Rock improve working capital by 30 percent and cut supply costs by 22 percent in four months." Follow up each statement with a link to a case study that summarizes how you worked with that client to achieve those results.

GUERRILLA TACTIC: GET DOWN TO BRASS TACKS

State your solutions and results as specifically as possible. Use your clients' names, if you have permission. Everyone pays more attention to and retains information about names they recognize.

Many consultants mistakenly believe that by describing their services broadly, they will appeal to a wider audience and acquire more clients. Actually, the opposite is true. The less specific you are, the less likely it is that clients will think of you when they need help with a particular problem. By being ambiguous, you also might attract clients who wouldn't be a good fit for your practice, which—at the very least—will waste your time and energy.

Providing details on solutions and results serves two important purposes, one for prospective clients and the other for you. For clients, it demonstrates what you have to offer and how you are different from your competitors. For the consultant, it weeds out those clients who may find your material interesting, but don't need the particular solutions you provide.

■ CASE STUDIES AND TESTIMONIALS

Case studies have long been a staple of consultants' proposals and, more recently, their Web sites. But many clients breeze right by them, believing them to be self-serving, puffed-up promotions of consultants' accomplishments. As a result, case studies have become an anemic tool for winning client work, instead of the powerhouse-marketing tool they could be.

Include links on your Web site to case studies for your most challenging and successful assignments. Make it easy for visitors to download them. These documents can answer the number one question clients ask consultants: How will your team work with our team to achieve the results we need? Case studies also clarify approaches, strategies, and resources that you have successfully employed on other projects.

Infuse the materials that you post on your site with a sense of the challenges and obstacles involved. Explain what, why, and how you and the client attacked issues. Always stress that the solutions came from working together.

Keep case studies short—no longer than one or two pages. For each case study, name the client company, if possible. Some clients prefer confidentiality, and you must honor that trust. But case studies have more punch if the company is named, instead of being referred to as a "large, industry-leading plumbing supply client." Exclude the name of your contact in the client's company, but be willing to disclose it in response to inquiries.

SEVEN ELEMENTS OF A GUERRILLA CASE STUDY

1. Tell a story; don't just list facts.
2. Place the client's success, not yours, at the center of the story.
3. Define the problem the client faced and your role in solving the problem.
4. Describe how you worked with the client's team to achieve results.
5. Don't overstate results.
6. Keep it short.
7. Provide access to references whenever possible.

Include a limited number of testimonials on your site. Instead of an extensive testimonial section, post a list of all your clients and let visitors select whomever they wish to call. They can give you the names they select and you can arrange for the calls. Testimonials are of questionable value because everyone knows you won't let them near a bad reference. However, visitors expect to see them on your site and some will still be impressed by notable names on your list.

■ HOW YOU WORK WITH CLIENTS

Another critical question for prospective clients is "How will the consulting team interact with us on the project?" Devote a page on your site to show how you work with clients. This page does not define the tools, methodologies, and approaches you use—it describes how you work with clients on projects.

Many clients know they have problems, but they worry that hiring consultants will give them even greater headaches. They may have good reason to worry that a pack of disruptive consultants planted in the middle of already overcrowded offices will sap productivity and monopolize key employees' time.

Use case studies to illustrate that you know how to avoid disrupting clients' operations. Some consultants never leave their offices to visit clients, while others move right in with the client and remain there for months and even years.

Before they sign on to work with you, all potential clients want to know what the projects will cost and how long they will take. Most clients realize it is impossible to provide that information until a proposal has been completed. In the meantime, though, they will want to know the answers to other questions:

➤ What is the typical size of a project team?

➤ Will client staff serve on teams?

➤ If so, how much of their time will be involved?

➤ Will staff need training?

➤ How will you administer projects?

➤ What are your reporting and communication policies?

➤ How do you determine when the project has been completed?

➤ What tools and methods do you generally use?

This section of the site helps clients understand your firm's personality and culture. For many clients, these attributes are among the top criteria for selecting consultants.

■ WHAT'S YOUR STORY?

As mentioned, clients are not as interested in the pedigrees of your consultants as in their results. Even so, you have to include some personal information on your site about your key consultants and your practice. Tell visitors who you are, what you do, and describe your background and achievements. Detail how and why your practice was formed, how it grew, and list its accomplishments. Show how your clients have helped you succeed and include some of the hurdles you have overcome.

Make your story the personal, noncorporate, part of your Web site. Give visitors a sense of the people behind the practice. Use this page to stress the human element of your practice so that visitors can identify with real people who care, and do not feel as if they are dealing with a faceless corporation. If possible, include pictures of your staff, with short statements about their backgrounds, the clients they have served, the awards they have won, and some of their personal interests.

■ ALLIANCES AND AFFILIATIONS

Many consulting firms have powerful alliances with universities, research groups, and other consultancies that add depth to the consulting team and value for clients. Alliances with strong partners enhance the image of a practice, as people tend to judge us by the company we keep.

Particular alliances can also help firms fill in the gaps in the solutions they offer. If a firm needs additional expertise in designing new product packaging, an alliance with a prestigious professor who focuses on materials development can mean the difference between winning and losing a project. Consultants should seek affiliations that can help their clients and stress those affiliations on their Web sites.

If you have alliances with highly recognized individuals and organizations, post them on your Web site. Also include any memberships in industry or professional associations, but don't expect clients to be overly impressed by these credentials.

■ MEDIA CENTER

Your media center is the source for press releases and other information about your practice. Its purpose is to make it as simple as possible for members of the media to acquire newsworthy items about your firm. Since this page targets professionals, keep the information fresh or the media will leave your site and you'll lose potentially valuable publicity.

The information in your site's media center must be easy to access through e-mail and print. Your media kit should include, at a minimum:

➤ *Press releases.* Provide a list of all your firm's press releases, listing the most recent first. Create links and make them printer friendly so that visitors can download each press release. Give the name of the member of your firm who handles publicity and public relations, along with contact information.

➤ *Articles written about the firm.* List all articles written about your firm, the subject of those articles, and the publication that they appeared in. Include all articles that were published in the past several years. Provide links that allow visitors to download articles and easily print them.

➤ *Company history.* Write the company history in story form and detail the genesis and steps involved in its becoming successful. Don't make it a blatant commercial. Stick to the facts, but give it human interest by stressing the role that key personnel and clients played in building the firm.

➤ *Basic financial information.* Provide background on the size of the practice, number of consultants, clients, and revenue (if possible). Some firms are uncomfortable publishing financial information but if you keep it current and accurate, it gives clients a good idea of the breadth of your firm.

➤ *Biographies of key personnel.* Consultants' biographies should stress their accomplishments, their positions as experts, and details on their areas of expertise. It should also give their backgrounds, training, and experience as well as their social and community activities. All bios should be written in a personable tone.

➤ *Articles and appearances.* List all articles that your firm's members have published and the subject of each article. Provide printer-friendly links that allow visitors to download copies. If you speak frequently, include a list of your speaking engagements for the past two years. Note if you were the keynote or featured speaker. If you speak less frequently, list your major appearances over the past five years.

➤ *Speaker information.* Give speaker information for each firm member who gives presentations. Briefly describe speaking topics, the duration of presentations, target audiences, and the results achieved. State that copies of speeches are downloadable, provide links to them, and make sure they are printer friendly. Provide, or offer to provide, audio or video recordings of all speeches and presentations.

➤ *Calendar of upcoming events.* Provide a calendar that shows the dates, times, and places of upcoming events that the firm or its members will sponsor or participate in. The calendar should list presentations, workshops, seminars, interviews, and appearances. Create downloadable links that allow visitors to obtain more information about each event.

➤ *Endorsements and testimonials.* If you decide to include endorsements, provide the best endorsements you have received from the most well-known and respected endorsers. Do not include more than two pages of endorsements.

➤ *Client list.* List your clients' names. You may choose to sort this list by industry or alphabetically.

➤ *Frequently asked questions.* Present frequently asked questions (FAQs) and their answers. Be creative; include questions that clients and the media ask and anticipate others they might ask. Include questions on issues facing the industry and on recent changes and developments that are affecting the industry. Keep your answers short. Use this section to show your knowledge, creativity, and problem-solving ability. Also write questions on the background of your firm, its size, areas of specialization, and objectives, even if it repeats material provided in other sections.

Keep in mind that the information and material you include in the media center is intended to reach potential clients. Make members of the media feel welcome on your site so they will understand what your practice is about and give you good press.

■ RESOURCE LIBRARY

Knowledge is the consultants' currency; it is their stock-in-trade and what clients pay hefty fees to obtain. Very few consulting firms hold

GUERRILLA INTELLIGENCE: YOUR INTELLECTUAL STOCKPILE

Build a store of highly relevant intellectual assets that can become part of your marketing activities. The top items form the content base of your Web site:

- ➤ Articles and compilations of articles
- ➤ Presentation and speech transcripts, slides, and videos
- ➤ Client case studies
- ➤ White papers and special reports
- ➤ Survey results
- ➤ Client and industry interviews
- ➤ Archives of newsletters, zines, and blogs
- ➤ Webinars
- ➤ Workbooks or Assessment Guides
- ➤ Perspective pieces on industry issues
- ➤ E-books
- ➤ Methodologies and tools
- ➤ Audiotapes of speeches or articles
- ➤ Book excerpts

many physical assets. After its consultants, a firm's most valuable property is its intellectual assets—its stockpile of collective wisdom, experience, tools, methods, and other intangibles. Your site's resource library is the repository of the assets you wish to share with clients, prospective clients, and the media.

The best resource libraries provide both consultant-developed material and access to other independent thinkers on the topics covered. So your library should also include lists of relevant reference books, academic experts, journal articles, industry and research site links, and other resources that will allow clients to round out their knowledge.

■ TERMS OF USE

We live in a litigious world. So, your site must have a page that describes the terms of use that visitors to the site must observe. On this page, focus on your privacy policy and state that you are not liable for how visitors use the information they obtain from the site. Review

GUERRILLA TACTIC: SHARE YOUR SECRETS

Some consultants resist sharing their intellectual assets over the Web for fear of losing their competitive edge. The world is awash in so much information that you will look stingy and paranoid if you don't give up at least some of your secrets to let clients see how you really work, what you know, and what you can do. If you're uncomfortable posting all your intellectual assets, by all means, hold some back. Check other sites' information-sharing practices to see how they handle the dilemma.

Clients know that people must implement changes, and without experienced consultants at the helm, costly, time-consuming disasters frequently occur. That is why they hire consultants to implement the ideas and approaches they believe will best solve their problems. Most clients are unlikely just to take your ideas and run. If they do, be there to bail them out when they get in over their heads.

several sites to understand the terms-of-use clause and then decide if you need legal counsel to help draft a statement that will protect your practice.

■ BUILDING YOUR WEB SITE

Trust is the key to whether prospective clients race past your site or stay on it. Most visitors want to see evidence that you have a trustworthy site, even if they haven't read its content.

A study by Princeton Survey Research Associates[2] indicated that only 29 percent of Internet users trust Web sites that sell products or services. Compare that with the 58 percent of survey respondents who trust newspaper and television news, and the 47 percent who trust the federal government. Since 80 percent of Web users believe it is "very important to be able to trust the information on a Web site," trust must be a major design component in every page you publish.

Seven guidelines will help make visitors comfortable with your site and your practice:

1. Clearly state your privacy policy.
2. Give access to visitors' e-mail addresses only to editors and others involved in creating and maintaining the site.

GUERRILLA TACTIC: SYNDICATE YOUR CONTENT

Draw potential clients to your Web site by syndicating the headlines of your zine, blogs, and other site content. All you need to do is add a small bit of computer code to your site and summarize your important content, and those headlines will be picked up by news syndication services called RSS (Really Simple Syndication). Web-based news aggregators sweep sites with RSS and deliver headlines to readers who have requested information on specific topics.

RSS is a spam-free, filter-free way to let interested readers know what is on your Web site. MarketingSherpa.com points out that the 250,000 people now using RSS are ". . . active information-seekers, not passive e-mail readers. And, their numbers will grow rapidly as RSS becomes more user-friendly and as more people get fed up with spam and irrelevant e-mail."

Here are two sources for further details on RSS: NewsGator (www.newsgator.com) and Bloglines (www.bloglines.com). The technology and services for RSS are changing rapidly. To read up on the subject, you can type "RSS" into your Web browser and take it from there.

3. If advertising is on the site, prominently label it as such.

4. Describe any financial relationships you have with other firms, organizations, or vendors.

5. Provide sources for research and links to source documents, if possible.

6. List those responsible for the creation of site content.

7. Promptly correct errors in a prominent place on the site.

Don't expect to impress visitors if your site is little more than an online telephone book or a sales brochure. The clients you hope to attract and the peers you want to impress are savvy businesspeople, and they want solid information. Don't waste their time with marketing babble.

GUERRILLA TACTIC: CAN YOUR WEB SITE PASS THE FIVE-CLIENT TEST?

Before you release your site to the public, ask five of your clients to review it. Ask them to be brutally honest (well, maybe constructively critical) in their reviews and to answer these seven questions:

1. What is distinctive about the site?
2. Is the content valuable?
3. Does the site convey a clear understanding of what your consultancy does?
4. Would the site's content be helpful in addressing clients' issues?
5. Is it focused on clients' needs?
6. Would you bookmark the site?
7. Would it encourage you to call?

The results of the client reviews will tell you how to make your site an effective marketing tool. Repeat the test at regular intervals to be sure your site stays fresh and relevant.

Remember that guerrilla clients demand more. They want professional sites that give them solid information about who you are, what you do, how you think and, most importantly, how you can benefit them. Providing anything less on your Web site will eliminate you from their list of candidates for their consulting projects.

Chapter 7

Boost Your Web
Presence with a Zine

In 1971, an unassuming computer engineer named Ray Tomlinson sent the world's first e-mail message—to himself. Tomlinson and the others who tinkered with this invention sensed that e-mail could have practical uses, but they had no idea it would lead to a revolution in how people communicate.

Now, more than 30 billion e-mail messages are sent on the Internet every day, and e-mail has become a dominant force in our lives. According to a survey by META Group, 80 percent of the businesspeople polled said that e-mail is a more effective form of business communication than the telephone.[1] And 75 percent of executives surveyed expect e-mail to be their primary source of business information by 2005.[2]

E-mailboxes are direct conduits to buyers of goods and services, and marketers have been so aggressive that government agencies have stepped in to protect consumers. One offspring of e-mail—the electronic newsletter, or *zine*—has exploded as a dynamic marketing vehicle.

WHAT IS A ZINE?

A zine (pronounced "zeen") is an electronic newsletter; an e-mail-based publication that is sent on a specified schedule to subscribers who have agreed in advance to receive it.

■ TO ZINE OR NOT TO ZINE

Because zines are everywhere these days, consultants may think it's mandatory to have one. Not true. Zines are not for everybody. Producing a zine takes talent and resources that may be better spent on other marketing activities, such as updating your Web site, delivering speeches, or conducting surveys.

Carefully weigh the possible benefits of a zine against its challenges. If you decide against it, you can still speak directly to clients on your Web site with blogs, articles, reports, and case studies. Or, you might prefer to publish a hard-copy newsletter instead of an electronic one.

■ THE UPSIDE OF ZINES

A zine is a low-cost, high-impact marketing tool that can be a building block in an integrated guerrilla marketing campaign. At a fraction of the cost of other tools, such as direct mail, a zine can heighten your visibility in the marketplace, build your reputation as an expert, and open dialogues with prospective clients. A zine has enormous potential for generating leads for your practice.

The continuous nature of zines is ideal for consultants because so much of their business depends on building long-term, ongoing relationships. The continuity of zines gives guerrillas a systematic way to remain in contact with clients by providing them with vital, timely information, analysis, and feedback. A zine keeps you on clients' radar without the intrusiveness of telephone calls or the need for in-person visits.

Clients are eager for knowledge that can help them solve pressing problems, find out what is going on in their industry, and learn what the competition is up to. But the pace of business is fast, and most clients don't have the opportunity or the perspective for the independent analysis that an expert can provide. Zines can benefit clients by summarizing relevant information and delivering it to them quickly.

Consulting projects tend to have long sales cycles. A zine can help you make a strong impression during that process, and can provide ready topics for discussion with clients from initial meetings about a project, through the proposal and negotiation phase, and beyond.

Zines help you turn prospects into clients and clients into advocates. They allow you to maintain ongoing dialogue with readers that you would not otherwise have. You have complete editorial control, so you can customize your zine quickly in response to the feedback you receive.

The search for zine content will stimulate you to think more creatively about how the issues of the day influence your clients' success. That search will give you a focus and point of reference as you sift through the overwhelming amount of information that affects the business world today. The insights you develop in the process not only will make your zine valuable to clients, but will be equally useful in all your other marketing activities, from speeches to proposal writing.

You can publish a zine with little cost and minimal resources. All you need to start is a computer, an e-mail program, and subscribers. At first, it will take time to build your zine, but as you progress, it will become easier. You always have the option of outsourcing some parts of the zine or the entire publication (more on this later).

■ ARE YOU UP TO THE ZINE CHALLENGE?

Even a one- or two-page zine takes considerable effort to produce. And you will need patience to make a zine effectively generate leads for your practice. With a zine, you're entering the publishing business, which is markedly different from, and will take time away from, your consulting business.

To publish a zine, you must commit resources to design and periodically update it. You need access to great content or the ability to develop it—you must have enough content to fill each issue. It takes writing and editing skills plus a bit of artistry to gather and analyze information, write articles, and lay out a zine.

It takes discipline to publish every issue of a zine on time and to respond quickly to questions and feedback from readers. You must also be willing to promote your zine and be patient while your circulation grows. The continuous publishing cycle of a zine means that you or someone in your firm will always be working on the next issue. That can make you feel as if you've got a perpetual, low-grade fever.

The most daunting challenge of zines is competing for clients' attention with the flood of e-mail they already receive. You will have to fight, not only to win a place in their e-mailboxes, but also to get your subscribers to open and read your zine.

Most businesspeople today are sophisticated users of e-mail and the Internet. Of the 60 million U.S. workers who have Internet access, 98 percent of them have e-mail. They are selective about what they read and are quick to hit the delete button—even if they subscribe to an e-mail publication. In fact, according to research by Quris, Inc., over 40 percent of permission-based e-mail is deleted before being read.[3]

■ STEP UP TO THE PLATE

To hit a home run, your zine must generate leads for your practice. For guerrillas, that's the definition of a successful zine; leads are the justification for your zine's existence.

■ CREATE TRUST

You must build trusting relationships with your subscribers just as you do with your clients. Subscribers have to trust your integrity as a publisher. They must be convinced that you are honest in reporting

> ## GUERRILLA ALERT: NO SPAMMING ALLOWED
>
> Guerrillas know that they gain nothing from sending un-wanted e-mail, including zines. Learn about and follow both the spirit and the letter of the laws that govern e-mail. In your zine and on your Web site, state clearly how to subscribe and unsubscribe to the zine, and make it easy to do. Be sure to use a "double opt-in" system so subscribers have to (1) sign up for your zine and (2) confirm that they want to receive it. Also, you must include the editor's name and *physical* address in a logical place in the publication.

and interpreting the facts. They must have complete confidence that your content is accurate and up to date. Readers must feel comfortable relaying information in your zine to others and using it for business decisions.

Trust is vital to e-mail users, especially with the proliferation of spam. Having subscribers' e-mail addresses creates a confidential relationship. Subscribers must feel assured that you will respect and protect their privacy and not disclose their e-mail addresses or personal information without their express consent. A written privacy policy is essential. Be sure to include a link to that policy in your zine.

For subscribers to trust you, they must respect you as an authority in your area of consulting, as a writer, and as a publisher. They must believe in the quality of your zine as a trustworthy source of information. To keep subscribers' trust, maintain that quality with every issue, and always deliver your zine to their e-mailboxes at the scheduled time. You want loyal readers, and loyalty follows trust.

■ DELIVER VALUE

To reap benefits, your zine must provide real value to subscribers. Without value, your zine is nothing more than junk mail. Many zines are indistinguishable from sales brochures; they exist solely to promote the publishers' products and services. Your zine won't keep subscribers if you only publish promotional material that masquerades as news. Instead of sell, sell, sell, guerrillas inform, inform, inform.

For many readers, the most valuable feature of your zine will be your analysis of how recent developments could affect their industries and businesses. Inform them about new laws that might affect

> ### GUERRILLA TACTIC: MINIMIZE SELF-PROMOTION
>
> A definite line separates a useful, informative zine from a pro-motional piece. While savvy readers expect and tolerate a certain amount of promotion, limit self-promotion in your zine to 10 percent or less of each issue. Otherwise, readers will think of your zine as a blatant sales pitch and delete it. Don't spend half of the zine promoting your current seminar or your latest book. Let the value of your content promote your practice and products.
>
> The intent of a zine is to pull clients toward your practice, not push your latest service on them. Concentrate on intelligently discussing the topics of greatest interest to your readers. Provide links to your Web site in selected spots in the zine so readers can find out more about you and what you have to offer.

them, judicial or regulatory decisions, mergers, acquisitions, financial trends, breakthroughs in technology, or upcoming events. But don't just report decisions and statistics; examine the implications of events and trends for your readers.

Zine subscribers also value interviews, columns by featured guests, articles on new strategies or business processes, individual and company profiles, or success stories. Here are some more suggestions for content:

➤ Present a problem and suggest a solution.

➤ Tell a story about a consulting project.

➤ Offer tips, alerts, or market intelligence.

➤ Conduct a poll and report the results in a subsequent issue.

➤ Point out resources, including books, research studies, and Web sites.

➤ Editorialize and analyze.

➤ Ask subscribers to contribute articles (within your editorial guidelines).

Your zine can include any of the preceding elements, or you can come up with other ideas. But develop a high-value formula for content that works for you and stick with it. And be sure to archive past issues of your zines on your Web site, indexed by subject categories.

■ STIMULATE DIALOGUE WITH READERS

The point of your zine is to engage your audience in conversation and build relationships. Many zines are boring and don't provoke much reaction. You should ask for feedback from readers in every issue. You might want to include a question at the end of featured articles like, "Was this item useful to you?" and provide an e-mail feedback link for response.

It's essential to get feedback on every aspect of your zine, including content, quality, format, and frequency of publication. You should regularly ask subscribers for their opinions on these elements. But asking for feedback is not enough.

Guerrillas stimulate responses from readers with a combination of personality, style, and point of view. Readers are more likely to respond to your zine if they feel that they know who you are. So give your zine a human voice; write your zine in a personal tone as if you are speaking to friends. Think of yourself as a radio or television show host whose listeners tune in because they like the host's engaging personality.

Make your articles and features lively; get to the point quickly and avoid stilted language and corporate-speak. Assume that your readers are intelligent and never talk down to them or take them lightly. When appropriate, inject humor into your zine—but never force it. Do:

➤ Include plenty of white space in your zine to make it easier to read. Tightly packed prose, however brilliant, is intimidating and less likely to be read by busy professionals.

➤ Bullet important points so they jump off the page.

➤ Create sidebars and emphasize key words.

➤ For longer articles, put brief summaries in your zine with links to the full texts, which can be stored on your Web site. Readers who want to read the full versions can do so.

➤ Avoid superboring features like statements from your CEO or president.

Your zine should be visually engaging, with some graphics and color to liven up the look of the publication. Easy does it, though—your readers are all using different hardware and software to access e-mail. Extensive use of graphics, colors, or special formatting can make a zine so slow or difficult to load that readers may delete your zine before it sees the light of day.

You'll know you're on the right track if your zine produces feedback from readers. When readers want to discuss issues you've raised,
consider it a compliment and respond as soon as possible. Prompt,
thoughtful responses build goodwill, loyal readers, and eventually
clients. Use feedback to discover what your readers want and give it
to them.

■ EXUDE PROFESSIONALISM

Zines must be professional in appearance. Design matters—in fact,
it's critical. Readers want publications that are well laid out, easy to
read, and don't look cheesy or homemade. They expect zines to be delivered on schedule and to load quickly and easily.

Guerrillas want wide circulation for their zines. An unprofessional looking issue or one with even a minor inaccuracy can damage your credibility and your reputation.

Readers also appreciate ease of access. Provide a prominent link
to a printer-friendly, text version of your zine on your Web site so
subscribers can download and print it at their convenience. They will
then be able to read your zine anywhere and at any time, and pass it
on to others.

The professional image of your zine depends on consistency of
editorial standards. Consider including a statement of editorial policies at the end of your zine. Be consistent in the following areas.

➤ Content

Whatever content formula you choose for your zine, use essentially
that same formula and place features in the same place in every

issue. Readers like the familiar, the predictable. Make your zine error-free. Always double-check facts, figures, grammar, report or book titles, and the spelling of people's names. Create a style sheet for your zine and distribute it to everyone who works on the publication.

➤ Frequency of Publication

Zines can be published on any schedule, including weekly, monthly, or quarterly. To maintain a continuous presence in your readers' minds, you should publish at least once per month. The trick is to strike a balance between maintaining visibility and inundating your subscribers with more than they want. In a survey by Quris, Inc., 68 percent of respondents cited "too frequent" mailings as their top grievance about e-mail marketers.[4]

As to what day of the week is best for publishing a zine, opinions differ among the experts, with little hard data to support their preferences. Pick a weekday, publish on that same day every time, and indicate in your zine what day that will be. You might want to indicate what time zone governs your publishing schedule, as your zine may appear on a different day in some countries.

➤ Length

Most zines are two to eight pages long. The length of your zine will depend on how much information will be regularly available to you and the frequency of publication you choose. If you decide to publish your zine every week, even one page will be a lot of work. For guerrillas, a tight, two-page zine is usually sufficient. Aim for the same length with every issue; don't mail two pages one month and ten pages the next.

➤ Format

Publish your zine in Hypertext Markup Language (HTML) rather than text format or Portable Document Format (PDF). These days, 90 percent of browsers can read HTML, and your printer-friendly, text version will take care of those that can't. The HTML format offers significant advantages in design features and measuring and reporting capabilities.

Text format is harder to work with, has much less visual appeal, and provides no reliable way to find out how many subscribers are reading your zine. PDF looks better and preserves the format and graphics of original documents.

The HTML format allows you to track important data, such as how many readers actually open your zine (open rates), how many click through to your Web site from your zine (click-through rates), how many forward your zine to others (forward rates), and how many readers subscribe and unsubscribe.

Whatever format you choose, keep in mind that industry and readers' standards for e-mail publications are getting higher all the time. Subscribers will have little patience for zines that don't look right on their e-mail programs or don't correctly display on their monitors.

➤ Advertising Policy

Marketers frequently place ads in successful zines. However, like self-promotion, outside ads can detract from the image of your zine. They can also raise questions about conflict of interest on your part. Ads can defray the cost of producing your zine, but they may not be worth it in the end. Instead, propose link exchanges with reputable marketers of products and services that would be of interest to your readers. If you do take ads, identify them clearly as paid advertising.

➤ Subscription Fees

You will attract more subscribers if you don't charge for your zine. You may need to consider a fee if the expenses of designing and publishing your zine prove too great a drain on the resources of your practice. Some consultants don't charge for their zines, but give readers brief summaries of their articles in the zine, and then charge for access to the full text. Unless your full report is quite substantial, most readers will find this practice annoying.

If your zine is in great demand, you may want to charge a high fee for subscriptions to limit your audience to a select group. For most zines, though, free access is the best way to get and keep subscribers.

➤ Administrative Matters

You or someone in your practice must consistently attend to administrative activities for your zine. Make it easy for readers to subscribe, unsubscribe, put their subscriptions on hold for vacations or other reasons, change their e-mail addresses, and tell you what they think.

People expect speed, so respond to change requests within 24 hours. You want to keep the goodwill even of those who unsubscribe—they may be back. Don't ask for too much information from people signing up for your zine; keep it to a minimum. Send standard, but polite and personable letters to confirm any changes a subscriber makes.

For initial subscriptions, your confirmation letter should welcome readers, tell them when to expect your zine to arrive, and how they can unsubscribe. You also should refer them to your privacy and editorial policies. Stay on top of administrative matters to make a good impression on your readers.

Consistency with all the preceding elements will ensure that your zine gets the respect it deserves. Another way to improve the professional aspect of your publication is by outsourcing some of its production.

➤ Outsourcing

Guerrillas emphasize collaboration, and publishing a zine can be much easier if you have help. Do you have the resources to produce your entire zine in house? If not, many services are available to help at reasonable costs. The two most likely candidates for outsourcing are graphic design and list management.

Hire a talented graphic designer to translate your vision into an easy-to-use template for your zine. Many designers will help you through the process the first time or two and will set you up with Web-based tools that allow you to build your zine with ease, step by step. Some designers also provide services to help you find content for your zine. Design services are not that expensive and an appealing design is well worth the money.

Find a competent list management service to handle subscribe and unsubscribe requests, store your confirmation letters, host your zine, send it out on your signal, and keep statistics for you. A service will keep your subscriber list up to date; handle duplicate subscriptions, e-mail address changes, necessary interfaces with various Internet service providers (ISPs), bounces (returned or undeliverable e-mail); and allow you to send mail to subscribers with a click of the mouse. Good list managers are preapproved by the major ISPs (on what's called a "White List"), so your zine won't be filtered or blocked by e-mail programs as spam.

GUERRILLA INTELLIGENCE: OUTSOURCING

Publishing a zine can be challenging; unforeseen problems always seem to arise. Once you commit, you have obligated yourself to continue publishing your zine and that can be hard work. To ease your burden, consider outsourcing the graphic design of your zine and the ongoing management of your list of subscribers. Find reliable sources of help and stick with them. Good help is hard to find.

List management services are economical and will free up your time for more important activities, like finding and writing the content of your zine. Plus, a service takes the most mundane aspects of being a publisher off your hands.

Outsourcing design and list management will add to the professionalism of your zine. You may want to consider outsourcing more aspects of your publication, but be sure to maintain editorial control. And don't get too far removed from your readers or your zine will not provide an opportunity to establish relationships with them.

➤ Get Legit

Add the stamp of authenticity to your zine by registering the publication with the appropriate agencies. Apply for an International Standard Serial Number (ISSN) from the Library of Congress, and send copies of your zine to the Library's Register of Copyrights. Place a link in your zine to the statement of terms and conditions of use on your Web site. Include copyright and ISSN notations in your zine.

■ HIT YOUR TARGET MARKETS

Even if you publish the world's most engaging, valuable, professional-quality zine, it won't do your practice any good if no one knows it's available. Promotion is essential to reach potential readers and to build a base of subscribers. That effort starts, naturally, on your Web site.

Include a prominent sign-up box for your zine on every page of your site. If subscriptions are free, make that clear. In the text of your home page, highlight the main features of the current issue of your zine and tout the coming attractions for subsequent issues. Also, make it easy to access the archives of past issues from the home page.

Avail yourself of the many free ways to promote your zine. Use free directory listings and propose link exchanges with other consultants and industry associations. Ask clients to list your zine as a resource on their sites or intranets. If you conduct interviews, ask interviewees to add links on their sites to that issue of your zine. You can also take the following steps:

➤ Write articles for other publications and include in your signature file your Web site address and zine name.

➤ Include the basics about your zine on your business cards and in speech and presentation materials.

➤ Make hard copies of your zines to distribute at meetings, conferences, and conventions; keep a stack of the current issue on your desk and in the reception area of your office.

➤ Tell friends, relatives, and colleagues about your zine. Ask them to sign up and to spread the word.

Especially in the start-up phase, it's worth the investment to list your zine with zine directories, major Web search engines like Google, and on other Web sites, such as Business.com. You will have to pay small fees for some of these listings, but your investment will pay dividends in the form of new subscribers. You can also pay for subscribers by making arrangements with companies that promote zines and send e-mail subscribers to you. Often, though, these subscribers are untargeted and not likely to become clients, so tread lightly with this option.

■ CREATE A REALISTIC BUDGET

Promotion is not your only zine expense, but it will be an ongoing cost. Create a realistic budget for your publication that includes design (including periodic modifications), preparation, list administration, technical assistance, promotion, and content (for example, if you have to pay for access to reports). Keep track of what you spend so you will be able to accurately judge the success of your zine.

■ MEASURE SUCCESS

After putting forth the effort of publishing a zine, how will you know whether it is working? Sometimes, you will know that business came to you from your interactions with subscribers. More often, you won't be able to see obvious connections. Since lead generation is the primary goal of your zine, the best way to gauge success is by keeping a close eye on statistics, which your list management service will track.

Monitor open rates, click-through rates, forward rates, and unsubscribe rates on a regular basis. Keep a record of all feedback from readers. These data will indicate whether your readers value the zine. If you see a negative trend, revise your zine until you get the results you want.

Chapter 8

Talking Heads

The Cost of Free Publicity

Media outlets are always on the hunt for new content, and consultants are a ready source of fresh topics and perspectives. But, committing the time and energy to cultivate media relationships, prepare newsworthy material, and train for and make appearances means that being a talking head is anything but free.

And contrary to conventional wisdom, in this era of 24/7 news, there *is* such a thing as bad publicity. Just ask 2004 presidential hopeful Howard Dean. One overzealous speech after the Iowa caucuses—replayed and talked about over and over again—damaged his image at a critical time in his campaign.

WHAT IS PUBLICITY?

Random House Webster's Unabridged Dictionary defines publicity as "the measures, process or business of securing public notice." Consultants might define publicity as free media exposure for their practices.

If you want notoriety, any publicity will do. But like all marketing tools, the purpose of publicity for guerrillas is to grow their practices. Guerrillas look for results, not glitter.

> ## WHAT'S THE POINT OF YOUR PUBLICITY?
>
> Your publicity program could include the following objectives:
>
> ➤ Developing your firm's market identity
> ➤ Building your networks—of potential clients, collaborators, industry contacts, and media representatives
> ➤ Identifying leads for new projects
> ➤ Winning new clients
> ➤ Giving something back to the community

To capture a worthwhile return on your investments, your publicity campaign must have a well-designed strategy and be skillfully executed. In keeping with the "One Size Fits None" principle of guerrilla marketing, consultants must first decide what role, if any, publicity will play in their marketing plans, and they must decide on the objectives of publicity for their practices. Both will vary from firm to firm.

Some consulting firms make publicity the center of their marketing efforts; others just react when a media request is lobbed over the transom. For some firms, it makes sense to have a small publicity program running at all times. Or, you may decide that you don't want any media exposure. Part of the decision involves cost, in both time and money. But the role of publicity may also depend on the type of consulting you do—whether the business you are in lends itself well to media exposure and if you stand to gain from it.

If you decide to pursue publicity, developing objectives for your program is critical for two reasons: first, so that when you're in the spotlight you can remind yourself why the heck you agreed to an interview; and second, so you'll be able measure results.

■ ASK WHAT PUBLICITY CAN DO FOR YOU

Publicity offers tremendous benefits for consultants because it can generate a high degree of trust. People tend to give greater credence to items they read in newspapers, hear on the radio, and see on television because they are provided by independent sources that the audience perceives as being objective. The mere fact that you appear on television or are interviewed by the press automatically positions you as an expert in the minds of most people.

Publicity can produce extraordinary benefits for consultants who use it skillfully. In addition to establishing you as an expert, it can create leads for your practice, build your visibility in your industry, and generate business. Though not really free, publicity can be less expensive than other forms of promotion, such as advertising and direct mail.

Media coverage can strengthen your other marketing materials. Use the publicity you receive to enhance your client presentations and proposals and to add punch to your Web site. Reprint articles in which you were interviewed or featured and distribute them at speaking engagements, at industry functions, and at meetings with your clients. A big plus of publicity is that it has a long shelf life; it can lodge in peoples' memories and pop up long after a media event.

■ ARE CONSULTANTS IDEAL MEDIA DARLINGS?

Scan any major publication or periodical and you're likely to find a consultant quoted. Consultants are natural sources for the media because they have

- ➤ specialized expertise;
- ➤ independent opinions;
- ➤ strong communication skills;
- ➤ documentation to substantiate their statements;
- ➤ well-reasoned positions and insights.

On the flip side, though many consultants are highly informed experts in their areas, they are often too long-winded for the media. Consultants are used to giving clients what they want—detailed answers and thorough, well-reasoned analyses. That mode of communication is suitable for clients, but makes consultants poor interview subjects. What works for the media is not dry recitation of facts, but short, snappy, direct replies that instantly connect with audiences.

Guerrillas train themselves in the art of media presentation to make sure the media will value their input.

■ CONSIDER THE TRADE-OFFS

Although you don't have to buy airtime or pay when features about you run in newspapers, getting publicity isn't simple and doesn't bear fruit overnight. You'll need repeated media exposures to gain the visibility that will get clients' attention. And keep in mind that publicity items don't stay in your control: Once representatives of the media have an item, they can do whatever they want with it.

To obtain results, you must learn about publicity, cultivate your media presentation skills, and build and sustain media relationships. You also have to write and distribute articles, press releases, media kits, and publicity materials. As with all marketing tactics, guerrillas look carefully at the trade-offs between the benefits publicity can provide and the time and effort it takes away from other marketing efforts and client service.

Be patient and persistent. Don't waste your time trying to get publicity on a one-shot basis; it simply won't work. If you participate in an exceptional event or development, you may get your 15 minutes of fame, but the hoopla will die down quickly and you will end up essentially where you began.

■ THE COST OF FREE PUBLICITY

To integrate publicity into your consulting practice, you must expend time finding, courting, and developing solid relations with the right media people. You also may incur costs for media training as well as for preparing and distributing materials to the media. Media training is essential because in addition to covering the news, the media wants to give its audience highly entertaining features. If you are a well-trained subject, you'll make yourself substantially more attractive to the media.

Hiring an expert to help you learn about getting publicity can be expensive. In the beginning, you may want to hire a public relations consultant to teach you how to create media lists, write press releases, and use appropriate directories, as well as instruct you in proper media etiquette. Books such as *Guerrilla Publicity,* by Jay Conrad Levinson, Rick Frishman, and Jill Lublin[1] can also give you a solid understanding of the industry. Building a publicity program isn't rocket science, but it does involve managing numerous details.

■ USE PUBLICITY EFFECTIVELY

To be effective, publicity about you must reach your client markets. The best way to accomplish this is with a focused Rolodex of media contacts. The media list you develop should reflect quality over quantity.

CHARACTERISTICS OF A GUERRILLA PUBLICITY PROGRAM

To ensure effectiveness, a guerrilla makes sure a publicity program:

➤ Includes clearly defined objectives and a way to measure success

➤ Targets potential and existing clients

➤ Brings coverage from appropriate media outlets

➤ Entails minimal out-of-pocket expense

➤ Has a systematic approach, instead of relying on one-shot publicity events

➤ Strengthens client, community, and collaborator relationships

➤ Makes a valuable contribution to clients, your industry, or a good cause

➤ Helps clients understand your firm's capabilities, instead of just recognizing its name

➤ Undertakes activities that play to your firm's strengths

➤ Results in leads for new projects

Targeting a select group of well-placed contacts will use your time more efficiently and yield better results than seeking contacts from a huge generalized list.

Consultants in the natural resources industry, for example, may fare better with coverage in the *Journal of Forestry* than in the *New York Times*. If you're a consultant for the auto industry, being published in the health care press won't help you attract the clients you want.

The next step is to translate thought into action by combining the preceding elements with your objectives. The list of potential publicity activities on the next page can serve as a starting point for your program.

■ MANAGE YOUR MEDIA EXPOSURE

To benefit from media exposure, you need to educate yourself about how the media works and how best to use your media connections. You must identify yourself as a resource for the media and understand the media's needs.

GUERRILLA TACTICS: POTENTIAL PUBLICITY ACTIVITIES

➤ Publish articles or letters to the editor.

➤ Conduct a survey and send results to targeted media outlets.

➤ Propose speeches to local business organizations.

➤ Hold a seminar on a relevant topic and alert the media.

➤ Cultivate media relations.

➤ Sponsor an event for your targeted clients.

➤ Undertake a project for your industry association.

➤ Join the board of a local community organization.

➤ Undertake a pro bono project for a community organization.

➤ Appear at a trade show.

This list is not exhaustive, but should give you some ideas. Optimize any activity you undertake by making sure your media contacts know what you are doing. The point is to get good press from your activities.

➤ **Become a Media Resource**

The media needs a constant stream of news and information for features it runs. Despite the flood of information now in circulation, the media still needs more. Its people are always looking for additional stories to keep the public informed, entertained, and up-to-date.

To be a media resource, become recognized as an expert in your chosen area. You want to be the "go-to person" the media seeks out for information, insights, and quotes on features in your field. If your expertise is in human resources, your objective should be to become the first expert the media contacts for stories that involve employee layoffs, downsizing, transfers, and related matters. Make your media contacts think of you whenever news breaks in your field.

Try to anticipate when the media may need your help. Think in terms of pithy quotes and clever headlines. Learn to write one-liners that will instantly grab people's attention. If the media considers you a "good quote," your phone will be ringing.

Always deliver accurate, timely, and complete information. Build a reputation for having unique insights as well as access to terrific contacts in your field—other people who can provide great quotes.

Verify all your sources, and if you have the slightest doubt, tell your media contacts. Send the media well-written press releases that they can publish verbatim, adapt, or excerpt as they wish. Write attention-grabbing headlines; insert tight, informative leads; and bullet-point your important facts. Have backup documents or research on hand if they need additional material or verification.

Ask your media contacts about the items they are working on and see how you can help. If you can't help but you know someone who might, give them that person's name or arrange for them to speak with that contact. Suggest stories; fill them in on exciting trends and developments that they should watch. Extend yourself for the media and they will help promote you.

Think of yourself as a news source. Issue press releases about your business and your clients. Send releases when either you or your clients win awards, have other successes, introduce products or services, or have financial news. Inform the media when you are

GUERRILLA TACTIC: SAMPLE PRESS RELEASE

Program to Forecast Profits Announced

Thursday, December 2, 2006   Contact: Jeff Bing at jbing@pcg.com

Plastics Consulting Group (PCG) will announce its newest consulting service, **The Profitability Quotient,** to over 800 attendees at the World Plastics Conference next week in New York. The Profitability Quotient is the first service to examine the impact on company profitability of forecasted changes in worldwide market prices for polymers. PCG will use data from its proprietary research, competitor analysis, world supply/demand analysis, and price forecasting models to pinpoint clients' future earnings.

According to Ruth Grant, Managing Partner of PCG's New York office, "The addition of this new service allows PCG to provide specific and valuable planning information for our clients. This service goes beyond the product perspective to help each company plan its overall strategy in the context of global supply and demand."

PCG provides strategic business planning services for the worldwide plastics industry. The firm maintains offices in New York, Paris, Tokyo, and Sydney. Find out more about The Profitability Quotient and PCG at www.pcg.com.

moving your practice, going into new businesses, building a new identity, getting a new logo, and hiring new people.

Send press releases to promote events that you are sponsoring. Tell the media when you are providing services or your clients are donating their products or services for a charitable cause. In your releases, find a unique angle or tie it to news or upcoming events.

Sponsor contests and events and award interesting prizes to the winners. Reporters prefer to cover events that provide good photo or video opportunities.

➤ Develop Newsworthy Content

Publishing articles that display your knowledge and express your opinions can be an outstanding publicity vehicle. Start by submitting letters to editors on subjects about which you have unique knowledge. The "Letters to the Editor" section of publications is a good place to be controversial, to take a stand, and to express your opinions. It gives you a forum to begin what can become fascinating exchanges that will help get your name and positions known.

Identify specific topics on which you can provide information that can get you publicity. Make a list of the subjects you know inside and out. Include the issues involved in current projects or those you've recently completed. Ask yourself how you would reply to a friend who inquired, "So what are you working on now?"

➤ How would you make your current project seem interesting to an outsider?

➤ What facets of the project would be of interest to your friends or to a segment of the public?

➤ What elements of the project fascinate you?

➤ What unique, creative approaches have worked for you?

➤ What parts of the project have unusual or far-reaching implications that would interest your media contacts and their audiences?

Usually, topics will pop right into your mind. Be forewarned, however; issues that captivate you may put others to sleep. Or, they may interest only a small niche or group that you may not be able to reach.

To find ideas for stories, review information in your computer, your briefcase, and your e-mail. Check all news sources to see if the issue is being covered and, if so, the slant they took. Use Internet information-gathering sources such as the Google News Service, or the numerous news crawler software programs that are now available.

Try not to get sidetracked by the lure of broad audiences. Frequently, broad media concerns won't be interested in your submissions anyway. Focus on media outlets that concentrate on the segments of the industry you serve. Remember—your primary objective in publishing is to obtain business; fame is a secondary bonus.

Target your markets precisely. Submit only to publications that will reach your target readers. Don't approach a food writer with a sports story.

It takes practice to spot publicity opportunities and develop content that will interest others. But before long, spotting opportunities will become second nature.

➤ Build Your Network of Media Contacts

Approach your media list as you would client relationships. Start by identifying writers and reporters who have covered stories in your field. Conduct research to find out how long they've been at the job, their work history, and the areas they cover. For media outlets, find out what they publish: their requirements, policies, and preferred approaches. Get copies of their earlier pieces and read them. Look for common threads, their "spin," favorite topics, and what they won't touch. See how extensively they use experts in their pieces and how liberally they include quotes.

Use online services like Media Finder (www.mediafinder.com), Bacon's Media Lists Online (www.medialistsonline.com), and Burrelle Luce (www.burrelles.com). They provide names, addresses, telephone and fax numbers, e-mail addresses, and Web site addresses for newspapers, radio and television stations, newsletters, and magazines.

Create a list of target media sources. Include contact information and notes on individuals' backgrounds, experience, and accomplishments. Create profiles of writers, editors, and producers with whom you would like to work. Summarize features they have authored or produced, when and where they ran, and the perspectives that were presented. Read their articles and watch or listen to their shows. Many media people will ask you directly if you are familiar with their work. If the answer is no, the conversation is likely to go downhill quickly. Update your list at least every three months because media people constantly move.

When you read an article, or see or hear a feature on your area of expertise, send the writer and/or producer a note or an e-mail stating how much you enjoyed the piece. Offer additional information, anecdotes, insights, and ideas for follow-up pieces. Set forth your expertise and encourage them to call you if they need quotes, sources, or other information. Don't write a book; simply provide enough information to bait the hook and hope that you'll get a bite.

Dedicate a specific time each week to work on publicity. Use that time to identify subjects and prepare materials to send to the media. Also use it to contact people in the media and to update your media lists.

➤ Aim for the Perfect Pitch

Approach a media contact in the same way that you approach a client meeting. The media is inundated with press releases and promotion requests; they get truckloads of them. So make your pitch sound compelling, exciting, or unique. Don't waste your time sending run-of-the-mill press releases.

Build your pitch around a compelling hook. If you send a press release, stress that hook in your headline and explain it in the lead sentence. If you capture a media person's interest or curiosity, you may get a call asking for more information.

If you call or send an e-mail to a media contact, write a summary of your pitch that you can say in 10 seconds or write in one sentence. "Our study found that employee turnover can be cut in half, at no new cost to employers, by following three easy steps." Then have a fuller explanation on hand that you can reel off in 20 to 30 seconds or two or three more sentences.

Send a short e-mail that includes your summary statement and lists each item that you're sending. Make it a brief cover letter. It should be direct and easy to read. Don't include lengthy materials such as surveys, white papers, or media kits, but have them on hand if the media requests additional information.

Prepare both online and hard copies of all documents. Direct your contacts to the media section of your Web site. Be prepared to send information in whatever format is needed.

➤ Give Them What They Want

Understand, respect, and be prepared to accommodate the special dynamics and requirements of the media:

> ➤ *News.* First and foremost the media wants news. The media reporter's basic question always is, "Will our audience care about this story?" If the answer is no, little else matters.

GUERRILLA INTELLIGENCE: TIPS FOR THE PERFECT MEDIA PITCH

Members of the media are pulled in many directions each day. Without a perfect pitch, you'll have a tough time getting any attention for your story. Here are five quick tips for a great media pitch:

1. *Talk trends.* Connect your story to a current social, business, or political trend. Instead of pitching your new consulting service that helps hospitals design more efficient emergency rooms, find information that supports the need for this service, like the rapid rise in emergency rooms as the primary health care facility for many patients.

2. *Go against the grain.* When big stories break, there's usually a chorus of similar opinions on the implications. While others are spouting off about the economic justification of moving business operations to other parts of the world, pitch a story about companies that are reversing course and bringing jobs back to their home bases.

3. *When in doubt, roll out the facts.* Credible statistics and surveys on relevant topics grab reporters' attention. If you have a substantial study, for example, showing that Internet shopping is declining in several major purchase categories, you're likely to get a call about the survey and questions about what retailers can do to reverse the trend.

4. *Align with the seasons.* During holidays, you may well find some slow news days that are perfect for your idea. If you propose a story about how to reduce graffiti during Halloween, it's likely you'll get a call.

5. *Remember the audience.* As you pull together your ideas, keep in mind a clear profile of the audience you hope to reach with your story. If you pitch a story about a new process for handling returned merchandise to a reporter who focuses on issues facing banks, you've wasted your time.

➤ *Picking your brain.* Like it or not, you are a source for information addicts. As an expert, you must gladly let them pick your brain. Consider every opportunity a chance to show that you're a reliable resource of continuing value to them.

➤ *Quick action.* Media contacts are always facing deadlines so they don't have time to dawdle or engage in small talk. Give them information quickly and when you promise more, deliver it on time, and as promised.

➤ *Constant help.* Because of their crushing workload, media people always need help—identifying stories, finding good angles, putting stories together, documenting and substantiating them, and meeting deadlines. In other words, they need help with virtually every step of the process.

➤ Follow-Up

If you've contacted the media but have not received a response, follow up with a call or an e-mail. Ask if you can answer any questions or help in any other way and leave your name and telephone number, but keep it brief. Busy media people usually won't listen to long telephone messages or read lengthy e-mails. Extended communiqués will only irritate potentially important contacts.

Don't badger your contacts with endless follow-up attempts. Assume that after a call or two, your message got through. Thereafter, keep on the contact's radar screen by sending periodic e-mails or information. However, only send material that is related to subjects of interest to your contact. Unsolicited, irrelevant submissions are the equivalent of spam, so avoid them. Keep your name in their minds, but don't be a pest.

Many ideas won't result in stories. Many of your media contacts won't include your quotes. Much great information gets cut. Don't take it personally; move on.

When media contacts reject your pitch or cut you from an article, accept their decision. Don't try to convince them to change their opinions. Concentrate instead on maintaining good relations. Turn your defeats into opportunities. After rejections, thank media contacts for their interest and ask if they can give you names of others whom you could contact. If they provide information, get permission to use their names.

If you haven't established a close working relationship with a contact, never say, "You owe me one." Never forget that the media doesn't exist to promote your business.

➤ Prepare for Interviews

Okay, so you've studied up on the media and what they want, made your pitch, and your media contact thinks it's a great idea. An interview is arranged and you are set to go. But are you really ready? Before you do an interview, the single most important step is for you to

---

GUERRILLA TACTIC: TWELVE STEPS BEFORE A MEDIA INTERVIEW

1. Complete media training.
2. Anticipate questions the interviewer might ask.
3. Rehearse quotable answers.
4. Prepare data and examples to support your major points.
5. Develop a focused theme for your message.
6. Compile additional sources to amplify your points.
7. Review your notes on the interviewer's past work.
8. Make sure you know the publication's audience.
9. Understand the slant or main theme of the story.
10. Clarify in your own mind what you *don't* want to say.
11. Find out when your quote, story, or interview will appear.
12. Confirm the date, time, and attendees of the interview.

---

get some media training. Training can give you both the confidence and the insider information you need to handle interviews by telephone, in front of a microphone, or in front of a camera. You'll learn what colors not to wear for the camera and where to look; how to judge the tempo of the interviewer; when to speak up, and when to wait patiently.

Preparation for an interview can be summarized in the 12 steps above.

After an interview, call or write your media contact to say thanks and offer to help put the piece together. Your help may not be needed, but the offer will be appreciated.

■ WHEN TO AVOID PUBLICITY

Publicity opportunities may arise that cannot help you. In fact, they could hurt you or place you in an awkward position. When a chance for media exposure teeters on the edge of your expertise, walk away—fast. Invariably, you're looking at a no-win situation in which you may have to bluff or repeatedly say, "I don't know." Broadcasting even the implication that you are uninformed or not up to speed is poison for a consultant and not worth the risk.

Don't accept an opportunity when you lack adequate time to prepare for it. Again, you risk coming off as being poorly informed. Don't take a chance when you feel uninformed on the key points that are likely to be raised. Also consider whether to appear when you haven't rehearsed your presentation or have not had time to find out about the interviewer. Most media members will try to make you look good. However, a few have agendas and have built their careers on demolishing guests. So think twice about going forward when you don't know enough about the person you're dealing with or you're on shaky ground with the material.

Cautiously respond to requests for comments on your clients' business. First, it's not your role; you are a consultant, a secondary source, and if they want reliable information, they should go to the source. Second, as close as you may be to your client, you may not know everything about that particular situation, including your client's plans and motivation. Your answers could be wrong and might embarrass or jeopardize your relationship with the client.

Also avoid media opportunities if you have had insufficient media training. Frequently, this occurs the first time that you must give a press conference on negative or damaging developments. Prior to new situations, get help; call in professionals. Don't go it alone.

The glamour of publicity can be alluring, especially when your past efforts have been successful, fun, or both. The temptation to repeat past successes is hard to suppress, and publicity efforts can provide a welcome break from the unrelenting pressures of your practice.

■ CONSIDER PROFESSIONAL HELP

Sometimes you need professional help with your media adventures because you don't have sufficient time or expertise to properly handle your publicity efforts and your core consulting business. Frequently, when you attempt to do both, you do neither well. Consider what your practice can gain from using a public relations firm.

PR firms and consultants can be invaluable in helping you get started. They can teach you about publicity and lay out what's involved. As experienced professionals, they usually have knowledge and ideas that might take you years to acquire, if you ever could. They also may have contacts that can cut straight through the electronic fences that make members of the media so difficult to reach.

GUERRILLA STRATEGY: SHOULD YOU USE A PUBLIC RELATIONS FIRM?

The most obvious consideration about using a PR firm is whether you have the funds to support an outside service provider. Such services can be pricey, depending on how you use them. A PR firm or consultant can:

➤ Save time in developing your publicity strategy and objectives

➤ Provide expertise in planning and implementing your campaign

➤ Help create publicity materials, such as press kits, media lists, and press releases

➤ Obtain media introductions for you

➤ Arrange interviews

➤ Gain momentum for your publicity program

➤ Assist with story ideas

➤ Provide media training

➤ Assist in evaluating your media success

Experienced PR professionals know the best media outlets for you or how to quickly find them. They are equipped to perform tasks that could be hard for you. They include developing story ideas, writing press releases, preparing media kits, planning and staging events, and building momentum for your campaign. They can provide you with media training as well as book you for and produce interviews and appearances.

Selecting the right PR firm can be as hazardous as picking the right consultant, and you face almost as many options. You can choose between firms of all sizes and different individual practitioners.

Choose your PR firm carefully and use its services judiciously. Be precise about your needs and your budget. You could easily blow your whole publicity budget on a professionally orchestrated campaign. And you may not need such comprehensive service. Decide what you need professional help with and what you can do on your own. Use the pros to fill in the gaps in your experience and knowledge about publicity.

GUERRILLA INTELLIGENCE: EVALUATING PUBLIC RELATIONS FIRMS

Evaluate PR firms by asking basic questions:

➤ What's the quality of their relationships with the media? Can their team help with access to the media representatives you need?

➤ Who would actually do the work? In some firms, senior PR professionals handle client matters for the firm's largest clients, while smaller assignments are handed off to less experienced staff. Understand where you fit in the client pecking order and who will work on your account.

➤ How are limits set on scope and costs? PR campaigns can be complex, requiring the time of many people. Even with the best intentions, the scope and cost can easily creep beyond your expectations.

➤ Who else is out there? It's wise to shop thoroughly. Like consulting firms, the number of firms offering PR services is staggering and the quality of service they offer varies widely.

■ ARE WE THERE YET?

An effective way to use a PR firm is in evaluating the results of your publicity program. Do you remember the objectives you chose for your program? Well, don't neglect to circle back and determine whether your media exposure is fulfilling its purpose—to bring you business and grow your practice. If it's not, the cost of all that free publicity is too high.

Chapter 9

When It Pays to Advertise

If you aren't going to make a case for profound, dramatic superiority, NEVER advertise.

—DAN KENNEDY[1]

When we hear the word *advertising,* we tend to picture glitzy, high-budget television commercials for cars, beer, or movies, or full-color print ads for pharmaceuticals. Such advertising seems extravagant for consultants and questionable at best. While mass media advertising (for example, television ads) can help build brand awareness and may be effective for large, multinational firms, it isn't a good investment for most consultants.

Most consulting practices build their brand identities on the strength of their performance for clients, and referrals for new work follow. If word of mouth and your networks are not enough to sustain your practice, some paid advertising can help. But, instead of throwing around huge sums of money for splashy, expensive ads, consider using an assortment of affordable advertising programs that reach your desired clients, not the universe. Remember, the primary purpose of guerrilla advertising is to generate leads for new consulting work; brand building is a secondary concern.

■ GUERRILLA ADVERTISING

When properly executed, advertising is a powerful guerrilla weapon, but it can also be an expensive crapshoot. It's possible to reach your precise target clients with timely and compelling offers that get prospective clients to pick up the telephone and call. It's just as easy, though, to create ill-timed ads that potential clients ignore.

With most paid advertising, you start at a disadvantage. Most consumers simply don't read or trust advertising because so many claims have proven to be exaggerated or untrue. Consumers have been bombarded with so much advertising that they've become desensitized and instinctively skeptical of ads. So, most skip right over or, at best, scan them.

And ads can be costly to create and run. A one-third page, black and white ad in a national business magazine costs more than $20,000 each time it runs. And the costs of design firms, production resources, and writers mount up.

Putting together an ad campaign and then measuring its results can be complex, costly, and time consuming. And to work most effectively, your advertising must be integrated with all your other marketing efforts.

But advertising has its place in the guerrilla's marketing arsenal and can draw clients to your practice using the tactics outlined below.

■ GOING POSTAL: DIRECT MAIL

Initially, the suggestion that consultants advertise via direct mail might not seem like a great use of money, especially if you're mailing to a large list of unknown prospective clients. Most people don't like to receive junk mail, and response rates for direct mail are usually low.

Consultants have differing opinions on the value of direct mailings: some use it, but others don't. The guerrilla does use direct mail, but only under the right circumstances. For example, when the government issued new patient privacy regulations for health care providers, consultants used direct mail to inform clients of the upcoming changes and offered to help. Recipients read those mailings because the content was relevant, timely, and valuable. When public companies had to comply with the Sarbanes-Oxley rules for financial reporting, many consultants used direct mail to offer assistance with compliance programs.

In both instances, clients had immediate needs that direct mail addressed. In response to a mailing, one firm secured dozens of clients who needed help implementing changes required by new regulations. The mailing wasn't a generic recitation of the firm's qualifications, but addressed an immediate business problem. Unless you target an immediate and known demand, direct mail is not an effective use of resources.

Here is a case in point. A personnel agency that specializes in providing interim salespeople to companies looking to augment their sales forces sent direct mail to dozens of partners of a large consulting firm. Each mailing arrived in a large, straw-filled box that contained a full-sized dartboard, a set of darts, and a personalized letter. One of the darts was lodged in the bull's-eye of the dartboard with a Post-it note attached promising that the agency would "Hit your sales targets every time."

Not only was this expensive mailing hokey, it was not relevant to the recipients. And the mailing was so large it gummed up the consulting firm's mailroom. The personnel agency's name went on the firm's "do not use" supplier list.

Direct mail doesn't always backfire. It has many advantages: You have total control over the look, content, and distribution. You can make direct-mail pieces personal, friendly, businesslike, humorous, hard hitting, or subtle and give them any look you choose.

Direct mail is ideal for making announcements and keeping relationships alive. It's an easy, inoffensive, and inexpensive way to give clients and prospective clients gentle reminders about you, your recent accomplishments, and what you can do to help them.

Direct mailings can be a cost-effective way to follow up with those you meet at speeches or other events and to build traffic to

GUERRILLA TACTIC: USING DIRECT MAIL

➤ Mail only to highly targeted lists, preferably a list you have created, not rented.

➤ Use caution with rented mailing lists because you have no idea if they will reach your target clients.

➤ Focus the subject of the mailing on a timely, specific, and urgent matter, not just your firm's qualifications.

➤ Be sure you can quickly follow up with every lead that the mailing produces.

➤ Handwrite some part of the mailing.

➤ Test the results of a small mailing before committing to a mass-mailing campaign.

➤ Send specialty items—like dartboards—with extreme caution.

your Web site by drawing attention to your news reports, articles, white papers, and information on seminars, workshops, or trade shows. Direct mailings can also make effective thank-you notes. With so much e-mail flooding the world, a handwritten note is often greatly appreciated.

■ READ ALL ABOUT IT: NEWSPAPER AND MAGAZINES

For the big firms, a full-page ad in the *Wall Street Journal* can help build brand awareness, but if you ask 25 people who saw the ad whether they remember the firm or what it stood for, you're likely to get blank stares. Most newspaper and magazine advertising run by consulting firms is unimaginative, dull, and a poor use of money. In one recent full-page ad in a national newspaper, a firm's claim to fame was, "We Get It Done."

If you choose to use magazine or newspaper advertising to build your brand, stick with it consistently. One or two ads, no matter how creative or valuable, will not penetrate the imagination of most readers. One public relations consultant has run a full-page ad in an industry publication for years. She is now well known among a small group of professionals, but it took years and a tidy investment. If you go this route, be prepared to commit to a long-running ad campaign that will help you get through all the advertising clutter.

Unless you have a vault of money, it's wiser to use the print media to publish short articles, position pieces, reports, survey results, and announcements. If you need to promote an upcoming event, like a seminar, a print ad in highly targeted publications can be the best way to go. With some research, you can create professional print ads for relatively little money.

If you decide to use print ads, conduct research to find the publications read by your target market and make sure your ad runs in the right section or issue. Position your ad with other relevant subjects.

GUERRILLA TACTIC: WHAT DO YOU WANT THEM TO DO?

Ask your ad's readers to take some action in response to your ad. Ask them to call your toll-free number, visit your Web site, or send you e-mail. This simple tactic will help you generate leads, measure the effectiveness of your ad, and suggest ways to improve it in the future.

You don't want your seminar on logistics consulting to run in the garden section.

For newspaper advertising, consider using your own designer instead of one provided by the newspaper. Every element of your ad should be perfect, and hiring your own designer will help you achieve that standard.

■ TELEVISION AND RADIO

Some of the large consulting firms can't resist the allure of television advertising. Urged on by their creative agencies, many of these firms ape beer, car, and fast food companies and take to the airwaves to build their brands. However, as soon as the ad appears, many television viewers are either off to the kitchen for a snack or zapping with the remote control.

Guerrillas love the exposure television provides, even if it reaches some who may not be their targeted clients. If you want to use television, work toward being a guest on news panels or targeted talk shows. Contact the producers and inform them of your expertise and your availability to discuss a particular subject. If you're an expert on how businesses can cope with funding company pensions, approach the producers of well-known business news shows with an offer to alert their viewers on the important issues about pensions. Appearing as a program guest eliminates the costs of producing commercials and buying airtime and gives you better exposure. As a guest, you're treated as an expert authority, not a pitchman.

The same rules apply to radio. Bring your expertise to radio listeners, not your latest pitch. If you are a tax consultant, volunteer to be interviewed on tax tips to save people time and money. Your expertise will be appreciated and rewarded because radio producers are always looking for interesting and informative guests.

Television and radio ads are expensive to produce and run. The costs include outlays for talent, crews, production companies, equipment, sets, and airtime, to name just a few. If you've set your sights on being a media star, use your expertise, not fancy ads. You'll go farther and will spend a lot less money.

■ TRADE SHOWS AND CONVENTIONS

Most industries have an annual bash (or a series of them) in the form of a trade show, where practitioners, suppliers, and others gather to learn, sell, buy, and make contacts. At these large get-togethers, consultants can strut their stuff, meet new clients, catch up with old friends, and monitor the competition. Be sure to attend the annual trade show for the industry you serve.

If you're unsure which show is right for you, check www.tsnn.com, one of the largest trade show locators on the Internet. You can search for shows by industry, function, geography, and schedule. You'll get a description of events and instructions for registering.

A consultant's ultimate objective at trade shows is to speak at the general session, a panel, or one of the many seminars offered. Approach the conference organizers several months in advance to secure a spot. If you offer to speak on a compelling topic, it can land you an opportunity. And, if you give a good speech, you'll walk away with at least a few leads.

Decide whether you want to have a display booth at the trade show. It's increasingly common to see consultants with sales booths, so don't rule it out. To decide whether to invest the time and effort in a booth, consider several factors:

➤ Will the show's attendees include a fair percentage of decision makers?

➤ Can you get an affordable location that isn't in the northernmost outpost of the hall?

➤ Can you assemble a booth that adequately represents your firm, its culture, and capabilities?

If you choose to have a booth, you'll have access to thousands of contacts and potential clients in a very short period. Most trade show attendees fly down the aisles, so you need to offer something dynamic that captures their attention. Consultants can feature their current research, offer miniseminars on specific topics, and distribute gifts. You may not have as many visitors as the booth featuring a movie star signing autographs, but you'll attract people with an interest in your business.

A trade show booth can be time consuming and costly, particularly for multiday shows. Here are a few tips for getting the most out of your investment:

➤ Get training on trade show etiquette. If you haven't hosted a booth, you'll find it valuable to understand how to approach attendees and when to leave them alone.

➤ Don't be pushy. People will turn off if they think you're giving them the hard sell. Be respectful and courteous.

➤ Rotate your booth staff frequently. It is tough duty greeting people for hours and hours, so give your staff regular breaks.

➤ Turn off your cell telephones.

➤ Make sure visitors take something with them. Whether it's a research report, a key chain, or your business card, make sure they don't leave empty-handed.

➤ Take criticism lightly. Occasionally, an attendee will give you grief about something. Shake it off with a smile.

➤ Don't sit down. Attendees will feel as if they're interrupting you and may hesitate to approach the booth.

➤ Follow up promptly. If you make a promise to an attendee, follow up as fast as possible. Memories of trade shows quickly fade after visitors go back home.

➤ Conduct a competitive assessment. When you're not working the booth, scour the trade show and collect as much competitive intelligence as possible. You will rarely have a better opportunity to understand exactly what the competition is doing, so make the most of it.

Trade shows can be a rich source of leads for prospective clients, whether you have a booth or simply visit the event. So, go to trade shows, work like crazy to get on the speaking agenda, and consider the costs and trade-offs of sponsoring a booth at the show.

■ PRINTED BROCHURES GATHER MOLD

Guerrillas don't invest much in preprinted brochures that sit in a box in the closet. Instead, they develop the capability to create customized brochures. With currently available presentation software, it's easy to prepare and print brochures for specific uses.

If you are headed to a client meeting, create a brochure for that client and print a limited number of copies. Include the client's name on the brochure and align the content with the client's business needs.

Keep a small supply of brochures on hand in your office to send out in response to telephone or mail requests. Constantly revise and update the content of your brochure to reflect current topics. Those that just rehash your qualifications and service descriptions are a waste of money and paper. Brochures should be issue-based and should reinforce your marketing message on how you can solve clients' problems.

■ PROFESSIONAL DIRECTORIES

It all began with the Yellow Pages. Traditionally, businesses conveniently placed ads where many people were sure to look when they needed help. Some businesses don't need anything more than a Yellow Pages ad to attract all the business they want. For consultants, though, it's a different story.

Don't neglect the Yellow Pages, or white pages, but add other professional directories to the mix to get wider exposure for your firm and its expertise. Today, both print and online directories list businesses by their specialty areas. The chief virtue of directories is that they keep your name in the public view. Directories are mainly research tools: They give prospective clients convenient places to find your contact information or to gather information about you. It's important to be listed to show that you're a player in the game.

Arranging directory listings is easy: All you have to do is obtain a submission form, complete it, submit it, and your information will be published. Once your listing is published, your work is done. You usually have nothing more to do except update your listing periodically and pay the renewal fee. It's smart to pick a few paid directory listings.

For accessing journalists, talk show producers, and editors, consider a listing in the *Yearbook of Experts*. The publication is sent to leading print and broadcast journalists across the country. The companion Web site, www.yearbook.com, boasts a million hits per month. You can also list yourself in the Radio-TV Interview Report (www.rtir.com), which purports to be the largest database of authors and experts who are available for live and telephone interviews.

Depending on your specialty, you may also consider a listing with HG Experts.com (www.hgexperts.com), one of the largest Internet directories of experts, consultants, certified attorneys, expert witnesses, mediators, arbitrators, speakers, and medical and legal specialists.

As a member of other professional associations such as the Institute of Management Consultants, the National Speakers' Association, or the American Society for Training and Development, you can include a current directory listing for your practice. Your investment in directory listings will not be your mainspring for sales leads, but if you land one or two interviews or leads that result in projects, your ROI on those investments will be acceptable.

Some directory listings are free and valuable for consultants. The Open Directory Project, www.dmoz.org, is a Web directory of Internet resources that operates like a huge reference library. DMOZ includes listings for most businesses and is the largest human-maintained, free directory on the Web. The beauty of a listing in the Open Directory

Project is that it serves as a feeder site for large search engines that want to fill in their databases. A listing in DMOZ usually lands in smaller search engines.

A few well-placed directory listings are a cost of doing business for consultants. If you're looking to save money, this isn't the right place to do it.

■ START YOUR SEARCH ENGINES

Nearly 90 percent of all Internet traffic begins at search engines such as Google, Yahoo!, America Online, or Microsoft Network. At these sites, users enter search terms and receive a list of Web sites that they can visit. Therefore, consultants' sites must be listed on the most heavily trafficked search engines. The more prominently your site appears on search engine listings, the better the chance that a prospective client will click through to it.

Your site can be listed on Google at no charge. Other search engines also provide free listings, but the process can be time consuming and they don't accept all sites or guarantee when they will be posted.

You can accelerate getting your site listed on the major search engines by paying an annual fee. For example, www.teoma.com will list your site on several major search engines for a moderate fee. Microsoft's www.bcentral.com has a similar service for submitting your site to the search engines. The fees for these services vary with the number of pages you submit, but generally, you'll renew your submissions annually.

Other services claim to submit your Web site to thousands of search engine sites simultaneously. Their fees are often small and the promised results big. Be careful with these services. If you are using search engine submission services, stick with the big guys.

You'll also find firms that will claim to optimize your site so it is guaranteed to land at the top of the list when a user enters the right keyword. Search Engine Optimization (SEO) consulting is a big business that helps you develop strategies to get top placement on the search engines. These firms can help you select the keywords that will trigger a search engine to display your site in response to a search query from a user. Research these firms carefully before choosing. Look at their clients, call references, and come to a complete understanding of their prices. Some of the SEO firms are quite good, but others are a waste of money. The industry changes rapidly. Be thorough in your analysis and update it at least every year.

GUERRILLA INTELLIGENCE: KEEP YOUR SITE AT THE TOP OF THE LIST

Once you've submitted your site to the search engines, don't ignore your listings. Check periodically to see where your site shows up when you enter particular keywords. Ensure that your site rises to the top of the search engine list by monitoring and, if needed, changing the keywords you use.

■ PAY PER CLICK (PPC)

On most search engines, you can arrange to display a text-based ad when a user enters particular keywords. The keywords you should submit to the search engines are often obvious. For example, insurance consultants would include "insurance consultant" and "business consultant insurance" as keywords for their listings on search engines.

When a user types one of your search terms into the search engine, your ad appears with a description of your services and a link to your site. Each time a user clicks through to your site, you are charged a specified amount. Google, Yahoo!, and many other search engines offer this service, which is called Pay per Click, or PPC.

An auction process often determines the amount you pay for each click. Advertisers compete to have their ads placed at the top of the list that users see. The advertiser willing to pay the most per click will own the top spot. Fees can range from 15 cents to several dollars per click. You can run a campaign for as long as you'd like and change, at any time, how much you're willing to pay for each click.

Using PPC to generate leads is only effective if you can measure the conversion rate of click-through to leads and sales. Try this technique gradually to see if you are paying for semi-interested browsers, real potential buyers, or competitors trying to deplete your budget by clicking through to your site.

■ ONLINE MAGAZINES

Most business magazines have companion Web sites that will gladly accept your ads. The prices for these ads can be high, so stick with other alternatives such as trying to get an article published. You'll save money and demonstrate your credibility more effectively.

■ LINK STRATEGIES

Some organizations will agree to post links to your site on their sites, particularly those that focus on providing resources and information to their visitors. Frequently, they'll want a link on your site in exchange. If you have a zine, ask other relevant publishers to trade links in an upcoming issue. It's an easy, free way to cross-promote your practices. You can use the link to announce upcoming events, offer a recently released report or just let readers know you have a zine that might interest them.

A large consulting firm recently spent over $75 million for an advertising and branding campaign that featured ads in the highest circulation newspapers and magazines around the globe. For guerrillas, that kind of investment is sheer folly. The campaign may bring the firm's consultants to the table when a project is up for grabs, but it won't get them any work if their ideas, relationships, and sales processes are flawed.

Invest wisely in an assortment of targeted advertising programs. And remember, your primary intent is to generate leads and, secondarily, to build a brand. That's how to make your advertising investment pay off.

GUERRILLA INTELLIGENCE: SIX RULES OF ADVERTISING FOR CONSULTANTS

1. Advertise to generate leads. Build your brand through your work with clients.
2. Advertising expense and advertising effectiveness are not related. You can draw profitable clients to your practice on a shoestring advertising budget.
3. Make your ad stand out. Consultants' ads tend to look alike and are jammed with platitudes that don't impress readers.
4. The best ads offer service and encourage readers to take action.
5. Never attack your competitors.
6. Explain the services you offer and the value they provide.

Chapter 10

Write This Way

There's something I've been trying to say to you/But the words get in the way.

—GLORIA ESTEFAN[1]

Marketing literature recommends that consultants write and publish reports, articles, and case studies so they can dazzle clients with their brilliance and attract business. But like most conventional marketing wisdom, publishing can backfire and leave consultants with little or no return on their marketing investment.

To benefit from writing and publishing, you must make a long-term commitment to publishing *continuously*. You must also concentrate on your area of expertise and carefully aim your writings at your target audience. Your publishing efforts may improve your writing skills but if they don't bring in new clients, it's not worth the effort.

Publishing one or two pieces may produce short-term results and those shiny reprints look good in brochure folders, but for guerrillas, that's not enough; guerrillas publish to get client leads.

■ WHY PUBLISH?

Clients call consultants as the result of referrals, but they also find consultants as a result of materials they read. It only takes one good idea to motivate a potential client to pick up the telephone and ask for help. And your record of thought leadership can make the difference between winning and losing the job.

GUERRILLA INTELLIGENCE: WHY PUBLISHING MATTERS

Publishing is a great way to *demonstrate* your value to clients in a nonselling manner. Do you wonder if publishing that white paper you've been thinking about will yield results? According to a report by Bitpipe and Forbes.com, 77 percent of corporate and IT executives pass on white papers to colleagues, and 68 percent use them to contact distributors and vendors.*

Six Reasons to Publish

1. Establish your expertise with prospective clients.
2. Enhance your relationships with existing clients.
3. Generate leads for work from new and existing clients.
4. Improve your name recognition.
5. Demonstrate your competence.
6. Build your stockpile of intellectual assets for future use.

*Statistics on use of white papers is from "2004 Forbes.com and BitPipe Study: Readership and Usage of White Papers by Corporate and IT Management," p. 2.

Being published gives consultants instant credibility; it automatically qualifies them as authorities. It's natural for clients and prospective clients to be attracted to consultants who are thought leaders in their fields.

Strangely, the flood of information we receive has intensified, not satisfied, the demand for high-value information. Clients are always hunting for objective insights into how their performance and business operations stack up against others and what the future holds for their industry. Publishing your work, though time-consuming, is a cost-effective marketing tactic you can use to give clients the value they seek.

Guerrillas view writings and published pieces as fungible, reusable assets that will provide an ongoing return on their investment. A consultant's writings can be used to support future proposals, press releases, media kits, zines, and Web site content.

Shape your writings for multiple purposes. Write pieces that can be converted into speeches, white papers, books, audios, or videos. Think of your writings as a database that you can reconfigure and tailor to a variety of needs.

■ A PUBLISHING STRATEGY

With so much information circulating these days, a one-shot or scattergun approach to publishing won't even register in your targets' minds. Publishing an article in an industry journal once or twice a year won't attract many clients.

Establish an ongoing presence by publishing frequently each year. Make sure that your writings target an audience that will enhance your consulting business; otherwise you'll be spinning your wheels. Don't scatter your pieces all over the place; concentrate on submitting them only to those outlets that reach your target audience.

To build name recognition, visibility, and attract clients, commit to writing a regular column or pieces for a newspaper, magazine, or for a Web site that your clients are likely to frequent. Your objective is twofold: to build a following of readers who will be your advocates; and to amass writings that convey the value of your ideas to clients and become assets for future use.

A systematic and continuous publishing strategy is the best way to both build your base of intellectual assets *and* exhibit them. When properly implemented, a well-planned publishing strategy will give you clear guidelines on what to publish where and for which audience. A systematic approach will also carry you through the sometimes agonizing process of writing and publishing because you'll have your goal firmly in sight.

You should commit at least one-third of your marketing budget to publishing. That may seem high, but your strategy must comprehensively cover every element in the publishing process:

➤ Finding hot topics

➤ Researching those topics

➤ Writing, editing, and rewriting

➤ Finding the right publisher

➤ Marketing your work

Publishing has drawbacks. Writing and publishing can detour you from your core business. It's easy to get bogged down with necessary evils like editing, meeting deadlines, and coordinating with sources, editors, printers, agents, and publishers. And it may be a challenge to find time in your already insane schedule.

Most consultants think that the writing experience they have gained from project work is sufficient for writing articles. But their writing may not be in the style or voice appropriate for most publications. Don't assume you can just transfer your client writing skills into polished prose that will satisfy an editor. It rarely happens.

For example, redundant words creep into consulting prose like vines in rainforests. In his classic book, *On Writing Well,* William Zinsser calls clutter "the disease of American writing" and says that we are "strangling in unnecessary words."[2]

Consider these bits, drawn from consultants' writings: "a 5 percent positive revenue increase"; "two parallel paths"; "Your satisfaction is our main priority."

You are writing to draw readers to your practice, so look for help if you need it. By working for even a short period with a writer or editor, you can learn how to eliminate jargon and consultant-speak and to write clear prose that readers can easily grasp.

The fear of writing for publication prevents many consultants from ever getting started. Writing—like most disciplines—can be learned, but it usually takes effort and practice. It doesn't help that having pieces rejected is a standard part of the publishing business. But guerrillas take rejection in stride and eventually break through to become published authors.

■ PUTTING FINGERS TO KEYBOARD

You can make writing easier for yourself by mastering the following steps.

➤ Focus

Consultants are famous for advising clients to focus on those things they do best and leave the rest to others. The rule of focus applies equally to writing. Before you begin to write, identify a topic that you're truly qualified to write about, focus on exactly what you plan to write, and develop your point of view on that topic.

Don't start writing if you only have a vague or general idea and hope that the central theme will emerge. Start only when your focus is clear and when it's something you're ready to share with the world. Then plan how to go about it.

➤ Maintain a Clippings File

Create a clippings file where you can save articles, quotations, reports, and other information that you cut or copy from newspapers, magazines, and newsletters. Also include information that you print from the Web. Make sure that each clipping has the date and name of the publication. As your collection of clippings grows, organize it by subject matter.

➤ Outline

We all cringe at the thought of outlines with Roman numerals, sub-points, and other creativity-sapping techniques. Even so, it's imperative to begin with an outline of some kind. Find a method you're comfortable with, whether it is mind-mapping or writing key words and phrases. Don't stick with Roman numerals just because Mrs. Kelly, your seventh-grade English teacher, said that's how it's done.

Whatever technique you use, make a list, in no particular order, of all the important points you want to cover. Write either key words or complete sentences (whatever helps you identify essential ideas). Then organize the entries you compiled in the order that you plan to address them. If you feel that you have too many items for the article or for your target publication, consolidate or delete.

➤ Give It a Name

When you've completed your initial outline, name each section and under each, list in detail the information you want to discuss. Identify all facts, information, or leads that you need to research or check further. Jot down where you would like to include a quote, anecdote, illustration, sidebar, or other device. At this stage, you should be able to create a brief abstract of the piece that potential publishers can review.

➤ Identify Targeted Publications

The old saying "all dressed up and nowhere to go" applies to unfocused, nontargeted articles. As you put together your thoughts, identify the publications that might be suitable for your piece. The rules and schedules for submitting articles to publications vary. Some require you to submit a query letter asking if the article is suitable for publication; others don't. Some publications have yearlong lead times for publication; others can get you in their next issue.

If you understand the rules of the publications that you target, it will make your job as an author easier. Contact publications to obtain their requirements for submissions—what type and what subject matter they accept, the style and format required, and their return policies. Determine which publications accept pieces from freelance writers, who owns the rights to published works, and if the staff prefers to communicate by e-mail or postal mail.

Numerous resources can help you identify appropriate publications. One useful reference is *Writer's Market,* which is available in print or online and includes information on thousands of editors.

➤ Create a Research and Writing Schedule

A consultant's to-do list is usually overwhelming and your desire to research and write often falls to the bottom of the list. There never seems to be enough time. Consultants often find it difficult to write for publication simply because they don't set aside enough time for this task.

It's usually preferable to complete all your research before you write. With the Internet, however, you may be able to do both simultaneously. For most people, writing goes more smoothly when their research is complete. But proceed according to your own preference and style.

Block out the days and hours that you'll actually write and what you plan to accomplish in those time blocks. Build in sufficient cushion for editing, which invariably takes longer than expected, and the many other delays that always seem to arise. They include postponed interviews, difficulty getting crucial materials, those pesky client commitments, and the unavailability of others on whom you depended. And frequently, you have to go back and do additional research and fact checking.

You can write anywhere, so seize on all opportunities. If you're waiting for a flight, standing in a supermarket line, or attending a meeting, take a few minutes to jot some notes or organize your thoughts. Although it's nice to have multihour blocks of time, you can train yourself to write effectively in short intervals.

➤ Be Flexible

As you're writing, you may find that one of your key concepts no longer holds true, that your organizational structure misses the mark, or that a celebrity's quotation, around which you built a major point, is simply too stupid to print. Be prepared to make necessary adjustments that will maintain the integrity of your original idea and the value you're trying to deliver.

■ THE WRITING PROCESS

Noted journalist Gene Fowler once commented, "Writing is easy. All you do is stare at a blank piece of paper until drops of blood form on your forehead."[3] While we have more writing tools at our disposal today than Fowler could have imagined, writing hasn't changed all that much. What has changed, though, is how readers actually read.

In your writings, provide practical information in an easy-to-read format: "Five Ways to Lower Group Health Costs," "A Foolproof Quality Control System," or "Reasons to Always Promote from Within."

Compose headlines that will capture readers' attention and make them want to read further. Don't try to say everything in the headline, but try to find a clever or interesting way to convey what your article reports. Follow up your headline with a lead sentence that reveals the most important information and then elaborate on those points in subsequent sentences and paragraphs.

Most business readers scan rather than read. Usually, they glance at the headline and lead sentence and race through the remainder in search of key words or phrases. When they spy those keys, they read in more depth, but often only for a sentence or two.

Assist readers by bulleting key points. This device quickly summarizes your important content and signals readers when they should read further or more closely. When you build a reputation as a writer, readers will scan less; they'll dive right in because they want to learn your views.

Keep your language simple and your sentences short. Try to inject humor and enthusiasm, but above all make your writing clear. Never forget that your goal is to communicate, not to show off how many multisyllable words you know or how poetic, clever, or funny you are.

Freely provide examples that illustrate your points. Examples make lessons come to life. Whenever possible, include case studies

GUERRILLA ALERT: NO HORN-TOOTING ZONE

In writing for publication, eliminate self-promotion. Many editors won't publish pieces that they consider commercial. At the end of your feature, include only your name, firm, telephone number, e-mail, and Web addresses. If readers feel that your piece is self-serving, they will stop reading it. Furthermore, blatant self-promotion will diminish you in their eyes and could ultimately prove harmful to your practice.

If you get a byline or are otherwise identified as the author of your work, readers will get the message loud and clear. They will judge you on the quality of your ideas and if they are top rate, you and your practice will be regarded accordingly.

that describe the situations under discussion. Case studies are an excellent device to help readers retain information.

Keep your writing as brief as possible. Eliminate unnecessary repetition; assume that you're writing for intelligent readers who lead busy lives.

Avoid dense pages by including lots of white space. Thin margins and tightly packed pages intimidate readers and don't provide convenient havens where they can stop to comprehend what they just read. Break up your text with headings and subheadings that inform readers what is to come.

When appropriate—and only when it's actually how you feel—be provocative. Controversial writings garner more interest than those that echo collective wisdom. Express a strong point of view and don't be afraid to take a different angle or position. If most recent articles warn about the dangers of debt financing, set forth the advantages. Taking an uncommon or unpopular position will attract the attention of editors, agents, and readers. It will also be of interest to the many independent thinkers in positions of power and influence.

Provide an explicit call to action that tells readers what to do with the information you have provided. If you have proposed a new way to reduce factory overhead costs, be sure to include a three-step program for getting started. If your article extols the virtues of new tools that speed the delivery of customer orders, be sure your readers know how to find them. Calls to action confirm that you understand the problem, especially its practical aspects, and that you have solutions.

GUERRILLA INTELLIGENCE: TEN ATTRIBUTES OF A GREAT ARTICLE

1. Informs, educates, and entertains the reader
2. Has a distinct point of view
3. Is jargon-free
4. Is easy to read
5. Solves a problem or saves time
6. Is simple, but not simplistic
7. Can be used for other purposes such as speeches or special reports
8. Contains a call to action
9. Has a way for readers to contact you
10. Creates interest in your other work

Adopt a consistent format for all the writings on your Web site by using similarly designed pages. Design each page to be consistent with your firm's overall visual identity, business cards, and promotional materials. Create templates so that all your pieces have a uniform format when printed or displayed on the reader's computer. If all your articles have the same look, they'll be suitable for binding, which will extend their life. Consistency with your visual identity will help you look professional and promote your brand.

You need to maintain uniformly excellent quality and content in your writings. If your articles are not vastly superior to the usual run-of-the mill stuff, you will be wasting your time. Anything less than first-rate work will damage your reputation and defeat the purpose—growing your business.

■ MARKETING WHILE WRITING

Finding time to conduct research and prepare items for publication is always difficult when you must balance those activities with a tough client assignment. Guerrillas take advantage of this apparent dilemma by including clients in the research and development process. Once you've worked out a core set of ideas, discuss your emerging concepts with clients and solicit their feedback. They may help solidify your ideas, add a dimension that you missed, or give you quotable examples and statistics.

If your piece is about a new way to organize a sales force, seek opinions from several clients who are involved in that part of their business. Clients usually welcome the opportunity to help, and most appreciate being quoted. Plus, you get to show clients that you are always thinking of ways to help them, and you have an opportunity to explore any other issues that may arise during the conversation. By involving your clients in the writing process, you remind them once again about you, your firm, and your interest in their company.

■ SELLING WHILE YOU SLEEP

Guerrillas are always on the lookout for a return on any investment, including the time and effort it takes to develop intellectual assets. One possibility is to offer your particularly valuable material for sale. Some consultants offer premium content to clients for a fee by permitting special access to in-depth reports, collections of articles, and other tools that clients find helpful. The consulting firm, McKinsey & Company, makes this service available to clients and others with great success.

Other consultants compile articles, speeches, and even videos into a cohesive package on a relevant topic and offer it for sale through their Web sites. One sales consultant offers an advanced sales training package of three videos, a workbook, a three-CD audio program, and an e-book on his site.

The revenue from these sales can be substantial and, assuming the material is of the highest quality, consulting assignments often follow quickly.

■ THAT'S THE IDEA

In the past, a well-designed brochure, a good sales pitch, and a respected reputation were all it took for consultants to reel in new clients. Well, those days are gone.

The consulting business is based on ideas and solutions; writing about and publishing your ideas can reinforce your expertise with existing clients and attract new clients. Whatever the size of your consulting practice, publishing great ideas is a competitive equalizer in the market that will help you win projects for your firm.

Chapter 11

Five Steps to a Winning Speech

Be sincere; be brief; be seated.

—FRANKLIN D. ROOSEVELT,
ADVICE ON SPEECHMAKING[1]

Whether it's leading a seminar or delivering a keynote address, speaking presents unique long-term marketing opportunities for consultants. A speech places you face to face with a roomful of prospective clients who have signaled their interest in you and your topic by showing up. You have the rare chance to meet and address people who want to learn about you and what you have to say. And you don't have to find them—they come to you. As a marketing opportunity, what could be better?

As a bonus, speaking expands your network of contacts, positions you as an expert, and generates leads for new business. And your speech material will add to your store of intellectual assets and can be marketed in other formats, including audio and video offerings, CDs, slide presentations, and articles. Your material might even form the basis of a book.

Speaking, after all, is the perfect marketing tactic for consultants, who communicate for a living. And as Nick Morgan, author of *Working the Room,* puts it, "There is something essential about the intellectual, emotional and physical connections a good speaker can make with an audience that . . . no other medium can reproduce."[2]

Remarkably, most consultants fail to capitalize on the marketing potential of speeches because they narrowly define a speech as a single, isolated event. They go to an event, present their speech, and then disappear. To realize the full benefits of speaking, the guerrilla manages a speech, not as an event, but as a marketing process.

Before you begin, honestly assess your speaking skills. Most consultants haven't focused enough time or energy on the craft of public speaking and are uninspiring speakers. The best advice on speaking for consultants is that if you can't do it well, don't do it. Instead, use your marketing resources on other tactics. Recognize proficiency as an entry barrier to the speaking arena.

■ TRAINING AND PRACTICE

If you are going to pursue public speaking, find out about training programs for speakers. Join the National Speakers Association, where you can take courses, practice, and make great contacts. Consider taking a few lessons with a speech coach who can tape your practices and give you tips and constructive criticism. Watch great speakers, in person or on video. Some consultants hone their speaking skills by teaching at local colleges and universities.

Look for a training program that will teach you speaking platform skills, methods for turning the natural fear of speaking into positive energy for your speeches, and effective rehearsal techniques, especially video feedback. Find a systematic way to develop speeches. The Decker Grid System, created by communications expert, Bert Decker, is an example of an effective approach.[3]

Lack of rehearsal is a noticeable problem with most consultants' speeches. When asked in an interview about his thoughts on rehearsing, Nick Morgan said, ". . . the vast majority of business speakers under rehearse woefully. Typically, they don't rehearse at all. . . . That is a disaster."[4] Practice may not make your presentation perfect, but it can make the difference between excellence and disaster.

■ A SPEECH IS NOT A SPEECH

Proficiency in speaking is essential, but it's not enough. To ensure that a speech is an effective tool that will draw clients to your practice, think of it as a five-step process:

1. Develop compelling content.
2. Get a speaking engagement.

3. Prepare your presentation.
4. Attend the big event.
5. Participate in postevent activities.

Keep in mind that you are marketing your practice in each step of the process. A speech is not just a speech—it's a marketing continuum.

GUERRILLA ALERT: DON'T BE A BORE

Audiences have heard it all, so you must stretch to keep them from scurrying for the exits. You're not putting on a Broadway musical, but the audience members won't find out what you can do for them if you don't command their attention:

➤ *Avoid fact-intensive presentations.* Consultants tend to give audiences more statistics than they can absorb. Limit statistics to a few facts and figures that directly support your major points.

➤ *Best practices are passé.* For many clients, best practices mean warmed-over tactics others have tried. And, what's best for one client may be a disaster for others. Listeners want to hear about novel approaches, innovative ideas, and techniques they haven't tried. When explaining a new solution, point out potential risks you can anticipate, but encourage your audiences to think creatively.

➤ *Stay on course—keep to your main route.* If you do wander, get back on track fast. Like most experts, consultants can ramble endlessly on subtleties that are of little interest to anyone else.

➤ *Your speech is not a commercial.* Sell your ideas and know-how, not your firm's services. You can present one slide of your qualifications, but that's it. Let the person who introduces you blow your horn.

➤ *Don't be a book report speaker.* Reading a book or two does not qualify you as an expert, and summarizing the content of books, no matter how great they are, is boring. Only speak on what you expertly know; that is what will interest your audience.

➤ *Learn to be an engrossing speaker.* Tape your speeches and analyze them later. An audiotape or CD can be a great tool to help you become a better speaker and avoid being dull.

➤ Step 1: Develop Compelling Content

The Yawn Factor

Every day, thousands of speeches are given. Most fail to move their audiences to do anything other than yawn. Most consultants excel at addressing clients across a desk, but when they speak publicly, they often register new highs on the yawn meter.

Speeches must provide first-rate content and engage listeners' attention. According to a survey by the National Speakers Association,[5] what audiences want most is education and skill building. More than 75 percent of speakers are hired because they provide education and training. The most sought-after topic is performance improvement. Industry trends, by the way, are at the bottom of the list.

Audiences appreciate hearing about tools, processes, or systems that will help them solve their problems. Try to give them solutions that they can apply right away. Explain how others have solved similar dilemmas and provide innovative answers to complex problems. Solutions should be a prominent feature of your presentations. Once again, delivering value is the key. Translate your knowledge, experience, and synthesis of issues into understandable and actionable steps for the audience.

Once you identify three topics, call your network contacts, your clients, academics, and industry experts and ask for their thoughts

---

GUERRILLA TACTIC: WHAT TO TALK ABOUT

Pick topics according to the following rules:

➤ The subject must be relevant for your clients.

➤ It has generated buzz.

➤ It has captured your deep interest.

➤ It is in your area of expertise.

➤ You can explore new angles that will interest your audiences.

Identify hot topics by reviewing magazines, newspapers, radio and television programs, academic journals, industry newsletters, and issues discussed at industry events. Look for subjects on the Web sites of trade associations, businesses, and other consultants. Use your client experience to develop ideas for topics.

on the subjects. Design a few informal survey questions. Asking survey questions is a good way to expand your network, so include people you don't know. Plan to use the results in your speech, along with information from more formal surveys (with proper permission, of course).

Follow Your Expertise

Talk about what you do and know best; it's your competitive edge over rivals with less experience. Audiences will recognize that you are knowledgeable and credible. Plus, it's easier to prepare talks on subjects you know and easier to concentrate during your presentations.

All businesses share seven fundamental characteristics that you can build speeches around, as suggested here:

1. *A plan for the business:* how strategy and tactics improve profits
2. *An organization:* seven ways to streamline your organization
3. *People:* improving productivity while forcing employee turnover
4. *A planned outcome:* six ways to stretch your distributed network
5. *Activities to make the plan work:* management techniques for large-scale projects
6. *Performance measures:* building reporting measures that work
7. *Future or emerging trends:* five trends that will shape consumers' shopping experiences

If you're a business process expert, you can examine any process for ways to enhance performance, consolidate activities, or compare and contrast performance or organizational models. You can compare the activities of leading organizations to identify breakthrough strategies. Or you can talk about the future of a process.

A change management consultant might fashion a speech on how change will impact an organization's people or its organizational structure. Or, you might focus on change to the organization's long-range plans.

Turn Your Back on the Sunset

The most creative photographers say that when everyone else is capturing the image of the sunset, you should turn around and shoot behind you for an entirely different, but stunning view. As you think about your point of view for your topic, try to look at it in a new way. Your speech will be much more interesting to meeting planners and audiences if you zig where everyone else zags. Take a stand. Stimulate audiences to think.

What the Heck Are You Saying?

Once you have selected a topic and decided on a point of view, isolate the core message of your presentation. What do you want to stick in the minds of your listeners when they leave? Try to summarize your core message in one or two sentences. Build the rest of your presentation around that theme.

Once upon a Time

So much has been written about including stories and humor in speeches that you'd think we'd all be master storytellers by now. Sadly, we are not. Yet stories are critical to connecting with your audience. Mark Victor Hansen, coauthor of *Chicken Soup for the Soul*, points out, "Storytelling helps speakers make a lasting impression on their listeners." He says that's because we ". . . understand *everything* through the context provided by story."[6]

Grady Jim Robinson, premier storyteller and author of *Did I Ever Tell You about the Time*, says, ". . . story, with its potential for symbolism and use of innate universal archetypes, is a powerful way to deliver your message, whatever that message may be."[7] Robinson advises speakers to use personal stories that ". . . contain just enough self-revelation that your audience will begin to feel comfortable with you, understand a bit of your past history, and sense where you are coming from."[8]

Like public speaking in general, effective storytelling is a skill that doesn't come easily. But both can be learned with training and practice. And if you can effectively weave a story and humor around your core message, it will resonate with audiences and stick in their memories.

➤ Step 2: Get a Speaking Engagement

The word is out. The advantages of public speaking are no longer secret, and the competition is fierce. Thousands of want-to-be speakers are now vying for a limited number of slots, and many are accomplished performers who put on highly entertaining shows. Industry events need great speakers. Many events are built around the quality of the speakers they present, and without them, their attendance would dwindle. That demand sustains an industry of professional speakers who have impressive credentials and decades of experience.

A research report by the National Speakers Association found that 35 percent of respondents had been speaking for 11 to 20 years and 28 percent for 6 to 11 years. That's some stiff competition. The good news is that consultants have qualities that audiences and event planners crave:[9]

➤ *Expertise:* Audiences want to hear from the best. That's why more than 75 percent of all event speakers are industry experts.[10]

➤ *Value orientation:* Consultants understand what constitutes value to the clients and industries they serve and can frame their presentations accordingly.

➤ *Up-to-date information:* Consultants can provide audiences with the latest information. They can also provide current data within the historical context of their specialty areas.

➤ *Insider's perspective:* Consultants speak the language of the industry and know the players.

Referrals and Other Resources

Referrals remain the best way for you to get speaking engagements, especially recommendations from people who have heard you speak. Therefore, it's vital to build a network of people who will recommend you as a speaker to their contacts.

Industry associations, corporations, and nonprofit organizations regularly need speakers. Check Web sites for events and look for directories with information on groups. The Directory of Associations, which is published by the Concept Marketing Group, provides information on over 35,000 organizations.

Organizations frequently issue requests on their Web sites for proposals (RFPs) from speakers. They state that they're looking for speakers on various subjects and ask you to submit your biography with a brief summary of your speech. While you're looking for RFPs, also check schedules of upcoming events for other opportunities.

Many sponsoring organizations require potential speakers to furnish an audio or videotape of past presentations. If you expect to be paid, you will need to submit a videotape to even receive consideration. Keep in mind, however, that a professionally made video showing you in the best light can be a substantial investment and a questionable use of your resources if you don't plan on becoming a professional speaker.

GUERRILLA INTELLIGENCE: WILL YOU GET PAID?

The National Speakers Association survey found that meeting planners were somewhat more likely to use unpaid industry experts (59 percent) than paid ones. Of those speakers who did get paid, almost 75 percent of them received less than $5,000 per speech. The big paydays—$15,000 and up—went to just 5 percent of speakers.*

The goal you have for a speech will help you decide what level of compensation, if any, you want. You may be willing to do it for free for the right audience.

---

*"Speaker Usage Monitor: Wave 1," National Speakers Association (June 2003), p. 10.

Ask meeting planners if they plan to videotape your speech. If so, negotiate to obtain a copy of the videotape for your future use.

Speakers' Bureaus

Speakers' bureaus or agencies book engagements for speakers. They are like bank loan departments: If you don't need the money, the bank will be happy to lend it to you. Similarly, when you are an established, popular speaker, bureaus will want to represent you. Celebrities are an exception, but unless you are well known or you have an impressive speaking track record, they won't be dying to represent you.

Bureaus charge commissions, which can be as high as 30 percent of the speaking fee. And keep in mind that they don't work for speakers, but for event sponsors. Bureaus have stables of speakers, some of whom may compete with you for the same engagements. Bureau agents are like commissioned salespeople.

Many bureaus require you, at your expense, to supply them with marketing materials, which can include a professionally prepared color brochure describing you and your credits, your photo, and videotapes of recent presentations. They then send those materials to event planners. Bureaus screen speakers and try to plug them into appropriate venues. Many bureaus also require that you have a "bureau friendly" Web site, which means that the speech and contact information links to the bureau, not the consultant.

Using a speaker's bureau is cost effective for well-paid speakers who are in high demand and have established speaking reputations. Unless you fit this profile, bypass these services.

➤ Step 3: Prepare Your Presentation

This step in the process can last for many months. Use the time to solidify your presentation and build relationships that will make your speech a worthwhile marketing investment.

Reconnoiter

After you've been hired to speak, arrange to meet with the event planners, including the host organization's executives and the event staff. They are usually well informed about both logistics and the makeup of the audience. Test your ideas on them and ask for their insights on how to customize your presentation. This is a chance to meet executives and staff when they are most receptive. After all, it's in their best interests to help you deliver a great speech. Think of event planners as clients, which they are.

Continue to network as you polish your speech. Some speakers send canned questionnaires to event sponsors in an effort to customize their speeches. Most of the information you'll need is available on the Web, and it's better to gather the rest by meeting with your clients and others who plan to attend the event.

Interview other experts in the field, including academics. Also try to meet with your client's customers. Discuss their problems and elicit their opinions. That will produce richer and more perceptive information, including first-hand experiences, on-point stories, and real-life solutions.

Obtaining such input will forge new relationships and strengthen existing ones because you are giving those you talk to a stake in, or even partial authorship of, your presentation. Their involvement can increase your support, visibility, and client referrals, and can lead to tips about future speaking possibilities. Be sure to mention that you'll tell the audience how the experts or clients helped with the speech, which will give them a return for their effort.

Add to Your Ammunition

As you polish your speech, look for additional ammunition to support your points. Find out what your fellow speakers plan to cover during the event so you can coordinate or differentiate your presentation. You may want to build on the themes of previous speakers; it's

GUERRILLA TACTIC: PRESPEECH CHECKLIST

Gather the following intelligence before your speech:

➤ What are the deadlines for submitting a summary or draft of your speech, photos, and other materials?

➤ Who is to be your main contact person leading up to your speech?

➤ What are the audience demographics?

➤ What is the theme(s) of the event?

➤ What are the key issues facing the host organization?

➤ Who spoke and who attended in the past?

➤ Who else is on the program and who will present before and after you?

➤ When will you appear on the program?

➤ How long are you expected to speak?

➤ Can you invite guests and how many?

➤ What will be your compensation—pay, access to the event, guest passes, hotel and airfare, master copies of audio and videotapes of your presentation?

➤ Who will own the rights to play and reproduce recordings or derivative works?

➤ What items, if any, will you be permitted to sell at the event?

highly effective and flattering to those speakers and can forge supportive relationships. On the other hand, you don't want to be repetitious. Speech titles can be deceiving so find out as much as you can, preferably directly from your fellow presenters.

Spread the Word
Publicize your appearance by alerting your clients, inviting peers, potential clients, and the media. Request passes for your guests from the event sponsors. Highlight your speech on your Web site and in your zine. Publish excerpts of your presentation or place announcements in other publications.

➤ Step 4: The Big Event

Many events run for several days. Plan your schedule so you can spend time at the event, not just to deliver your speech, but to participate in other activities.

Testing, Testing

Check out the room where you'll speak. Test all the equipment: lights, microphones, speakers, and projectors. Consult with the event staff and decide where to place handouts, article reprints, copies of your books, and other material. Explain to staff members how they can help. Speakers can be a pain for event planners. Don't be—be a pleasure to work with.

Check Out the Event

Attend as much of the event as you can: the host organization's receptions, dinners, exhibits, and other presentations. Find out what issues concern attendees, your peers, and the other speakers. Ask their opinions and discuss possible solutions. Listen and learn. Network, network, network.

Mingle before You Speak

In whatever time you have just before your presentation, be visible and meet people. Give them the chance to ask you questions and engage you in discussion. Make it a point to talk to event staff, especially those who coordinated the publicity. Staff can be extremely helpful, so treat them well.

It can be difficult to focus on getting to know people when you're mentally getting ready to speak, especially if you're not good at small talk. But it will pay dividends in the long run. You might even be able to mine bits you can use to personalize your speech. And being able to spot friendly faces in a roomful of strangers can ease your nerves.

Deliver a Great Presentation

Finally, the time has come to get up there and speak. This is when your research, planning, and rehearsal will pay off. If you have confidence in your content and know it well, you will be able to relax and enjoy your time in the spotlight.

Make eye contact with your audience. Don't rush. Gesture and move naturally. Pause silently when you need to, but avoid awkward, overly dramatic, or insincere movements or vocal inflections. Listen to and read nonverbal cues from the audience. Involve your listeners in your presentation.

GUERRILLA TACTIC: PROVIDE EXTRAS

Plan to give your audience extras: survey results, white papers, recommended reading lists, how-to articles, and Web addresses that are relevant to your topic. Don't give attendees souvenirs or trinkets—give them something useful. Include your contact information, but don't hold the materials hostage by requiring recipients to give you their business cards or other information to obtain them. Don't push; simply mention what additional items are available at no cost.

Visual Nonaids

Speakers are often tempted to use visual aids like slides and pointers. Used correctly, they can make the difference between a good and a great speech; in the wrong hands, they can be a disaster. PowerPoint is a helpful, but misused tool. Slides can be effective, but they can

---

GUERRILLA INTELLIGENCE: POWERPOINT RULES

➤ If the audience can't read every word on a slide, turn off the computer.

➤ Aim for no more than three words or a single image per slide.

➤ If a slide is too dense, apply the 50 percent rule twice: Remove half of the slide's content, then look at it again and remove another half.

➤ Every slide must be clear, readable, and coordinated with your presentation.

➤ An effective PowerPoint presentation takes practice and rehearsal, especially the transitions. Just because it worked like a charm last week doesn't mean it will again. Before subjecting audiences to needless distractions, rehearse with your slides.

➤ Include your Web site address on each slide (that doesn't count in your three words).

➤ Avoid animation—it detracts from the point you are making.

also be a crutch and a distraction. Don't use slides as speaker notes or as an outline for your speech. Nothing is more boring than a speaker reading bullet points from slides for an hour. Use them sparingly. They are most useful for visually enhancing your main points.

What's the Question?

Decide in advance whether you will answer audience questions during your speech or at the end, and let the audience know the plan. Taking questions as you go along can inject insightful observations and spontaneity into your presentation.

On the other hand, some questions can be distractions and a waste of everyone's time. It takes practice to make judgment calls on the fly about how long to spend on a question and how to get back on track. Be prepared for questioners who try to hijack the floor by posing endless questions. Skillful speakers know how to bypass long-winded questions.

Questions are an ideal way to get feedback about your clarity, find out what's on listeners' minds, and gauge the level of their knowledge. Questions also provide you with great examples that you can use in future presentations. Answering questions is important for the audience, but is often more valuable for the speaker.

Some speakers prefer to set aside a designated part of their presentations for questions and answers. A separate Q&A period avoids interruptions, and you usually get better questions when your audience has heard your entire presentation. It's a personal preference.

If you opt to take questions in a separate period, hold your conclusion until after the Q&A. When you've finished answering questions, deliver a strong closing. In that way, you won't leave the audience hanging; you remain in control of the finale and can finish your presentation on a high note. Also, having the last word gives you the opportunity to incorporate an issue that was raised during Q&A into your concluding comments.

Stick Around

Many speakers leave events as soon as they've given their speeches. In doing so, they lose valuable marketing opportunities. Occasionally, a scheduled speaker cancels unexpectedly. If you're still around, the sponsors might ask you to step in, which will win their gratitude and give you more visibility.

After your presentation, answer any further questions and swap contact information with attendees. Be generous with your time. If you don't have the time or the information to answer a question, make arrangements to do so later.

However long you stay at the event, thank the staff and the sponsoring organization's brass before you leave. If possible, and it's not too awkward, say good-bye to important attendee contacts.

➤ Step 5: Postevent Activities

Within two or three days after your speech, send handwritten notes to event planners and key members of the host organization thanking them for their hospitality and the opportunity to speak. Try to personalize each note.

Call the people who asked you to contact them about their business or to answer deferred questions. Strike quickly, while memories of the event are still fresh. People tend to forget as time goes by.

Organize for Future Reference
Organize the business cards and contact information you collected at the event. Make notes of any special information that may help you remember conversations. Keep a copy of your speech or your presentation notes in a file with the contact information. Add a copy of the event agenda or brochure to your file.

Maintain a master list of all your speaking engagements and include the name of each organization, the primary contact person, date and place of the speech, and your topic. Update the list after each speech.

Organize this information not only to remind yourself what took place, but also to facilitate transfer of important aspects of the event to your Web site and other promotional materials.

Stay in Touch
Plan how to regularly keep in touch with both the attendees and those who hired you to speak. Send e-mails with articles, information that might interest them, or a copy of the book you just wrote. Put entries on your calendar or planner to contact key individuals and make notes on what you might say.

Keep current on the subject of your speech and update or supplement it when appropriate. Send new information with a brief note to the contacts you made at the event. Occasionally, pick up the telephone simply to say hello. Stay on your contacts' radar.

Breaking It Down
Viewed as a process instead of a one-hour torture session, speaking provides excellent opportunities to market your practice. And most

---

GUERRILLA TACTIC: WRITE ALL ABOUT IT

Draft an article based on your speech. Distribute it after your presentation as a marketing aid. Include the piece on your Web site, in your zine, and on your clients' sites or intranets. Also send it to the media, industry association publications, and the host organization's publication. If you wrote an article publicizing your speech before you delivered it, revise it for additional publications.

---

consultants are well equipped to break that process down and master its elements.

The demands of speaking are substantial, but so are the potential rewards. Research[11] shows that, in selling, a demonstration is 50 percent more effective than the most glowing testimonial. A speech demonstrates what you know and what you can do. It also shows how you think and how you work. If you have trained, practiced, and performed well, it will show.

Chapter 12

Book Publishing

The Guerrilla's 800–Pound Gorilla

If I read a book that cost me $20 and I get one good idea, I have gotten one of the greatest bargains of all time.

—Tom Peters[1]

When Michael Hammer and James Champy published *Reengineering the Corporation* in 1993,[2] they launched a business revolution. The book, which called for the "rethinking and radical redesign of business," became a *New York Times* bestseller and the handbook for business transformation. Hammer and Champy were also swamped with new consulting business.

Authoring a book has marketing clout with clients and prospective clients. The right book, at the right time, invariably will catapult a consultant to the top of a client's list of favorites. However, writing a book is also a time-consuming, long-term commitment. For many consultants, devising, writing, and publishing a book takes longer than completing their longest client project.

■ THE POWER OF THE PEN

Few marketing weapons give as much bang for the buck as a successful book:

144

➤ *It establishes you as an expert.* On publication, the book instantly establishes you as an expert with your clients, potential clients, and peers. Authorship grabs the attention of prospective clients and experts both in your field and in other areas. They want to meet you to discuss your theories, their problems, and how you can help. Those who have read your book will know your ideas and approaches and may be looking for opportunities to work with you.

➤ *A published book provides a platform for speaking opportunities.* A book will get your name in front of those who hire speakers. With aggressive promotion, you should land multiple paid speaking engagements that can supplement your consulting fees and provide leads for new consulting work. With the right publicity strategy, the media will seek you out for interviews, quotes, and television appearances.

➤ *Your intellectual assets multiply.* You can condense the material in your book for multiple articles. Each chapter can serve as the basis for additional research and publication. You can create speech materials from the summary of the book's theories or individual parts of the book. You can create workbooks that help readers apply the book's concepts, audio recordings of the book, and book summaries of the basic ideas. The possibilities for using a book as a source for new intellectual assets are endless.

■ SHOULD YOU WRITE A BOOK?

For many, the *idea* of being an author is more appealing than actually sitting at the keyboard and working at it. It's fairly easy to envision a book-length work in your mind; it's quite another matter to get the whole thing on paper. You may have written dozens of consulting reports, but that experience won't always be helpful because many

GUERRILLA INTELLIGENCE: A BOOK'S VALUE TO A CONSULTANT
The greatest value of your book is the exposure it provides and the additional opportunities that follow. Look at your book as a platform and use it to create consulting opportunities and new contacts.

consulting reports are dry, fact-filled analyses of an arcane problem that average nonfiction readers would find painful to read.

A winning book shares some characteristics with a winning consulting project. You must have a compelling idea, a new way of looking at an old problem, or a unique twist on a new issue. To determine whether you should write a book, answer these seven questions:

1. *Do you have an idea that can fill a book?* It may be easy to imagine that a single, critical idea could fill a book, but that's not always the case. Do you have something compelling to say that will fill an entire book: an idea, a process, a story, unique position, or a combination of those elements? Drafting a rough outline of the projected book's table of contents will help you see whether you've really got a book.

2. *Do you enjoy writing?* Some consultants get heartburn when it comes to writing reports and proposals. If you don't enjoy writing, you shouldn't try to write a book.

3. *Are you willing to sharpen your writing skills?* Publishers want books that are less formal and easier to read than most consulting reports. Most readers won't slog through dense prose—they look for information that is presented clearly and concisely. You may have to change your writing style to appeal to business readers.

4. *Do you have the time and patience to master the details of preparing a book-length work?* Because of their expertise, consultants are often afforded great respect in the client environment. In the world of traditional publishing, the consultant is just another author, not a guru who commands high fees. You'll need time and patience to master the ins and outs of the publishing world.

   Realize that you'll spend considerable time finding and working with agents, lawyers, publicists, and others. Ask yourself if you have the time to write a book proposal, find an agent, endure contract negotiations, and undertake a long-term writing project.

   Writing a book usually requires a juggling act as you try to balance consulting assignments, your family, and your writing. Before you get too deeply involved, set your priorities and understand that everything will take longer than you think. Estimate the time you think you'll need—then double it. Then expect delays.

5. *Are you willing to write a detailed book proposal?* You will need to write a book proposal that meets stringent specifications because most literary agents won't discuss your project without such a proposal (see the discussion later in this chapter). Your book proposal, which can be a lengthy document itself, requires a substantial commitment. When you spend time writing a book proposal, you'll incur opportunity costs—you could have devoted that time and effort to other marketing efforts.

   A word of caution about book proposals is in order. Most consultants see the word *proposal* and believe they can knock one out quickly. A proposal is, after all, a routine activity for consultants. A book proposal is very different from a consulting proposal, so be sure to read up on how to prepare one. *How to Write a Book Proposal,* by literary agent Michael Larsen, is a good resource.

6. *Are you willing to forcefully promote the book once it's published?* Authors are responsible for promoting their books, so you must be willing to invest time, money, and energy in this activity as well as in writing. Some of the hardest work in the publishing process comes *after* a book is in print. If you want it to stay on bookstore shelves, you and your firm must be willing to pull out all the stops to promote the book, particularly in the first few weeks after publication.

7. *Can you handle rejection?* Many first-time authors make numerous attempts before finding an agent willing to support their book proposals. With patience, you'll develop a salable idea, but you may get a stack of rejection letters from agents before you find someone to help you sell your book to a publisher. It can be a humbling experience.

If you answered yes to at least most of these questions, you're ready to take on a book project. If you're unsure, consider first writing on a smaller scale and then moving on to beefier publications.

GUERRILLA TIP: THE IDEAL BOOK

As a consultant, the ideal book for you to write would focus on a topic you know cold, that's in demand, solves a problem, and promotes the services you provide.

Begin by authoring articles for newspapers, newsletters, Web sites, and other publications. Work up to longer articles or special reports for targeted publications. Over time, you'll polish your writing skills, generate some publicity for your practice, and be in a better position to decide whether you're interested in writing a book.

■ TAKING THE LEAP

Think about writing a book as a consulting project. You'll need to propose a salable and valuable idea, create a plan for completing the work and, once the project is done, sell your results. Unless you're self-publishing, your first sale will be to a literary agent or a publisher. Agents and publishers are only interested in books that will sell, so stress your book's sales potential in your proposal.

A book proposal sets forth a business plan for your book. You have to convince yourself and an agent that your book—the business in this venture—has profit-making potential. Build your case around the size of your market, the need for this particular subject, and the competitive situation your book will face once it hits the shelves. Review similar and complementary books. Their existence will prove to publishers that there are potential buyers for your book.

Examine both what's being published and what's selling in your book's category. Browse online and in traditional bookstores and identify the specific book category your book would fall under. Booksellers have to know where to put your book, so be sure you define its subject category. Then, determine whether that category is saturated or underserved. Tap into your client experience to test your ideas. Solicit clients' input and perspectives.

GUERRILLA INTELLIGENCE: WHAT ABOUT ROYALTIES?

Before you even consider writing a book, understand the full commitment of resources required. Although the rewards of publishing can be enormous, only a few books make money for their authors. Unless you're a best-selling author, your royalties may not even cover your book promotion expenses. The direct income you receive from writing a book may not be as great as you expect, but then again, the client projects you win can far outstrip any royalties you might receive from sales of the book.

Once you've done your preliminary research and settled on an idea, you're ready to start writing your book proposal. Even if you plan to self-publish your book, the rigor of preparing a book proposal will shorten the time you'll eventually need to write the book while giving you a good idea of the level of effort you'll face.

Many fine books have been written about the art of preparing a winning book proposal, and you should study them. You can ease the effort of preparing a book proposal by following the guidelines set forth by the publishing world. A fairly clear set of steps guide your way, so follow them. Buck the system too much and you'll find yourself rewriting your book proposal more times than you revise a controversial client report.

At a minimum, a book proposal must include seven major topic areas.

1. *The idea:* What is your subject and how will it grab readers? What's new or different about your treatment of the subject?

2. *The market for the book:* Who will buy the book? How large is the potential market for the book? And, how many books do you estimate you can sell?

3. *Comparable and competitive books:* Who else is writing on your subject? What are the strengths and weaknesses of those books and how will your book add to the subject? What books complement your proposed book and how will your book add to what's been written?

4. *Potential spin-offs:* What other avenues exist for publishing your material—book summaries, audiotapes, or companion field guides?

5. *Your qualifications to write the book:* Agents and publishers will look at how qualified you are to complete the book and how aggressively you will push it into the market. A professional chef who wants to write about the joys of making pottery had better have some real qualifications on the pottery wheel. Demonstrate your expertise by identifying a problem and showing readers how to solve it.

6. *Your plan to promote the book:* Agents and publishers place the lion's share of the promotion burden on the author, so show how you'll support the marketing of your book to meet the forecast you've set earlier in your proposal. Many agents and publishers view this section as the most important part of the proposal. A great book idea with a lackluster promotion plan will come back to you for revision.

7. *The details:* A book proposal must also contain the book's proposed table of contents, a brief summary of each chapter, and one or two sample chapters.

Painful though it can be, writing a proposal forces an author to define and state what the book is about and why a publisher should buy it. Many authors think this task is the most difficult part of writing a book. But once it's done, you have a running start on drafting the manuscript, so you won't spend as much time staring at a blank computer screen wondering what to write.

■ HAVE YOUR AGENT CALL MY AGENT

Most publishers won't accept unsolicited proposals and manuscripts, and those that do will have your submission evaluated by an overworked junior editor who will super speed-read it. So it's usually best to retain a literary agent to act as your representative with publishers' acquisition editors. Most literary agents are swamped with requests, so they can also be difficult to reach, but they hold the keys to the publishing world.

Since literary agents work on commission—usually 15 percent of the funds their clients receive—they won't waste their time on projects that publishers are not apt to buy. By submitting a proposal or manuscript to an agent, you'll get a mixed bag. Some will give you an expert opinion on the commercial merit of your book. Others may send you a thin letter in the mail stating only that they have decided not to represent you.

If you find an agent willing to take on your project, the best ones will advise you how to shape your proposal or manuscript to make it marketable. They'll also refer you to other resources such as proofreaders, editors, and researchers who can help you smooth rough spots.

Agents know the best potential publishers for your work and how and when to approach them. If a publisher shows interest, they'll negotiate on your behalf. Most agents are skilled negotiators and since they've got a vested interest, they'll fight for a good deal.

The greatest benefit of agents may be their role as advisors. They become your partners and may be the only people you can really talk to about strategy for your book. Agents know the publishing business, the markets, and your contract, and will protect your interests. If your book sales are good, they'll push the publisher for more promotion or perhaps a second book.

For more information about agents, see *Jeff Herman's Guide to Book Publishers, Editors and Literary Agents 2004*,[3] and *Literary Agents*, by Michael Larsen.[4]

■ YOUR PUBLISHING DECISIONS

The publishing business is undergoing major changes, and that's good for guerrillas. Today, authors have many options to bring their ideas to market. They can approach a wide range of traditional print publishers, from prominent publishing houses to smaller specialized firms with obscure names. If that route isn't desirable, they can self-publish their work, pay to have a vanity house publish their book, or publish an e-book. Today, with so many books being published, the trick isn't getting your book published, but getting it noticed in the market.

Here's a brief rundown on the options you can consider.

➤ Traditional Publishing

The mainstream publishing houses are like the shopping malls of publishing. They publish titles on subjects from advertising to zoos. Their business is highly speculative and marketing driven. Manuscripts have long development cycles and publishers must incur substantial upfront editing, printing, and marketing costs. Few publishers will offer you a contract if they don't believe that they can profit from publishing your book.

Producing artful books is great, but that's not the main objective of most publishers. Like other businesses, they survive by making money and tend to live by the stock investor's credo, "Buy low, sell high." As a result, they are efficient at controlling costs. They buy manuscripts as cheaply as possible and keep their editing, printing, distribution, and promotional costs down. A publisher's emphasis on profit can sometimes set up a creative clash with authors about things like book design, promotion, and distribution.

But the mainstream publishers provide highly polished, well-designed products and usually have wide distribution. Their books are well edited and frequently indexed. Although publishers help their authors publicize books, most want to see quick success and won't continue supporting books that start slowly out of the gate.

Because of the sheer volume of books produced by most large publishers, new titles seem to take forever to hit the bookstores. Book projects take longer than you might think, so remain patient. After you submit a manuscript to a large publisher, it will be many months before your book is published.

Being published by a major publisher certainly has cachet and can provide greater credibility than other publishing options, especially with clients who buy consulting services. So, don't shy away from this option, even though the process seems drawn out. However, that old canard "if your book isn't published by one of the big New York publishing houses, you're not a real author" is total nonsense. Never judge a book by its publisher.

➤ Smaller Publishers

Literally thousands of small publishers exist and many of them specialize in niches that could have great appeal for a consultant-author. Many smaller publishers have long histories and are highly respected.

Smaller publishers are usually able to bring manuscripts to the market faster than bigger publishers—often in half the time. They also tend to give books more personal attention and keep them in print longer. Many smaller publishers are experts at targeting their particular markets and can provide you with wise guidance on your book's content, approach, direction, and marketing strategy.

If you go with a smaller publisher, you still need to submit a proposal and usually have to go through an agent. Smaller publishers may pay low advances and low royalties, but they will bring your book to print.

➤ Self-Publishing

Self-publishing is the fastest growing segment of the publishing industry. Sophisticated hardware and software continue to make book production simpler and less costly. Self-published authors keep their book profits because they don't have to share profits with publishers. There is no need for a literary agent or a formal book proposal. The author has total control of the book's content, design, and distribution.

If you choose to self-publish your book, you've become more than an author. You're in the publishing business. Self-publishing requires authors to take operational and financial responsibility for every aspect of their books, which can consume that most precious resource, time. The good news is that people and firms can be hired at virtually every stage of the publishing process to help you edit, design, print, distribute, and promote self-published books.

Some of the world's best-selling books were originally self-published and later picked up by major publishers once the books became successful. The primary challenge facing most self-publishers is getting wide distribution of their books in bookstores and online outlets.

With the advent of printing on demand (POD), publishing your own book has become an even more realistic option. POD lets writers print only as many books as they need. If writers self-publish and get requests for 20 books, they can have their contract printer produce only that number and ship them wherever needed. POD avoids large up-front printing costs because you don't have to publish mass quantities and you don't have any storage costs.

The cost of POD for each book is slightly higher than printing in bulk because you are printing incrementally instead of in large print runs. However, it is easier on the consultant's cash flow not to print large quantities of unneeded inventory. Since traditional publishers dole out such meager royalties, especially to first-time authors, self-publishing can be very profitable.

➤ Vanity Publishers

Vanity publishers publish books for a fee; you pay them to publish your book. Essentially, vanity publishers are little more than printers, although some provide editorial services and limited distribution. You may hear vanity publishers referred to as joint venture publishers, co-operative publishers, subsidy publishers, and shared responsibility publishers. Some even call themselves self-publishing companies.

The quality of vanity publications varies from company to company and by how much you pay. Some of their products look like sales brochures on steroids. In most cases, books produced by vanity publishers are instantly recognizable. If you have a solid idea and a good promotional plan, you shouldn't have to pay a vanity publisher to print your book. You should consider one of the other publishing options.

➤ E-Publishing

The newest member of the self-publishing family is the e-book, which is a book that readers can download from an Internet site. E-books provide instant delivery to interested readers.

E-books are less expensive to produce than print books because you don't have printing or shipping costs. With e-books, you no longer have to wade through the laborious print publication process. You can simply sell the book on your own Web site or through e-book publishers. You can send your manuscript to e-book publishers electronically and they can help you get it ready for publication. Most promote the book on their site and some offer POD and direct downloads of the book. You'll still have primary responsibility for promoting your book, and you can sell it on your site and in other venues such as conventions and speaking engagements.

The advantage of publishing an e-book is speed. Once you create your book, it's easy to get it prepared for distribution via the Web. The best companies selling e-books offer much higher royalties than any other publishing option. But like their traditional publishing brethren, they'll reject poorly written manuscripts. So, apply the same rigor to an e-book that you would to any other publication. E-books are also easy to revise and update.

With e-books, readers can review your book, pay for it online, download it, and begin reading without leaving their offices. Not surprisingly, many e-book readers print out the file they receive so they can read the book more easily.

But e-books have disadvantages. Your royalties will be higher, but you will receive no advance. It can be more difficult to use an e-book to promote your expertise because you can't just lay the book down on the client's desk. Since your book won't appear in bookstores or in hard copies, it may be harder to use it to promote your practice with some clients.

As a publishing option, e-books are ideal for shorter works, chapter-length pieces, and speeches. Guerrilla author Seth Godin supplemented his book, *Purple Cow: Transform Your Business by Being Remarkable,* with the e-book *99 Cows,* which provides 99 examples of the points he raised in *Purple Cow.*[5]

GUERRILLA TACTIC: INCLUDE REAL CONTENT IN FREE EXCERPTS

Some consultants offer excerpts of their e-books or other work on their sites to encourage visitors to sign up for a zine or to make a purchase. If you offer such excerpts, be sure they provide real value. Don't frustrate potential clients by holding back helpful content. If you do, they may decide not to buy your book or cancel their subscription to your zine. Include some substance in a free excerpt because it can convince readers to buy the e-book.

■ PROMOTION

So many books are published each year that it's hard to distinguish your book and get it noticed, so guerrilla marketing tactics will come in handy. Most publishers have in-house publicity departments to promote your book. However, the reality is that in-house publicists are so overworked that they can't satisfy all their authors' needs. Besides, you should be eager to promote your own work. After all, it's your passion, and no one is going to sell your book better and more enthusiastically than you.

Most in-house publicists include your book in the publisher's catalog, take it to book fairs and expos, and send press releases about it to the media. Unless you are a big-name author or have negotiated a special deal, which is difficult to get, that's all you'll receive. In-house publicists have little time or funds to sufficiently promote your book. If you go with a large publisher, expect the publisher to assign your book to an overworked publicist.

■ THE GUERRILLA CONSULTANT'S RULES FOR PROMOTING A BOOK

➤ *Your book is a means, not an end:* Remember you have two objectives when promoting your book. First, you want the book to attract clients to your practice so your business will profit from your efforts. And second, you want to sell enough copies to earn back your advance, attract lots of readers, and make some money.

➤ *Promote early:* Begin a concerted, well-designed promotional campaign for your book long before the publication date. Your original book proposal included a promotional plan; so start

---

GUERRILLA TACTIC: GET HELP

Hire your own publicist. Invest a portion of your advance on publicity for your book. Many public relations firms specialize in book publicity and do outstanding jobs. They can plan and coordinate publicity campaigns with your publisher. And, they can usually get more from your publisher's publicity department than you can alone.

executing that plan early. Don't wait until your book is just about to hit the stores. If you do, it will be too late. Hire a publicist, begin working with the media, and alert your clients long before the book is scheduled for publication.

➤ *Do something daily to promote your book:* Bring attention to your book in some way every day. Whether you're preparing articles, speeches, or just making telephone calls to clients, get in a word or two about your book.

■ TWENTY-FIVE WAYS TO BUILD YOUR CONSULTING BUSINESS WITH YOUR BOOK

1. Promote the book on your Web site, include an up-to-date media kit, and make it simple for visitors to purchase the book from your site.

2. Create and promote a Web site devoted specifically to the book with author information, a sample chapter or two, speaking schedules, media kit, and a feature allowing readers to submit feedback. Include a feature for ordering the book. Promote the existence of this site on your firm's Web site.

3. Add a blog to the promotional site for the book that gives readers additional ideas related to the topic of the book. Include the latest news, tools, and tips. Include a link for ordering the book.

4. Create a high-quality summary of the book's major themes and allow visitors to download it.

5. Target 25 to 50 specific clients to solicit bulk orders for the book. If a client orders enough copies, the publisher can create a customized cover featuring the client's logo.

6. Send review copies to the top 100 executives in your area of expertise. Follow up with a request to meet and discuss the topic of the book. Include a customized letter, a book summary, and your contact information.

7. Be sure your prepublication book, along with a cover letter and press release is sent to the major book reviewers such as KirkusReviews.com, Publishersweekly.com, *ALA Booklist,* the *Library Journal,* and Bookreporter.com. Each organization reviews hundreds of books monthly that are widely read by librarians, publishers, agents, readers, and booksellers.

8. Take a client book tour. Contact each of your major clients and offer a personalized session on the problems addressed in the book. While you're in town, coordinate your visit with one or more local book signings, either at local bookstores or in the lobby of your client's building.

9. Make sure every person in your practice has a copy of the book, has read it, and understands how its content can benefit clients. Offer to give your colleagues briefings and Q&A sessions. Sign each of their copies with a personal note.

10. Create a postcard with an image of the book cover on one side and a summary of the book on the other. Mail these to key clients, but also keep a supply for leave-behinds at speeches, conventions, and bookstores. Keep a stack of the cards in your car—they will come in handy.

11. Contact every relevant trade and business magazine and discuss excerpting the book for readers in an upcoming issue.

12. Contact major newspapers and broadcast media to request media interviews on the book's subject.

13. Write articles for trade publications, client-based intranets, and relevant Web sites.

14. Create three presentations of the book's content—a one-hour keynote speech, a half-day workshop, and a full-day seminar. Promote the events through your Web sites, press releases, and to your clients. Include a copy of the book as part of the price of the session.

15. Send advance copies of the book to top industry association executives, university professors, civic organization leaders, and other consultants.

GUERRILLA TACTIC: DON'T FORGET THE OLD SCHOOL TIES

Notify your alma mater. In fact, notify all alumni organizations and publications for your high school, college, and graduate school. Former teachers, professors, and classmates can be your staunchest supporters.

16. Include a reference to your book in every marketing communication you produce, especially proposals.

17. Include a tidbit of information about your book in the signature file of your e-mails.

18. Attend the major conventions that focus on the issues in your book. If you cannot get booked as a speaker, use the event for networking purposes.

19. Instead of flying all over the country on a traditional book tour, consider reaching viewers via a satellite media tour.

20. Consider a press conference by telephone with a select group of reporters from around the country. Some publicists can arrange such conferences with members of the media who have audiences interested in the subject of your book.

21. Send press releases and notifications to library wholesalers like Baker & Taylor. They supply books to libraries and retailers worldwide.

22. Try to have your book stocked in both traditional and non-traditional book outlets. Many executives find their books in airport, hotel, and convention site bookstores. Don't ignore these retailers.

23. Submit your book to clubs like the Book-of-the-Month Club and the Literary Guild. These organizations reach millions of readers who may be interested in your book.

24. Attend book fairs. Each year, Book Expo America attracts thousands of booksellers, agents, publishers, and authors. It's an opportunity to plug your book and network with others in the industry.

25. Get a few high-profile testimonials. Send advance copies of the book to get prepublication blurbs that you can use for promotion. Once your book is published, solicit testimonials from some highly respected executives in the field who can describe how your book helped their organizations work through the issue you wrote about. Publish the testimonials on your Web site and in all your marketing material, including your speeches and articles you write.

■ PUBLISHING REALITIES

Writing a book is like breaking into any new industry: You're constantly learning from your mistakes. Like all new endeavors, you'll master this one, too. As you start, remember the book publishing business is celebrity based. Publishers seek authors whose names

GUERRILLA TACTIC: WRITING WHILE MAKING A LIVING

As your writing progresses, you may find that you need help. If you do, you can hire freelance researchers, editors, proofreaders, indexers, book designers, ghostwriters, and publicists. Try to get recommendations from your friends, literary agents, and network members, or contact writers' organizations to find the help you need.

Another way to ease your load is through collaboration: Share writing or research responsibilities, or both, with others. Split the writing or research by chapters, sections, or subject areas. One of you could do all the interviewing, or you could write together. The approach you take will depend on how much writing and research you want to do, as well as each of your strengths and weaknesses, preferences, and time.

audiences will recognize. If you're not well known, but hope to use the book as a vehicle to become better known, expect an uphill climb. Work to build your name by speaking, writing articles, and gaining prominence within your industry. Build a following that can support you and promote your book, even if it's just in your local area.

Writing a book can bring immense publicity and many new clients to your practice, so consider the option carefully. Keep in mind, though, that book writing requires concentration. It can disrupt your business and your life. It can also steal precious time, resources, and energy from your clients, your family, your friends, and yourself. Be sure to factor that reality into your plans.

A book and the status it provides are permanent. You'll be listed in the Library of Congress and elsewhere. When prospects check you out on the Web, your book is always attached to you. When your book has been published, you're considered an author even if you never write another word. You will become an expert, which will bring innumerable benefits to your practice.

Chapter 13

Survey Said!

Make Surveys and Proprietary Research Work

Surveys move markets. When the University of Michigan's Survey of Consumer Confidence is published, stock markets gyrate and consumer-buying behavior can change, impacting the overall economy.[1] The U.S. government's survey of leading economic indicators influences decisions from the purchasing of raw materials to the hiring of workers. Politicians follow every rise and fall in the polls as they formulate campaign or policy strategies. Surveys and their influence are everywhere.

What's ironic is that in a world awash in data, business leaders continue to bemoan the shortage of useful information to help them run their businesses. Most companies are constantly searching for more current, accurate, and sharply focused information to make strategic and tactical decisions.

Many businesses are swamped with so much information about their operations that it's hard for them to look outside their own walls and discover what's going on with their competitors, suppliers, and customers. Surveys can help by providing executives with the information they need.

Surveys are measuring devices. A well-executed survey can reveal the overall condition of an organization, problems in a promotional campaign, or the reasons for workers' dissatisfaction, to name a few possible results.

■ WHY CONSULTANTS SHOULD CONDUCT SURVEYS

When you collect survey data, analyze, and report on it, the results become a crucial part of your firm's intellectual assets. Surveys reinforce your firm's expertise, bring new ideas to your targeted clients, generate leads for new business, and expand your network of contacts.

A survey also provides you with market visibility. You'll interact with clients and prospective clients as you prepare a survey, conduct it, and present its results. Few marketing activities pack the punch of a survey when it comes to impressing and meeting potential clients.

Publicity you receive from surveys establishes you as the authority on your topics. When you are an acknowledged leader, clients will call you. Use the survey results to help build relationships with clients.

A successful survey is usually not a one-shot deal. Think of a survey as being more like a franchise, an ongoing initiative that you bring to the market at regular intervals. Over time, you stake out territory that your competitors can't match. You become the expert in resolving the issues addressed in the survey. Often, the results of consultants' surveys lead to the development of new services that consultants offer to clients.

GUERRILLA INTELLIGENCE: SLICE AND DICE

The data from a well-designed survey serves many purposes in addition to the initial report of findings. The information that you collect can be useful for preparing articles, speeches, and related reports. You can customize a survey report and present it to a particular client or a group of clients in an industry. Include provocative data from the survey results in proposals and on your Web site. Look for other media channels to distribute some or all of your survey results. Newspapers, television, radio, Web sites, and industry publications always need fresh and compelling information.

■ PROCEED WITH CAUTION

Conducting and marketing a survey can take on a life of its own, and surveys come in all types and sizes. Some consultants run unscientific polls on their sites by asking visitors for their opinions on a particular topic. They run the survey for a period of time and publish the results. If you'd like a snapshot of how your Web site visitors or zine readers feel about a topic, this method will work.

If you want to understand more substantive issues impacting the business community, you'll want to conduct a scientific survey, rather than an informal one. Even if you are an expert at survey design, development, and analysis, it can be resource intensive to move from your initial idea to the publication of your report. It is possible to outsource the entire effort to a polling firm, which can shorten the survey life cycle. But that will also cost substantially more than if you complete the survey yourself.

■ SEVEN CHARACTERISTICS OF A GREAT SURVEY TOPIC

The centerpiece of your survey project is the topic you cover. With a compelling topic, you can influence clients, contribute knowledge and answers to tough problems, and build your business. If your topic is repetitive or irrelevant, you're simply wasting your time. Find topics that hit the mark.

Review industry publications, local newspapers, and the Internet for ideas and interesting new angles. Interview your clients on the topics they'd like to see covered. Review the surveys that are currently underway so you don't repeat them. Consult with academicians, industry association executives, civic leaders, and even politicians. From these interviews, you'll develop a great list of potential topics.

Sort through your list and apply the following seven criteria to find a topic your market will respond to favorably:

1. *Uniqueness:* Is it different? Does the topic offer information on a new area or a new slant on an existing subject? Is it a compelling and valuable subject that would make readers pick up the survey report and read it? Resist creating another consumer price index.

2. *Popular demand:* Use your market research to determine whether demand exists for the topic. Remember the survey is not for you, but for your clients and others.

3. *Practicality:* The worst response you can get to a survey report is, "Oh, that's nice." If you are planning to use the survey for clients, give them findings that can guide their future actions. Make the results usable and actionable (for example, that 75 percent of the survey respondents are changing their mobile computing strategies). Many companies will be interested in that trend.

4. *Understandable data:* Some survey topics are too complex or narrow because they try to gather every possible shred of data. Make your survey easy to grasp, topical, and don't require respondents to go through training to fill it out. Make it simple and you'll get a higher and faster response rate.

5. *A focus on the future:* Readers want to get a glimpse of the future, so give it to them. When you ask questions about the history of a specific process or practice (for example, outsourcing), also include questions about the respondent's plans for the future (you might ask whether the respondent plans to spend more, less, or the same funds on outsourcing next year).

   Questions about the future give readers actionable items to consider, and the value of your survey franchise improves as a result. It also gives you an opportunity to measure how respondents acted when you obtain survey results in subsequent years.

6. *Continuity:* Choose a topic that lends itself to a recurrent survey. It will allow your clients to compare results on a year-to-year basis and understand how respondents are reacting to issues previously raised. The costs of a survey are higher in the first year than in subsequent years because of start-up expenses. As time passes, the survey process becomes easier and less costly. Plan to run your survey many consecutive years to gain economies of experience. Publishing your survey results annually also puts you in the limelight each year.

7. *Targeted topic:* Choose a topic of deep interest to your clients and target markets. Stay within your area of expertise so you will be a credible spokesperson on the nuances of the survey results.

■ TAKING THE PLUNGE

Before putting the final touches on your survey, consider several options for conducting the survey that will produce the highest impact at the lowest cost. In some cases, a client will sponsor an industry survey to ferret out the implications of a specific issue. Clients can help prepare the survey topic, identify the mailing list, and assist with analysis, if needed. Many consultants receive a fee for conducting the survey, preparing the findings, and presenting the results to the client's executive team.

When clients wanted detailed information on how retailers in their industry used trade funds, they commissioned consultants to conduct a survey. The clients participated in the survey development in the first year, and then allowed the consultants to carry on the survey in subsequent years on their own.

Cooperative arrangements work well. Some consultants create teams of experts drawn from consulting, academia, and the media to conduct surveys. When several parties share the costs and run a survey, it's usually completed more quickly and the results are more objective.

Outsourcing is now an option for virtually any activity, and survey design, development, and management are no exceptions. For a fee, you can commission a highly professional survey that requires little participation on your part. Some consultants use this option so they can focus on developing marketing programs to promote the survey, instead of dealing with the administrative details of survey preparation and analysis. Outsourcing can be costly; it will depend on the scope of the survey you plan to conduct.

Just as there are DIYers—do-it-yourself types—in the home improvement business, some consultants prefer to manage the entire survey process from beginning to end. With low-cost, online survey tools, like those offered by firms such as SurveyMonkey.com, conducting a survey is less costly than in the past.

GUERRILLA INTELLIGENCE: COLLABORATE

Collaboration with others is a hallmark of guerrilla marketing, and surveys lend themselves particularly well to productive partnerships. In one case, a consulting firm teamed with a local university and newspaper to conduct a survey on the city's future technology needs. The consulting firm, in conjunction with university faculty members, designed the survey; the local newspaper contributed use of its Web site to receive survey responses; and the consulting firm prepared the mailing list, analyzed the results, and published the joint report, which was featured for weeks in the local media.

GUERRILLA TACTIC: CHOOSING THE BEST SURVEY OPTION

There are many approaches to conducting a survey. Answering the following five questions will help you pick the option that is right for you and your targeted clients:

1. How much time do you have to spend on the mechanics and marketing of a survey?
2. How will that commitment affect other marketing initiatives?
3. How much can you invest in out-of-pocket expense?
4. Is in-house expertise available to manage the project?
5. Will your topic last for more than one survey cycle?

You'll still need a team to manage the process because surveys have many moving parts. They include developing the topic, preparing the list of names, creating the questionnaire, following up with respondents, and developing final reports. You'll also have to assign someone to handle the marketing program.

■ STEPS TO A SUCCESSFUL SURVEY

Test your topic extensively before beginning the survey. Consider testing to be a required part of your research. Run your choice of topics by clients, your associates, industry executives, and academics. Specifically ask them if they think that the topic needs to be surveyed. Would it be valuable for the industry or would it be unnecessary or redundant? If you learn that the topic has been surveyed, find out when and by whom, and study the results. Get copies of prior surveys to distinguish them from the project you propose. Ask someone objective to review questions to be sure they are unbiased.

During testing, ask your contacts to suggest any unique angles or approaches. If the people who help in your test have diverse backgrounds, they should come at the issue from different perspectives. This could flesh out the topic, which would make your survey even more valuable.

Identify your business and marketing objectives and clarify who will constitute your target audience for the final report. For example, is your target for a project on HMOs the chief executive officers, chief

operating officers, chief financial officers, prospective investors, or
possible management teams? When you've identified the audience,
ask whether your information will be compelling to them.

Decide which outcomes you hope to achieve. Are you looking for
visibility, to generate business leads, build new relationships, or any
combination thereof? What contributions do you expect your survey
to make and to whom?

Follow these rules in developing your survey questions:

➤ Keep questions short.

➤ Make all questions clear, simple, and quickly answerable. Try
to give respondents a straight line through the survey.

➤ Every question should be fully understandable at a single
reading.

➤ Eliminate any words or language that readers cannot immediately understand.

➤ Test the clarity of your questions on people who are not involved in the target industry.

Decide how to distribute the survey—via hardcopy, Internet, or
telephone. Ask permission to contact respondents with in-person,
follow-up questions. Clearly state the deadline for submitting the
completed survey.

It is often helpful to convene panels of respondents in a live setting, who complete the survey while discussing the issues it raises.
The input from the panel can add texture to the findings, and the
meeting can provide introductions to potential clients.

Before writing your survey questions, develop a working hypothesis that states what you want to test with the survey. For example,
you may hypothesize that the HMO industry is lagging behind academic medical centers in an important business process. After you

GUERRILLA TACTIC: WHAT'S THE POINT?

Write the survey so that respondents can answer all questions
quickly. Create an easy, logical flow of concise questions. Get
right to the point. Don't compose questions that require respondents to write essays; design them for short answers. Whenever
possible, include boxes that respondents can check.

have your hypothesis, identify the steps you must take and the specific questions you must ask to prove or disprove it.

Work backward from the final report to the survey questions. Before you write your survey questions, rough out the format for the final report, including the charts you'd like to include. Begin writing report outlines. This will ensure that you cover all the topics that the report should include. Sketching out what you expect to find helps identify all the data you need to prove or disprove your hypothesis, and can suggest questions you might miss, forget to ask, or pose differently.

Also identify the charts, illustrations, and comparisons you'll need when you receive the survey data. This will help you create survey questions that will simplify your report preparation.

Create a clear and compelling value proposition for the survey respondents. Explain in two sentences the real difference that the survey will make to a participant. In one case, a consultant promised to show a manufacturing executive how the company stacked up against 50 of its top competitors in areas like product development, manufacturing processes, and customer service. The client was interested enough in such valuable benchmark data that he participated in the survey.

Describe exactly what respondents will receive as a result of their help: a free copy of the report, a personal briefing on the results (if desired), or a customized data set showing how their situation compares with others. Providing a compelling value proposition will dramatically increase your response rate because survey respondents know they will receive highly useful information in exchange for their time.

Plan your marketing program well before the time when you expect to receive the survey results. Create a coordinated media campaign to maximize the impact of and publicity for your results. Early in the survey development stage, identify your marketing objectives and the best outlets to publish your results. Also determine where you can publish articles, editorials, and case studies, as well as where you can give speeches, workshops, and seminars. Since surveys have long lead times, time your project so you can release your results at conferences and other high-profile events. Also decide when to distribute the results to respondents.

Plan a systematic follow-up campaign. The media is deluged with survey data, most of which isn't high-priority news. Therefore, it's easy for your results to slip to the bottom of the heap. Plan a coordinated follow-up effort. Call two or three days after sending your results to media contacts to confirm receipt. Ask if they understand the results, their implications, and volunteer to explain whatever isn't

> ### GUERRILLA TACTIC: BEFORE YOU PUBLISH THE RESULTS
>
> Think about getting a separate review team to examine your findings. Recruit objective academics and experts who have practical experience in the field being surveyed. Make sure that they don't have a stake in the outcomes. Ask them to look for patterns in the data and for results that make them say, "Aha." Most surveys contain powerful information that will elicit such a response, but finding it often takes fresh eyes and time.

clear. Ask if they need any additional materials and give short deadlines; otherwise they'll take forever.

Give yourself sufficient time. Surveys invariably take longer than expected. Virtually every aspect of a survey can require follow-up and many details must be tracked. When you're dependent on others who are outside your control, response time increases. It's also tricky to put pressure on people whom you've asked for a favor. After the first cycle, the process gets easier, but during the initial go-round, something always goes wrong. Surveys provide spawning grounds for Murphy's Law.

Create firm privacy controls. Set your privacy policy early in the project so that it's completely in place when you approach prospective respondents. Privacy leaks can destroy your credibility, and the word will get out and kill future cooperation.

Assure respondents that you won't disclose information that they provide. If any part of the demographic information inadvertently reveals the identity of a respondent, mask that data. Potential respondents always want to know who else is participating in the survey, so give generalized answers that don't name the participants. Although your survey documents must provide a profile of respondents and demographic information, don't name people or companies.

■ GETTING THE SURVEY TO THE MARKET

Marketing your survey can be a tougher job than conducting the survey, so prepare your marketing program at the same time that you design your survey. Before you send a single press release about the survey, your first job is to be sure the survey results get into the hands of every survey respondent who requested one, along with an invitation to review the results one-on-one, or in small groups with other survey respondents.

GUERRILLA TACTIC: WHAT'S IN A NAME?

Surveys have a shelf life. The 2006 Annual Survey of Trends in
Hotel Management, for example, is less interesting to readers if
they first see it in the middle of 2007. Inform readers when the
survey was conducted, but do not use the year in your survey's
title. Instead, call the survey "The Annual Survey of Trends in
Hotel Management."

These one-on-one or small group briefing sessions fuel the marketing power of your survey. You have the opportunity to present the
results, listen to the concerns of the respondents, and build relationships that could result in future project work. It's not unusual to find
challenges to your findings in these sessions, so you also have a great
opportunity to refine the next survey and add or delete questions. As
you conduct the survey, approach industry association executives,
business leaders, and civic organization officials about sponsoring a
speech or small seminar on the survey findings. Many of these organizations plan their programs well in advance, so approach them
long before you complete the survey. Offer to write a summary article for their respective newsletters or Web sites, so members will
know the survey is available and a seminar is scheduled.

Arrange for publicity in as many appropriate media outlets as
possible, including television, radio, and the business press. Put the
results on your Web site and your clients' sites and intranets, if possible. Include survey information in your zine, blog, and any other
media where you publish.

Conducting a survey is among the toughest, but highest value
marketing activities in your marketing program. In a world swamped
by data, you'll find clients will welcome organized, new information
with enthusiasm. Treat your survey as you would a paid client project.
Use the same rigor and attention and your marketing effort will hit
its mark.

Chapter 14

The Power of Giving Back

We receive but what we give.

—SAMUEL TAYLOR COLERIDGE[1]

In these times of shrinking budgets and fierce competition for charitable contributions, consultants can give to their communities and benefit themselves by volunteering to help nonprofit groups accomplish their missions. Your expertise and efforts can advance the well-being of your neighbors and improve conditions where you live and work. In the process, you can enjoy positive professional experiences, hone your skills, build goodwill, expand your network, and advance your career.

Guerrillas derive numerous benefits from giving to others. But receiving self-serving rewards is not their main motivation. Your primary incentive should be a genuine desire to help others, not merely to develop your business. If you don't passionately want to help, your focus and momentum soon will fade. Lackluster results could hurt your nonprofit clients and damage your reputation.

You can contribute to worthy causes by making financial donations or by working on pro bono projects. Pro bono is defined as "work done without compensation for the public good." On pro bono projects, you can help civic, community, or charitable organizations address their most vexing, complex issues, and your technical expertise can make the difference between the success and failure of their projects.

■ BENEFITS TO CONSULTANTS

Few activities provide as much gratification as giving help to others or are as satisfying as solving important problems. Helping is our ethic; it's the glue that bonds our society, and it feels good to work for the benefit of others. Assisting the less fortunate is a way to share our success. By shifting the focus from our needs to the needs of others, we increase our appreciation for our good fortune and affirm our compassion for others.

Giving back to the community has several benefits:

➤ It solidifies your reputation as a consultant who cares about people.

➤ It helps build your brand with people associated with charities and in your community.

➤ You may attract new clients, but there's no guarantee. If you do receive new business, you can never tell when it might come. It could be just days after you make a great impression, or it might take years.

➤ You can enhance your consultants' skills. Pro bono projects are especially helpful for younger, less experienced consultants because pro bono clients are often willing to give consultants more freedom to perform and offer friendlier, noncorporate environments, which most consultants enjoy.

■ SEVEN SKILLS YOU BUILD

Pro bono projects can be exceptional training grounds where you can grow, build your communication skills, make important network contacts, and work with a variety of clients. Firms can take greater

---

GUERRILLA INTELLIGENCE: PRO BONO MARKETING

For consultants, pro bono work is nonmarketing marketing. It's a careful balance between the desire to contribute to the community and to build your business. To be successful, follow your passion for community service and the commercial benefits that accrue will be a bonus.

risks and put less experienced consultants in roles they might not consider with paying clients. When these consultants develop the following requisite skills, they are more effective in their work with commercial clients:

1. *Ability to work independently:* Pro bono projects are often understaffed because many of the organization's team members are buried in other endeavors or are performing other part-time volunteer work. As a result, volunteer consultants usually work independently, make tough decisions, and gain vital experience.

2. *Creativity:* Volunteer consultants usually have less access to funds, people, and other resources than they would on paying projects. So they often have to find more creative solutions to accomplish even the basic tasks. On a project to create a Web site for a nonprofit organization, a volunteer consultant had no one on his team who could design the graphics for the new site. To resolve the problem, the consultant called every Web designer in town and obtained the necessary volunteer help.

3. *Process consulting skills:* Many pro bono projects are staffed with part-time volunteers, consultants, and the nonprofit's employees. This creates the need for strong process skills like meeting facilitation, data analysis, and project management. Creating a cohesive and productive team from a disparate group is challenging and provides volunteer consultants with invaluable project skills for future assignments.

4. *Executive communication:* Often, the usual business hierarchy is minimal or nonexistent in nonprofits, so consultants must interact with people at every level, from part-time volunteers to board members. A consultant with less than two years of experience had to present her team's recommendations to a nonprofit's board that included the executive director, two state senators, a deputy mayor, and two industry CEOs. That presentation conquered her nervousness in dealing with high-powered executives.

5. *Leadership:* Consultants working on pro bono projects are expected to step up to leadership roles, even if it's a stretch for them. Three consultants led an education program that required them to manage the activities of 700 volunteers working in 23 locations. After that effort, leading other projects seemed tame.

6. *Collaboration:* Community and civic organizations draw volunteers from fields such as education, business, the arts, and politics. Diverse groups frequently must come together to meet common project goals. On an assignment to develop a management structure for a nonprofit's project to reduce urban violence, the team included consultants, former street gang members, the clergy, law enforcement officials, and several prominent politicians. The consultants, in collaboration with the team, found common ground among the team members that formed the basis of a solution. When the consultants subsequently had to deal with a dispute between a client's manufacturing and distribution executives, bringing the opposing parties together was a piece of cake.

7. *Getting it done:* Consulting projects may be extended because of scope changes or other external factors. With paying clients, extensions are usually acceptable because the clients pick up the bill for the extra services, but not in the pro bono world. Consultants must be dedicated to getting the expected results within the expected time frame no matter what other events create barriers.

When a firm was working for a local nonprofit, it learned that the executive director was being replaced. The effect of the change was to freeze the team's activities until the new director's priorities could be determined, which could take months. Knowing that after a few weeks it would be virtually impossible to reconstitute the team, the consultant sought the opinions of the nonprofit's board and the new director. With their help, the project proceeded uninterrupted.

Volunteer work, when performed well, can provide exceptional media exposure, build your business identity, and boost your community and business awareness. The willingness to do good deeds can differentiate a firm and bring it to the attention of potential clients. And volunteer service reminds us not to lose track of our values in the pressure-cooker world of business.

■ CHOOSING OPPORTUNITIES

When you look for ways to give back, you'll find that numerous organizations will welcome your assistance. Expert help is expensive and many nonprofits can't afford it. In deciding which organization to help, apply the following three criteria:

1. *Find the balance between the charitable organization's specific needs and your firm's areas of specialization.* For example, if your firm specializes in health care issues, search for pro bono health care projects. You will achieve better results if you build on and align your expertise with the charitable organization's problems.

   Use your skills in the most effective way. If your firm specializes in strategic planning and the local hospice organization wants you to beautify its facility's landscaping, that's not a good match. Using high-priced consultants to plant trees and bushes doesn't make sense. Volunteer to help the hospice with its five-year funding plan instead.

   After polling its employees, a consulting firm found that education was its staff members' top choice for nonprofit work. So the firm concentrated its pro bono work on education programs for grades K-12. Now, education is a main focus of the firm, and its members take great pride in helping children. One of the firm's areas of specialization was strategic technology planning, so the volunteers developed a districtwide strategy for training teachers how to use computers in the classroom.

2. *Understand the nonprofit's mission.* Find the charity that best fits your values. First, make inquiries with your associates, friends, and network members. Search the Web for additional information. Consider organizations that fascinate or interest you that you think can benefit from your skills. Working on uninteresting projects will bore you and may lead to burn out—so opt for stimulating opportunities with long-term relationship potential.

3. *Uncover the facts.* Reputable organizations clearly define their programs. They have measurable goals and concrete criteria to quantify their achievements. Be sure to compare charities that have similar missions. Also investigate the organization's culture; is it conservative, radical, aggressive, innovative, flexible, or staid?

In choosing a nonprofit to assist, trust your instincts. If you have doubts, don't agree to work with the charity. Instead, find another nonprofit that does similar work, where you can feel comfortable and wholeheartedly perform. Plenty of charities need your help and will be delighted to receive whatever time and effort you can spare.

■ PRO BONO RULES

Treat every pro bono project as if you're working for your best-paying client. Expect some pro bono efforts to be difficult because of red tape or personality clashes. Ironically, the worst nightmares always seem to occur when you volunteer your services or work for a highly discounted rate.

Qualify every pro bono project. Before you agree to help, make sure that you can do it effectively, that the scope isn't too broad, and that both the nonprofit and your firm will support your efforts. Try to select projects that fit in with your other commitments and that can produce results that will be worth your investment.

Get it in writing. As soon as possible, clarify exactly what you're expected to do and put your understanding in writing. It doesn't have to be a full-blown proposal or a long, detailed contract as long as it describes:

➤ Your role.

➤ How you're to work with others.

➤ The results that should flow from your activities.

Use the guidelines in Chapter 16 on writing proposals to prepare a statement of the work you'll perform. Also define measures of success by including what precisely should occur for the project to be successful. Define how you'll know when the project is completed and the nonprofit is satisfied. If you don't specify what constitutes completion of the work, you may never get out of the project.

GUERRILLA INTELLIGENCE: DON'T UNDERESTIMATE THE COMMITMENT

Before you jump in, be certain that you have sufficient time and resources to finish what you begin. Even if you have the best of intentions, don't commit until you're convinced that you can fully deliver. Don't go rushing into a nonprofit project and get its officials all fired up, begin the work, and not complete it. Don't underestimate the obligation you agree to take on and the time, effort, and costs it could entail. By not completing what you started, you could set the nonprofit back and make accomplishing its mission more difficult.

GUERRILLA TACTIC: MAKE IT COUNT

On pro bono projects, do something *significant*. Find a non-profit's toughest problem—a dilemma it doesn't know how to solve—and fix it. Use your skills to create solutions that make real differences. Think blockbusters. If an organization's finances are a mess, overhaul them or put in a new accounting system. If it is having trouble raising funds, implement a process that will enable it to increase contributions by 100 percent. Don't simply volunteer to collect tickets during a conference. Commit yourself to taking on important projects that bring meaningful change.

When highly skilled consultants provide nonprofits with the additional talent they need, the nonprofits frequently don't want them to leave. Charities truly appreciate the value of working with bright, dedicated consultants who produce outstanding results. As a result, they will keep stringing out projects because they're getting such great benefits at no cost.

Many charitable organizations are understaffed and need tight schedules and strong project management. Establish milestones. Create interim checkpoints throughout the project so you can monitor progress and make appropriate corrections promptly. Be responsive, easy to work with, and always meet your deadlines.

It's a good idea to give charitable organizations invoices to give them a sense of the value of your services. Clarify that the invoices are only for informational purposes and that you don't expect to be paid.

Tackling difficult pro bono projects will set you apart from the competition and provide you with interesting challenges. Your talents will be displayed and your accomplishments will be recognized, especially on high-profile projects. You will noticed by and interact with the organization's leaders and its most important supporters.

Performing wonders for worthy causes on big issues can also get you priceless publicity. It will earn you devoted friends and supporters in the community, and you will be helping a worthwhile cause.

Part

III

Guerrilla Selling for Consultants

Chapter 15

All Projects Are Not Created Equal

Time is a consultant's most valuable resource. Use it effectively by selecting the right projects to pursue; choosing wisely is essential to building a profitable consulting practice. The highly competitive consulting market is filled with firms that are willing to write proposals at the drop of a hat, which gives guerrillas a distinct competitive advantage.

Resist the temptation to outpace the competition by being the first one to write a proposal. Your speed and initiative might score early points with some clients, but you could just as easily misjudge a project and commit to a proposal that will cost you.

Instead of racing headlong into the sales process, systematically qualify each opportunity to make sure it meets two requirements: The client will truly benefit from your skills; and the project will help you build a profitable business. Don't pursue projects without those characteristics—you'll just be spinning your wheels.

The sales cycle for landing consulting projects can take weeks, or even months. During that period, clients routinely ask consultants to submit proposal materials, supply references, make presentations, and attend meetings. These efforts can be costly and time consuming, and they can interfere with your work on profitable engagements with other clients. So before you compete for business, objectively evaluate each opportunity.

GUERRILLA INTELLIGENCE: CLIENTS YOU'LL MEET

Buyers of consulting services generally fall into one of the following categories. To avoid those who have no intention of hiring you, no matter how good you may be, learn to recognize the following client types:

➤ *Serious buyers:* They have (1) real projects, not merely ideas they're toying with, and (2) they need outside assistance. Serious buyers carefully evaluate the services you and your competitors offer. They get involved: They work with consultants to design approaches for completing projects; they help with proposals; and they work hard to select appropriate consultants for projects. Look for these clients.

➤ *Tire-kickers:* Visitors to auto dealerships frequently circle new cars, slam doors, check out sound systems, and even take test drives—with no intention of buying. Some clients behave similarly. They'll invite you to meetings just to have a look at what you have to offer without any intention of using your services. Some take advantage of the opportunity to gather free competitive intelligence.

➤ *Benchmarkers:* In the proposal process, these clients set up one competing firm as the "benchmark" consultant. That firm's fees and approach are used as a baseline for leverage in the negotiations with competitors, especially the preferred firm. These clients use your proposal to induce preferred providers to lower their fees or provide more services for the same fees.

➤ *Idea shoppers:* Some prospects will ask multiple consulting firms to present their best ideas on a particular problem, such as how to enter a new market. Once consultants provide the information, idea shoppers assign internal teams to complete projects without hiring any of the consultants; they take the consultants' ideas and run with them.

➤ *Deflectors:* Clients have been known to invite consultants to submit proposals just to get rid of them. Perhaps the personal chemistry didn't work or the consultant's qualifications weren't right. Some prospects just aren't willing to tell consultants why they won't hire them; so they ask for a proposal, which they ultimately reject.

Identifying motives is not always easy. But if you evaluate prospective clients with the above types in mind, you will be able to focus on your targets—serious buyers.

■ THE CLIENT QUALIFICATION SEQUENCE

Whether leads are from new or existing clients, guerrillas use the following three-step sequence to qualify potential projects and pinpoint serious buyers:

1. *Prequalification:* Make sure it's a good prospect before investing your resources.
2. *Discovery:* Get the full story on the client *and* the project.
3. *Decision:* Add all the facts together and decide whether to write a proposal.

Too many consultants don't evaluate client opportunities with a thorough approach and are unpleasantly surprised later by under-budgeted proposals and poorly defined project objectives and scope. Following the three-step sequence described in this chapter prevents surprises and reduces the risk of chasing losing propositions. The better you qualify leads, the lower your cost of sales will be. Plus, you can pull the ripcord—bail out—at any point without damage to your reputation because you haven't made a commitment.

■ STEP 1: PREQUALIFY EVERY LEAD

If you've financed the purchase of a home, you know that realtors usually require prospective buyers to be prequalified or even preapproved for a loan before showing them property. As one realtor says, "It's standard for realtors to ask clients to obtain loan preapproval at the start of the relationship. I want to know that they are serious and that they are looking in the right price range before I invest my time and theirs in the search."

Guerrilla consultants view the prequalification step as similarly critical. When a client asks you to bid on a project, pat yourself on the back—your marketing is working. Then take a deep breath and ask the following nine questions before proceeding. The answers will help you decide whether to pursue the lead.

➤ What You Need to Know before You Proceed

1. *Can the client clearly articulate the objectives and anticipated benefits of the project?* An ill-defined project signals that the client is not yet far enough into internal deliberations about the project, which can readily result in a longer sales cycle and a high likelihood that objectives and scope will shift in

the middle of the proposal development process. If the client cannot explain why the project needs to be completed now, it is a telltale sign of a poorly defined plan.

2. *Has the project been approved and funded?* If the project doesn't have approval and funding, or there's no specific timetable for funding, the project doesn't yet exist. Help the client understand that these decisions must be made before you can participate in the effort; you may want to suggest strategies for getting the necessary approvals.

3. *Who is the client sponsor?* And, whose problem is it? Find out who the leading advocate for the project is and whom it will affect. If the project crosses boundaries between departments, territorial disputes may need resolution for the project to succeed.

4. *Who is calling the shots?* The number one waste of consultants' time and money is negotiating with those who can't make final decisions. If you won't have access to the decision maker(s) throughout the proposal process and the project, you will never know whether you are responding to the client's needs. Even if the client is using a group or committee to select the consultant, it's essential to discuss the details of the project with the ultimate decision maker(s). If that access will not be available, you might want to pass on the opportunity.

5. *Is a consultant-selection process in place?* Even though most clients answer yes to this question, a rational decision-making

GUERRILLA INTELLIGENCE: FIND THE DECISION MAKER

Be sure you understand the client's buying process. The real buyer of services may have delegated the discovery work to nondecision makers who don't fully understand the project's objectives and risks. It might be a member of the procurement department or a committee. Procurement and selection committee members may lack the authority to make a decision, but they often have veto power over candidates.

Meet and discuss the project with the decision maker so you can prepare the most responsive proposal for the project. Tread lightly, though, and reach the decision maker through those involved in the selection process. If you alienate them by going over their heads, you could find yourself out of the competition.

process for selecting consultants rarely exists. So ask the client who will select the consultant what criteria will be used, and if a deadline has been set for making the decision. From the answers, you'll know instinctively whether a selection process exists. If it doesn't, suggest one or more workable approaches.

6. *Does the client have an incumbent consultant who is bidding on the project?* Incumbents often have preferred status with clients for new projects, and you must know what you are up against. That doesn't mean you should pass on the project, but it could change your tactics.

7. *Is your firm interested in the work?* Ask yourself if the proposed project would be challenging and valuable for your firm. Identify the benefits the firm would receive in addition to fees. They could include building new client relationships, enhancing the consultants' skills, entering a new service area, or working with experts in a particular specialty.

8. *What are the potential opportunity costs?* When consultants pursue leads, they often forgo other projects. Perhaps you won't be able to work on a proposal for another client, develop a new service, or take a vacation. Though opportunity costs can be difficult to quantify or predict without a crystal ball, assess the possibilities and carefully weigh them before you begin the sales process.

9. *Why did the client call you?* Often, this is the most revealing question you can ask. The answer can tell you what the client thinks of your firm and if you're being considered to round out a field of candidates or because of some obligation. If the

---

GUERRILLA INTELLIGENCE: THE CONSULTANT IS A BUYER TOO

For consultants, pursuing a new opportunity is both a selling and a buying process. Of course, you have to sell your plan, proposal, and fee estimate to the client, which is never simple. But it's equally important that you be able to "buy" the information the client provides about the project, the barriers to completion, and its definition of success.

If the client holds back vital facts or gives you incorrect information, your proposal could be way off the mark and the project could end up in the ditch down the road. If that happens, you stand to lose as much as—or more than—the client.

client doesn't show great interest in working with you, politely decline the offer.

➤ **Now Can We Meet?**

If clients are satisfied with initial discussions, they'll usually ask you to visit their sites for face-to-face meetings. But remember, clients make no investment in your sales and proposal work. By completing the prequalification step, you will know if you have a reasonable shot at a profitable project before you travel to the client's site with colleagues in tow and devote your resources to further investigation.

A consulting firm, responding to a highly competitive Request for Proposal (RFP), spent two months with a team of five consultants preparing a detailed proposal to help a client create a new strategy for its flagging retail business. Working closely with the client's consultant selection committee, the team prepared a 75-page proposal, including appendixes, outlining how the client and consultant would work together to forge a winning retail strategy. The client found the proposal and team so impressive that they accepted the proposal. The consultants immediately celebrated this great victory.

The next day, the consultant called the client to confirm the project start date and other details, such as team composition and the early tasks needing attention. The consultant was shocked to learn that the project hadn't been funded. The start date was not established and wouldn't be for several months, if ever.

Remember the second question every consultant should ask in prequalifying client projects: "Is the project funded?" Don't proceed without an answer to that question.

■ STEP 2: DISCOVERY—THE REST OF THE STORY

The next step in the qualification process is one of mutual discovery. This is when consultants learn the rest of the story about the client's organization and the project, and when clients size up consultants. Often, projects are won or lost in the discovery phase. So diligently prepare for client meetings and leave nothing to chance.

Efficiently collect the information you need to assess the opportunity and follow the nine rules listed next.

➤ **Guerrilla Rules for Discovery**

1. *Set precise objectives and identify next steps.* Prepare an agenda that specifies what both consultants and clients will get out of discovery meetings. Some sales consultants suggest that you begin by citing an example of what you've done to help similar clients. That may be a waste of time if the client has researched you. Wait for clients to ask for details about you before volunteering such information.

Never leave a client meeting without agreeing what comes next. It could be scheduling your next meeting or setting up a series of interviews within the organization.

2. *Never wing it.* Before client meetings, review the client's annual report and other company literature. Then dig deeper to understand the executive relationships within the client's organization and the client's position in the industry. Call your contacts to get their perspectives on the company and its key people. Look at the company's competition to understand its external challenges, and research its customers, suppliers, investors, and employees.

3. *Skip the small talk.* On meeting a new client, it's natural to scan an office to get impressions about the client's interests and worldview. Go ahead and check everything out, but don't make lame comments about the deer head mounted on the wall and then launch into a tale about your experience hunting exotic animals in Africa. Make mental notes, but skip the small talk; it merely delays meetings and wastes time. Focus on using time to your fullest advantage.

4. *Bring the right people.* Make sure that the people you bring to discovery meetings can contribute. Bring only those who have

GUERRILLA INTELLIGENCE: DO YOUR HOMEWORK

It pays to do your homework. In a meeting about a project to help a national retailer improve its product return system, a consultant pointed out that the retailer was accepting return merchandise that it didn't even sell—goods that other vendors had sold. When the client challenged the assertion, the consultant left the room and returned rolling a worn-out truck tire. As the consultant hoisted the tire onto the conference room table, the retailer's return tag was clearly visible. Since the retailer didn't sell tires, the point was made. That demonstration sealed the deal, and the consultant was hired to improve the client's merchandise return system.

the professional expertise, poise, and ability to make intelligent observations. Don't include anyone who can't make a substantive contribution to your understanding of the proposed project.

5. *Forget the canned questions.* Sales textbooks frequently suggest that you ask silly questions to induce clients to talk about their most pressing issues. But clients have heard some questions so often that they simply give cliché answers. Don't ask questions like "What keeps you awake at night?" or "If you had a magic wand and could make the problem disappear, what would be in its place?"

Instead, ask questions that relate directly to the project, such as "What new issues might surface once you solve the immediate problem?" and "Where do you anticipate that it will be most difficult to overcome resistance to change?"

6. *Find out who's who.* It isn't always clear how people fit into the decision-making process within an organization. But it's usually possible to tell whether someone you're meeting with can make decisions. Through the discovery process, you must identify the buyer, even if a committee is handling the selection process.

7. *Recognize the client's priorities.* As you take part in discovery meetings with clients, accept that their first priority is to solve their problems. They don't care about your situation, your long history of service to the industry, your eye-popping brochure, or the bulletproof methodology you promised to customize for them. They want to know if and how you can help them, so focus on comprehending the full extent and ramifications of proposed projects.

8. *Ask thoughtful questions, then listen.* Incisive questions demonstrate your ability to quickly grasp and diagnose problems and offer viable solutions. Ask astute questions and listen fully to show clients how you assimilate data and think. Pour your energy and creativity into the discovery process so clients will get a preview of the vigor with which you will attack the project. If you find yourself talking more than 30 percent of the time, stop. You aren't listening or learning and, you're probably talking yourself out of a job.

9. *Create value.* As you learn more about the client's environment and issues, consider giving the client at least one preliminary idea that could help with the problem. Providing value during the qualification process will strengthen your

> ### GUERRILLA TACTIC: GET MUTUAL AGREEMENT
>
> Don't consider writing a proposal for a client until the opportunity is well qualified and there's mutual agreement between the consultant and the client decision maker(s) on objectives, scope, schedule, and expected outcomes for the project. In the end, this will ensure that the proposal is faster to complete and is aligned with the client's needs.

relationship with the client. Consulting expert Andrew Sobel calls this going "the extra mile" for the client.[1] It's a great practice to follow. Just be careful not to shut down the discovery process by leading the client to believe that you already have a solution in mind before you've considered all the facts.

➤ The Results of Discovery

Make sure you get the following findings from the discovery step in the qualification sequence:

➤ Clear and concise statement of the project objectives, including a quantified value for the expected benefits of the project

➤ Description of the desired end state the client wants to achieve when the project is finished and the consultant is gone

➤ Project budget and assurance that the project is approved

➤ Names of the project decision makers, especially those who are authorized to approve changes and expenditures

➤ Agreement in principle on all aspects of the consulting approach, scope, and schedule

➤ Assessment of potential risks of the project

➤ Conviction that the project truly addresses the client's problem

➤ Desire to work for this particular client

➤ Trust that the consultant selection process will be fair and honest

➤ A good picture of the competitive situation

➤ **What Clients Want**

Discovery is a mutual evaluation by clients and consultants, and clients have their own agendas for meetings during this period. Anticipate what clients want from discovery and help them get the facts they need to select a consultant and to make decisions about the project.

Clients are justifiably cautious about hiring consultants. After all, they may be investing big money, implementing a risky new system, or disrupting their operations. Plus, they have legitimate concerns about working with outsiders and perhaps jeopardizing their own careers.

Clients may not initially trust you; you must earn that trust one step at a time. The first discovery meeting is like a job interview: The client is considering hiring you, and you are assessing whether you want the job. That's a perfect time to get trust issues out in the open and address unspoken client concerns.

Does the Consultant Look the Part?
First impressions are powerful and long-lasting. Initially dress one level higher than the client, but don't show off. Find out about the client's culture and look professional. Your appearance in the first meeting often drives the remainder of the discovery and proposal process. If you don't know clients, it's helpful to briefly go by their offices in advance of meetings to get a sense of the people, how they behave and dress.

Is the Consultant Prepared?
During the first meeting, don't put on a dog-and-pony show. Instead, demonstrate that you understand the issues facing the client and that you have the background to address those issues. According to a study by the analysis firm, Ross McManus, the number one dissatisfaction clients have with consultants is that they don't fully understand clients' businesses.[2] If clients have to waste time bringing you up to speed on information you should already know, they'll wonder how much your lack of preparation will hamper your ability to complete the project.

Can These People Deliver?
Prepare, question, listen, and think creatively to show that you are credible and highly qualified to complete the proposed assignment. How you communicate, gather, and analyze information and suggest next steps will tell clients how you will perform on the project. It's not uncommon for consultants to have great meetings with clients

---

GUERRILLA INTELLIGENCE: QUESTIONS *NOT* TO ANSWER YET

During discovery, clients will want answers to seemingly harmless questions. But responding before the scope of the project is clear can obligate you in ways you may later regret. Be prepared for clients to ask you:

➤ How much will the project cost?

➤ What is your hourly rate?

➤ Will you send us a proposal?

➤ Will you discount your fees for a promise of future work?

➤ How long will the project take to complete?

You must answer all these questions eventually. But to avoid an unprofitable engagement or an unhappy client, wait until you have a complete picture of the client and the project before you answer. Most clients will push for answers to these questions right away. If you explain your position, they will usually recognize that it's in their best interests to wait until all the project issues have been thoroughly discussed before you answer.

---

but lose projects because they fail to demonstrate true understanding of those projects in their proposals.

How Well Do the Consultants Communicate?
Most clients give consultants the benefit of the doubt, at least for a while. They assume you are a credible professional who can help them—especially if someone they trust recommended you. That can change as soon as you open your mouth to speak.

Your credibility can go either up or down, depending on how you first address clients. No pressure here, but your initial statement can set the tone for a meeting or an entire project.

Discover beforehand the type of audience you will be addressing and the communication style of the client's organization. Communicate in a manner that is compatible with that style. When you know your audience, you can present yourself with confidence and competence.

Are the Issues Being Properly Explored?
Some consultants routinely suggest that all clients would benefit from their prepackaged services. It is premature to recommend complete

solutions during discovery, but some consultants just can't resist doing so. Clients are sensitive to what they may perceive as canned answers to their problems. They see their problems as unique and complex and may consider your quick cures to be simplistic and superficial.

Will We Get the Attention We Deserve?

Clients want consultants to be fully engaged and interested in them and their projects. They also want to be assured of their importance to your firm. If you dwell on the international companies you are serving, smaller clients may think they won't receive the attention you lavish on larger ones. Make clear that all your clients receive the same high level of service, regardless of size.

Who Will Actually Do the Work?

In some consulting firms, after consultants secure an engagement, they hand off the project to others who perform the work. If that is the case, disclose the fact to clients as soon as possible. No matter how much preparation you promise to provide to your project team, clients will believe that they will have to go over the same ground with the new people.

Allay this concern by bringing members of the project team in during discovery meetings. They don't need to attend every meeting, but they should have some presence during the process. Convince clients that you have a reliable method for quickly educating those who will be responsible for performing the work.

What Kind of Relationship Will We Have with the Consultants?

When clients are considering hiring consultants, it's reasonable for them to worry about how the consultants will interact with company personnel. Long-term projects can involve intense relationships that affect the company's success. Clients want amicable relationships based on competence and professionalism. They want consultants to treat everyone in the company with courtesy and respect.

Can We Manage a Consulting Team?

Clients often wonder how they will manage a consulting team in their midst. And they may find it difficult to both oversee the work of consultants and manage their own operations. Build status review measures into your projects and include some contingency for additional time or resources to reassure clients that your work will stay on target. Help clients plan for the inevitable disruptions consultants and projects will cause to their businesses. Set up clear lines of communication to handle problems as soon as they arise.

Will Consultants Be Able to Keep Fees under Control?

Clients are always concerned about the extent of their financial exposure. Though it's not advisable to hamstring yourself with fee estimates during discovery, you can explain the mechanisms you will employ to keep costs and fees to the point of your eventual estimate.

Be explicit about how you plan to stay on budget, how you monitor fees, and how often you will update the client on the budget. Discuss how changes to the project can increase costs if they require additional time and resources.

Conveying that you have controls in place will relieve anxiety about potential cost overruns and help advance your case for winning the work. The most effective way to allay clients' fears on this score is to include in your proposal that you will not exceed the project budget without their advance approval.

What Are the Risks?

When clients hire consultants, there are always risks to the client's business, to the consultants, and to those who hire them. If, for whatever reason, a project fails to meet its objectives, the consultants will always be blamed. But the fallout can readily extend to the client sponsor(s) of the project. People who questioned the need for the project or the consultants in the first place can be counted on to point fingers.

Understandably, clients want to know their business and personal risks before hiring you. They also want to know how you will react to the stress of failure. They may be thinking, "If the project goes sour, how will it affect my career? Whose interests will be protected?" Address this underlying current with a thorough assessment of the risks. Reach agreement with the client on how you will share those risks. In some situations, you may be comfortable asking directly how a project could impact a client's career.

Who Else Can Do the Work?

Regardless of how good you are, despite the outstanding quality of your work and dedication, expect clients to ask, "Who else could do this work?" Don't be offended—companies are always looking for a better way to achieve results. Clients may want to explore doing the work with in-house staff, or may want to look for new or cheaper approaches to the project. Don't try to talk clients out of researching other options. If asked, offer your objective perspectives on the alternatives. It's in your best interests for clients to satisfy themselves that they have weighed all their choices.

➤ Give Clients What They Want

You can't anticipate every question clients have, but addressing the ones that have been discussed here will go a long way toward giving clients what they want. The objective of discovery is to minimize uncertainty for both the client and the consultant.

■ STEP 3: DECISION TIME

How do you know if you have a qualified lead? Process the information that you acquire from the prequalification and discovery steps to determine whether the project is worth pursuing. Although every project, client, and consulting firm is different, if you can answer yes to most of the following questions, you should pursue the opportunity and submit a proposal.

➤ Client Qualification Checklist

➤ Are you qualified to perform the work?

➤ Has the budget been approved?

➤ Is this likely to be a profitable project?

➤ Are you comfortable with your relationship with the client?

➤ Do you have a complete understanding of the problem?

➤ Is the client ready to begin work? Or, do you have a date when the work will begin?

➤ Are your odds of getting the project greater than 40 percent?

➤ Are you in basic agreement with the client on timing, fees, scope, and objectives?

➤ Are the odds of a long-term relationship good?

➤ Are all nonconsulting resources readily available for the project?

➤ Is the proposed schedule realistic?

➤ Do you have access to the decision makers?

➤ Has the business case for the project been clearly articulated and approved?

➤ Has the client successfully worked with consultants in the past?

➤ Are key client executives supportive of the project and your firm?

➤ The Fruits of Due Diligence

Clients always seem to be in a hurry. When they call, they want action quickly and many consultants drop everything to oblige. Take your time and use the qualification process to your advantage. It can clear the fog that may shroud a project in uncertainty and improve your chances of winning more work with less marketing cost.

Thorough detective work during discovery will clarify the real costs of delivering the proposed service, in both time and effort. As a result, you will spend less time creating proposals. And the quality and accuracy of your proposals will be higher, improving the odds that you will be selected for the project. Plus, there will be few surprises once the project gets underway because your approach will be aligned with the client's objectives.

The discovery process gives you the chance to meet key members of the client's organization, which will build your network and could open up other opportunities. You also get license to walk the company's halls where you may spot additional problems that need attention. As you keep your eyes and ears open for potential opportunities, take the time to renew old acquaintances and start new relationships.

Chapter 16

"Send Me a Proposal"

Create Proposals That Win

I believe you should write a proposal after the client has decided to go ahead with the project.

—Jeff Thull[1]

Two bulky boxes land on the mailroom floor with a thud. The client cuts open the first box to find seven, five-inch binders bursting with a consultant's proposal. Sighing, he rips into the second box, resigned to finding more of the same. Instead, peering into the box, he spies several pieces of laminated wood and a plastic bag containing screws and bolts. The packet also includes the assembly instructions for the specially designed bookcase that the consultant thoughtfully provided for storing the voluminous proposal.

Sometimes it takes a bookcase full of binders to hold a proposal that meets a client's requirements; in other instances, a one-page e-mail will suffice. Whatever its dimensions, the consulting proposal is a powerful, yet misused marketing tool that often moves the selling process backward, instead of forward.

A great proposal can be a decisive factor in winning a project but it will not, by itself, secure the job for you. On the other hand, a poorly produced proposal can instantly unravel all the hard work you've done to persuade the client that you are the right choice for the job.

The words, "Send me a proposal" are music to many consultants' ears. Even though they might not enjoy writing proposals, most consultants jump at the chance because they believe that exciting, lucrative work might be right around the corner. The invitation to write a proposal is a milestone in the sales cycle—an opportunity to get one step closer to a client and a new project.

Writing a proposal is a high-cost undertaking. It diverts time and attention from your other clients and takes intensive effort. You should think of a proposal as the culminating product of the discovery sequence described in Chapter 15. Follow a systematic process to write proposals to ensure that they are top quality and will give you a high probability of obtaining the work.

■ THE REALITIES OF PROPOSAL WRITING

A few clients will hire consultants, sight unseen, bypassing the usual proposal and selling rituals. Some clients still start projects on a handshake, though that's becoming as rare as an unlimited consulting budget. Such informal arrangements are the exception to the rule, so pay attention to the following realities:

➤ *Clients reject boilerplate:* Include some standard language in your contract terms and conditions and in the description of your firm, but dump boilerplate whenever you're describing the results the client will achieve, the people you'll assign to the project, and your approach to working with the client. If you don't have a result clearly specified in your proposal, it's a loser.

➤ *Clients buy on emotion and justify on fact:* They make a series of emotional decisions about which group of consultants to hire. For many executives, it's about the gut feel they get once they've met the team. Your proposal provides the facts to back up the client's initial reactions. The foundation of this emotional response is developed during the discovery process, which takes place long before a single word is written in the proposal.

➤ *Clients expect proposals of increasingly higher quality:* Firms of all sizes now have access to the technology needed to create sophisticated proposals. Consultants are creating client-specific Web sites for proposals and delivering proposals in whatever way clients desire. To determine your capabilities, clients ask for greater disclosure of your ideas and approaches early in the proposal process instead of waiting until the project begins. Be sure your proposal delivery methods (paper, Web-based, CD, or other forms) meet professional standards.

➤ *A proposal is a simple document to define, but a complex one to create:* A proposal is intended to *help* you sell what you have to offer, whether it's a service, a product, or both. Your proposal is an extension of your overall sales process, not a lifeless recitation of your qualifications. It's often very difficult to describe the complexities of a project in an understandable way, but a proposal must summarize precisely the results you'll provide, over what time, and at what cost. That may sound simple, but it never is.

➤ *Time isn't your friend during the proposal process:* Given the resources you'll apply and divert to a proposal effort, you'll want as short a sales cycle as possible. As the selection process lengthens, your investment in business development grows. You'll have additional follow-up, travel expenses, and requests for more information. Also, as the sales cycle lengthens, the scope and objectives of projects tend to shift. It's essential that consultants stay very close to the decision makers to ensure that any project changes are included in their proposals.

➤ *The proposal process is a collaborative endeavor:* Most projects are complex; and results are often influenced by internal politics, the client's culture, or other factors that outsiders can't always anticipate or understand. To minimize potential snags, enlist the client's participation in all aspects of the proposal process: planning, research, preparation, editing, reviewing, and delivery. Use the client as a source of information and as a sounding board. Obtain the client's input, perspective, and agreement on all the major points you propose—project objectives, scope, approach, benefits, and fees.

➤ *When clients receive proposals, they don't like surprises:* As the proposal process unfolds, clients are always pulled in different

---

GUERRILLA INTELLIGENCE: PROPOSALS FOR EXISTING CLIENTS

Writing proposals for existing clients can be more demanding than writing them for prospects. Existing clients expect more because they think that you understand their operation, culture, people, and problems better than competing firms. They believe that you should be able to handle their projects more quickly, inexpensively, and insightfully, and will examine your proposal with a more critical and demanding eye. Existing clients will expect your proposal to be results oriented, without the marketing fluff they see in many other proposals.

---

directions, and the project may change from the time proposals were requested to the submission deadline. Therefore, it's crucial to stay in close communication with the client to keep your proposal on track and strengthen your relationship. If you are awarded the project, the information you gained and the relationship you built via collaboration will prove invaluable.

➤ *They're going to look at price first.* Even if you believe the project is presold through the discovery process, you must be sure that the decision makers know, in advance, the estimate of project fees and how you arrived at that estimate. Don't present a fee or range of fees that makes clients' jaws drop. This is where the meetings before the meetings come in. It's vital to discuss the estimated fees with selection committee members in advance to avoid sticker shock when the proposal arrives.

■ THE IDEAL PROPOSAL

The best proposal is one you don't have to write. Tip the competitive scales in your favor and try to eliminate the proposal process altogether. A competitive field reduces the odds of landing the business, so sidestep that challenge if possible.

It's less costly for you to write a letter *confirming* your services than to prepare a formal document *proposing* your services. Consultants rarely ask clients to award them the business without a formal proposal, so distinguish yourself and ask if you can start the work using a letter of confirmation. What do you have to lose?

A confirmation letter differs from a proposal in that it describes specifically what you will do, not what you are proposing to do. The confirmation letter will describe the objective, scope, schedule, fees, and results. But since it's not subject to competitive bidding, many other elements of a proposal may not be needed, such as a long list of qualifications, case studies, and detailed descriptions of your firm. Most importantly, the confirmation letter approach ends the sales cycle in your favor:

➤ Explain to clients why they also benefit from skipping the competitive proposal process.

➤ Point out that the consultant selection process takes their time and attention away from their business.

➤ Stress that you have the skills to get the job done, and that the lengthier the proposal process is, the more it costs them and the longer it delays the resolution of their problems.

In one case, a client asked a consultant how to improve communication between the client's engineering and manufacturing departments. The client intended to ask three other firms the same question and then solicit proposals.

Armed only with a white board and a marker, the first consultant led a three-hour discussion with the client team that dug out the real problem between the two groups, worked through a potential plan for creating the results the client needed, and proposed a schedule.

At the end of the meeting, the consultant asked for 24 hours to solidify the work of the group and prepare a letter confirming the work. The client agreed and awarded the work to the consultant the next day without a competitive bidding process.

If consultants have done their homework in qualifying the project and the client, a request to confirm the project should seem natural. You have nothing to lose in showing the client exactly what you can do and then asking for the work. Worst case, the client will say no.

■ WORDS TO AVOID IN PROPOSALS

Aside from failing to properly qualify a project during discovery, nothing ruins your chances of winning a project more than a jargon-laden proposal. Proposals brimming with consultant-speak drive clients to the competition faster than you can say "paradigm shift."

Scrutinize every word in a proposal and strip out empty phrases like "seamless connectivity," "strategic convergence," or "we deliver unparalleled solutions that create leverage for the enterprise." In the war of words, your most potent weapon is your computer's delete key.

■ THREE AILMENTS THAT CAN INFECT YOUR PROPOSAL

Consulting proposals suffer from one or more of three ailments that will drive clients into the waiting arms of your competitors—tired superlatives, buzzwords, and the plague of pronouns.

Superlatives are like weeds in a lawn: Unless checked, they tend to take over. Avoid prose such as "Our unsurpassed commitment to client service ensures your needs will be our highest priority." Does that mean the needs of other clients are a lower priority for the firm?

Consultants hope to get an edge by claiming to be the fastest, best, or most experienced in the field. Clients routinely ignore such claims as unproven hype. Unless you can quantify your claims beyond a doubt, strip superlatives from your proposal. Make each claim relevant to the client's issues and back it up with facts, figures, and testimonials. Without substantiation, clients will discount your claims and your proposal.

Instead of promising an "optimal solution for reducing customer complaints," say, "We will reduce customer complaints by 9 percent in 90 days." Then amplify in the proposal exactly how you will achieve that reduction.

Since proposals are often used to justify unspoken decisions made earlier in the sales process, include in your proposal facts that

---

GUERRILLA TACTIC: TIRED SUPERLATIVES TO DELETE OR JUSTIFY IN EVERY PROPOSAL

Most	Superior
Best	Maximum
Optimal	Minimum
Fastest	Unsurpassed
Shortest	Unrivaled
Easiest	Highest
Least	Unique

Nothing is intrinsically wrong with any of the preceding words, and we all use them in spoken and written communication (for example, "This is the fastest way to do that."). But in proposals, they are suspect, and you should use them sparingly, if at all.

validate your supporters' desire to hire you. Give them powerful ammunition to advance your firm's candidacy and convince others in the organization. Help them effectively sell you and your proposal.

➤ Ban Buzzwords

Every organization has its own set of insider buzzwords. In initial meetings with clients, parts of the conversation may go right over your head because of the shorthand they use to communicate.

When it comes to the use of mind-numbing buzzwords, consultants are among the worst offenders. When readers have to struggle through a muddy proposal, they become frustrated and may discard it.

Like tired superlatives, buzzwords sap strength from proposals and make them hackneyed, trite, and insincere—the exact opposite of how a good proposal should read. Drop the consultant-speak and replace it with words, terms, and phrases that clients instantly understand and can relate to. So many proposals are full of tech-speak that when one comes along that is clear and concise, readers will respond favorably.

The following typical statements were found in actual consulting proposals. Notice that they don't tell the reader anything of substance about what the consultants are proposing to do:

➤ Our seamless and integrated solution drives optimal business advantage far in excess of your investment.

➤ We deploy a cross-platform infrastructure that transforms mission-critical applications for maximum connectivity.

➤ Our value chain consultants enable clients to operationalize their strategies for the extended enterprise.

BUZZWORD HALL OF SHAME	
If Your Proposal Says . . .	*Consider Using This Instead*
Deliverables	Results
Enterprise-wide	Company
Human capital	People
Infrastructure	Foundation
Knowledge transfer	Inform
Thought-ware	Idea
Transformation	Change

Some consultants may understand these sentences, but it would be difficult for anyone else to translate this gibberish, unless of course the client reading it is a former consultant, who would likely get a good laugh.

If any words in the Consultants' Buzzword Hall of Shame appear in your proposal, replace them with more descriptive alternatives. If you cannot avoid using a buzzword, make sure that it's well defined, appropriate, and does not conceal an otherwise good idea.

➤ Words to Dump from Every Proposal

Reread your most recent proposal to see if it passes the buzzword test. The following words and phrases are so overused or meaningless that they should be banned from proposals. Eliminate them and say what you mean in plain English:

Best-in-class	Enterprise-wide	Ramp up
Best-of-breed	Frictionless	Real-world (*fill in*)
Best practice	Granular	Repurpose
Bleeding edge	Holistic	Scalable
Capability transfer	Human capital	Seamless
Change agent	Infrastructure	Synergy
Connectivity	Knowledge-based	Thought-ware
Convergence	Knowledge transfer	Time box
Cross-platform	Leading edge	Transformation
Cutting edge	Leverage	Value-added
Deliverables	Mission-critical	Value chain
Ecosystem	Offload	Win-win
Empower	Paradigm	World-class (*fill in*)
Enabler		

➤ Plague of the Pronouns

In the executive summary of one proposal, the pronoun "we" was used eight times in just six sentences. The client's desired result was barely mentioned. It's tempting to refer to yourself or your firm in a proposal with the royal "we": "We are uniquely qualified to complete the assignment." But these self-references are a trap that snares many consultants. Clients want your proposal to address *their* problems and the benefits they will receive, not to describe how great you are.

An accurate indicator that a proposal is straying too far from what the client needs is the frequent appearance of pronouns such as *us, we, our, me, my,* and *I*. Minimize your use of these pronouns and talk about your client's issues. Save the self-congratulatory stuff for the qualifications section of your proposal, where clients fully expect a hefty dose of self-promotion.

Although you can't always avoid first-person pronouns, use them judiciously and try to find alternatives such as individual or firm names, or rephrase the sentence.

■ CONSULTING ISN'T ROCKET SCIENCE

Scientists are notorious for using terminology and acronyms the rest of us stumble over. Sometimes when they clarify, that just makes it worse. That's okay, though, because it's not their job to communicate.

Don't make your clients ask more than once what something means. It will work to your advantage to strip buzzwords, excessive pronouns, and meaningless phrases from your proposals. After working hard to understand the client's needs, don't throw away your gains because of unclear language. Make your proposal one that advances your case to win the work.

■ BEFORE YOU BEGIN WRITING

Writing a proposal can deplete your resources. So carefully assess each opportunity before you undertake the process. It costs clients nothing to request proposals, and they can obtain substantial information without having to make a commitment. You, on the other hand, must make significant investments to prepare and write proposals.

GUERRILLA INTELLIGENCE: WHY DO THEY WANT A PROPOSAL?

Soliciting proposals allows clients to dip their toes in the waters and test what's available. Most companies want to see if consultants can solve problems that have stymied them. Some clients may feel that the impact of changes to their operation will be less severe if implemented by outsiders. Many companies request proposals solely to obtain price comparisons among consultants. Or they may begin the process with certain consultants in mind, perhaps incumbents that they want to keep on their toes. Nothing makes incumbents sharpen their pencils faster than competitive bids.

For many companies, hiring an outsider is a big step. It carries risks, and the costs can be steep. Review the types of buyer described in Chapter 15. Determine which type of buyer you're dealing with and try to understand the reasons for the RFP before you jump in.

Before you begin to write, consider these issues:

➤ *Examine the situation in which you've been invited to compete.* Don't agree to write a proposal until you thoroughly understand the client's needs and have figured out how to best address those needs.

➤ *Define at a high level your ongoing sales strategy.* Given the information you have, how will you use your resources to complete the proposal *and* get the work?

➤ *Find the root cause of the issue facing the client.* Often, the stated problem merely reflects symptoms, not the problem itself. Consider other areas that may be contributing factors but are not recognized as such by the client.

GUERRILLA TACTIC: KEEP IT SHORT

Keep your proposal as short as possible. A study by The Sant Corporation showed that when proposals are piled on a table, people pick up the smallest one first.* Recipients also tend to resent having to read through proposals that are stuffed with unnecessary information. Remember, you'll be competing with other consultants, and one of the factors on which you'll be judged is efficiency.

If your document is running long or you must elaborate on a particular point, submit two documents: your proposal and a separate appendix. This will keep your proposal short and reader friendly.

---

*The study result about proposals is from the interview with Tom Sant, "This Month's Featured MasterMind: Tom Sant on Creating Winning Proposals," *Management Consulting News* (April 1, 2003). Available from http://www.managementconsultingnews.com/newsletter_april_03.htm.

The Sant Corporation conducted tests with a group of people who make their living evaluating proposals. Sant said, "We gave them three proposals, one 25 pages, one 50, and one 100 pages long. We asked them to look for certain things, but we didn't really care about that. Typical psychological experiment—we just wanted to see which one they would pick up first. Almost without exception, they picked up the shortest one first because they wanted to get one out of the way quickly."

■ WHAT EVERY PROPOSAL MUST INCLUDE

Clients often want proposal content arranged in a specific order, and timing and scope differ from project to project. So, most proposals must be written from scratch. Every proposal request is different. For example, a pharmaceutical company had a problem to solve—fast. The clients were searching for a way to manage their inventory. The project manager called three firms and asked for a one-page proposal to be submitted the next day. The proposals were to describe tasks, results, fees, and resources the clients would have to dedicate to the project.

A manufacturer hoping to improve labor productivity throughout its network of manufacturing plants issued an 82-page RFP that included seven pages of precise instructions for completion of the document. The RFP also included predefined computer spreadsheets that consultants were to complete and submit with their proposals. Any deviation from the stated instructions was cause for immediate disqualification.

No matter what kind of proposal you're writing, you'll need an organizing framework to get the job done. Whether it's 2 or 200 pages, you'll find yourself using most, if not all, of the following proposal categories.

➤ Executive Summary

The most important part of the proposal is this section, which everyone will read—especially decision makers. The executive summary demonstrates your understanding of the issues and succinctly describes the results the client can expect. The summary is not the place to focus on technical descriptions of your approach and methods, but you may describe your strategy and differentiators.

The summary is likely to be the part of your proposal that is most widely distributed and read. So make it clear, concise, jargon-free, and well written. Focus squarely on the client's desired results, not the consultant's commercial.

Keep the executive summary to one or two pages, if possible. For complex or long proposals, use your judgment, but err on the side of brevity.

➤ Background

Briefly describe why you are being asked to submit a proposal. Consultants like this section because they can demonstrate that they understand what the client wants. The background statement of one proposal read, "After several quarters of improving on-time shipping performance, the client has asked a consultant to prepare a program to help other distribution centers in the company to achieve the same performance."

The length and detail of the background section will vary, but it's preferable to quickly get the reader through this section and show how and when the results will be achieved.

➤ Objectives and Scope

This is the "what" section of the proposal; it identifies what the consulting team will do to deliver the promised results. In one proposal, the objective was "to reduce the costs of third-party warehouses within 120 days to free up $500,000 annually in working capital for modernizing a corporate training facility. The scope of the project is to focus efforts on cost reduction in third-party warehouses, not other areas of the client's organization."

As you draft the objectives and scope, be sure to obtain the client's agreement. Often, the client will want to change objectives or expand the scope once the proposal is on paper. Once you've written the objectives and scope statement, confirm one more time that you've got it absolutely right.

On a recent proposal effort, a consultant followed precisely the objectives and scope statement included in a client's RFP and confirmed it with the client two weeks before the proposal was due. In the time between the consultant's confirmation and the proposal's due date, the client made substantial reductions to the project objectives and scope without notifying the consultant. The result was a disaster. The consultant brought the wrong team to the client meeting, upset the client for wasting time, and lost the work.

Always be safe. Confirm objectives and scope early and often. Don't expect the client to let you know about project changes—it doesn't always happen.

➤ Results

Describe in detail the results you will deliver for the client. Specify, in concrete terms, the outcomes, results, measures of success, and time frames involved. Effective results are specific and quantifiable, and can be given a value. For example, "The project will result in a 20 percent reduction in employee turnover in the customer service function within six months, which will reduce new employee training costs by $50,000 annually and will improve customer satisfaction ratings." This project result is specific and quantified and provides a way to measure success.

Here is another example: "The project will result in a 3 percent increase in cosmetic sales in the next seven months due to improved inventory management in each store location." The result is tangible, is measurable, and includes a time frame.

You must back up the results you promise with references and testimonials, but without a precise delineation of those results, your chances of winning drop precipitously.

➤ Project Approach

In the objectives and scope and result sections, you make promises about *what* you'll do once the project kicks off. The approach section of the proposal states *how* you will deliver those promises. Clients pore carefully over this section.

Many clients hire consultants for projects they cannot do themselves because they lack either time or resources. So there is always great interest in how consultants propose to achieve the results they promise. For proposal writers, creativity, ingenuity, experience, and client knowledge are vital.

Consultants have many problem-solving methods and approaches, including project management tools, standard interview templates, and preconfigured work plans. But like an artist creating a collage, the proposal writer must put together a combination of tools, people, and processes that will work effectively for the client. The consultant must carefully think through every element of the approach to ensure that results can be delivered in the agreed time frame.

Be sure to explain how the work will be performed, including the responsibilities that will be assigned to consultants and to client team members. Proposals must state precisely what clients are expected to contribute. Spell out how much time clients will be required to spend on a project and the skills they will need. If you omit this information, you can be sure you'll be asked about it.

Create a work plan for the activities that will be completed and the tools and strategies that will be used. This section will test your understanding of the project and convince clients that you have the best solution for their problems.

Consulting firms frequently present proposals that include detailed work plans accompanied by colorful charts and graphs. Although they may look good, they're usually cut and pasted from other proposals and often miss the mark. Some consultants prefer to dazzle clients first and work the details later. But it's better to work closely with the client from the start to customize an accurate plan that addresses the project's objectives. The resulting plan will identify the

GUERRILLA TACTIC: THE CONSULTANT'S BALANCE SHEET

If possible, in either the executive summary or the results section of the proposal, note how the benefits of the project align with the fees for the project. In many cases, consulting fees are a fraction of the benefit clients receive, so bring that fact to the client's attention.

level of effort needed to complete the assignment and will be essential in deciding what fees to charge.

➤ **Team Members**

Describe the members of the team with sufficient detail to show clients how each contributes to the result. List all team members, set forth their qualifications, and their roles in the project. Don't list "to-be-named team members," but state their actual names.

In proposals, consultants routinely promise to assign their best and brightest to the project. Chuck the hype and let team members' qualifications speak for them. Provide a detailed resume, customized for this assignment, for each team member.

Many clients will insist on meeting the team members before approving the project. Anticipate this request and plan to have the client interview your team members as part of the proposal process.

➤ **Timing**

This section (also known as "the schedule") sets forth the time period for completing the project, and each component segment. Be realistic and don't make promises you can't keep. Link all projected time frames to the availability of your resources, the client's team, vendors, suppliers, and others who may be involved. Incorrectly estimating the length of a project, or a component segment, can jeopardize profitability and your relationship with the client.

Build the schedule with extreme care, diligence, and the client's collaboration. Take into consideration the client's issues, politics, culture, and seasonal demands. And remember that your client's employees also have company jobs to perform. Don't overlook vacations, holidays, and inevitable sick days, which can wreak havoc with the best-laid plans.

Describe the controls that you will employ to monitor timely performance and to keep the project on time. Show how you plan to make sure that the project will start on time, stay on schedule, and make up for any lost time.

➤ Fees and Risk Reversal

On receiving a proposal, recipients always go straight to the fees section to check the bottom line and learn how much the project will cost. Pricing is discussed in detail in Chapter 17, but here are some basic rules about how to present fees in a proposal.

The fees you quote in a proposal must be clear and unmistakable. You may present the client with a range of pricing options depending on how the project is staffed or the results to be delivered. It is helpful for clients to see options.

Some consultants like to describe their fees using the term investment, as in "Your investment in this project is $100,000." Clients see right through this nonsense, so tell them straight up what the project will cost. If the project is an investment, clients will amortize the cost on their balance sheets. Let the client decide whether the project is an investment or an expense.

Give guarantees. State, "If our service fails to meet your expectations, we'll cut our fees in half." Every client takes risks when they hire a consultant; so let clients see that your price has a built-in risk reversal provision. A guarantee helps to ease nagging uncertainties clients have about hiring consultants.

Also specify how you expect to get paid for your services. State how much you want up front, in periodic payments during the project, and on project completion.

In most cases, it's appropriate to request a substantial part of the fees before you start the project; 25 percent to 35 percent is desirable. If your relationship with the client is solid, up-front payment should not be a problem. Most clients understand that consultants operate businesses and that cash flow is always a concern.

➤ Qualifications

Now you can toot your horn as loudly as you wish. Prior to this, your proposal should have focused on convincing clients that you understand their needs and on explaining your approach. Now it's time to sell yourself.

Bring to life why clients should use your services and why they should want you on their team. Highlight the challenges you faced working through similar problems, the ways that you resolved them,

GUERRILLA TACTIC: CUSTOMIZE YOUR QUALIFICATIONS

When providing their qualifications, most consultants simply take the latest version of their resumes and paste them into proposals. They may edit slightly, but for the most part, they submit the same tired information. That's a mistake. Instead, customize your resumes and qualifications to provide the best, most relevant, and client-focused information. Add appropriate stories, case studies, and testimonials; include names, dates, facts, and telephone numbers.

and the implications for the proposed project. Provide success stories, but temper them by not overstating your role; stress the results and client satisfaction.

Finally, emphasize the differentiators—the extraordinary qualities—that your firm brings to the assignment. Fully describe each special quality, quantify it, and state how it will serve and add to the project.

Many consulting proposals look exactly the same, so include three differentiators in your proposal that will set you apart from the competition. It's possible you have a special alliance with an academic expert that will contribute to the project; maybe you wrote a book on the precise subject of the project; or maybe your firm was the first to use a specific business process that is needed to make the project successful.

Most firms try to differentiate themselves on price or qualifications. Be creative about what makes your firm better, different, or first at something. It's a surefire way to win projects.

■ TWELVE TIPS FOR A SUCCESSFUL PROPOSAL

A public relations consultant sent a proposal to a client for the design of a small PR campaign that was to be a test for additional campaigns in the future. The firm presented a beautifully packaged proposal with a description of their qualifications, their understanding of the project, and their approach to completing the work.

After reviewing the proposal, the client noticed that the document footer showed a different client name, and in several places in the proposal, the previous client's name also appeared. The client threw the proposal in the round file.

To avoid that fate, follow these 12 tips before you send a proposal to a client:

1. Create a powerful, concise executive summary.

2. Focus on results, which matter more than methods and processes. Clients buy methods and approaches only when they know you can deliver results.

3. Be generous with your ideas; don't hoard them. Show clients how innovatively you think.

4. The length of the proposal doesn't win, but quality does. Projects are not awarded because proposals pass a weight test.

5. The proposal content must be about the client, not the consultant. Take a backseat and focus on how you will solve problems.

6. Your liberal use of "best practices" will label you as uncreative. Find the blend of outstanding practices and innovative solutions that fit your client's needs, not answers that worked for someone else.

7. Accuracy is essential. Validate all data and double-check to make sure it's right before you present it.

8. Sweat every small proposal detail, watch for typos, use high-quality materials and make sure the right people receive the proposal on time.

9. Rewrite your resume for every proposal. Highlight the skills in your resume that demonstrate your qualifications. Your boilerplate resume is rarely equal to the task.

10. Let your proposal sit for a day and then reread it completely before sending it out.

11. Let your personality shine through your proposals. Give clients a sense of the firm and your style of working.

12. Don't let your proposal claims outdistance your true capabilities. Write an honest proposal or you'll pay dearly in the future with blown budgets and unhappy clients.

The consulting proposal is a necessary evil. A great proposal can be decisive in winning a project; a poor one can cause you to lose a project, even if everything else in the sales process has gone flawlessly. Use these guidelines to a write a killer proposal every time.

Chapter 17

The Price Is Right

You may not get what you paid for, but you will pay for what you get.

—Maya Angelou[1]

The unsigned painting of a frowning, middle-aged peasant woman languished in a Tokyo auction house. The staff felt the painting was charming, but run-of-the-mill and not particularly valuable. They set its price at $83.

Before the auction began, the auction house owner asked a group of experts to take a closer look. Surprisingly, the experts determined that the portrait was actually a rare, unsigned painting by Vincent van Gogh, completed in 1884. At auction, it sold for $550,000.

■ THE COST OF A BAD PRICING DECISION

By insisting on a thorough assessment of the painting's value, that auction house owner narrowly averted a costly pricing mistake. For consultants, bad pricing decisions are just as costly—they can lead to unprofitable projects, damage your chances for long-term success, or even put you out of business. Like the Tokyo auction house owner, check every aspect of your project to assess its worth before you set your fees.

It's surprisingly easy to end up with an unprofitable project. Some consultants are blinded by the allure of large fees, high-profile jobs, or clients with fascinating projects. So they willingly accept pricing terms that can strap them for cash or force them to work for low profit margins.

Projects with low margins can be treacherous. They lock you into relationships that lead nowhere and drain your resources. Many pricing decisions that initially looked great turn sour as projects unfold, restricting consultants' financial flexibility.

■ THREE DILEMMAS OF PRICING SERVICES

➤ Dilemma 1: Whatever You Quote, They Want It for Less

The buying and selling of consulting services isn't like other shopping experiences—it's more like shopping in a bazaar than in a supermarket or department store. After all, you pay for groceries before you consume them and they have set prices; but neither of these conditions is true for consulting services.

Guerrillas are right at home in the consulting bazaar, where pricing is a process of give-and-take to reach agreement with clients on the worth, or value, of the consultant's services. But all too often, clients are not comfortable haggling over fees, and they can't connect their perception of value with the hefty price of most consulting services.

Interpretations of value vary greatly from person to person and time to time. Like the differing takes on the worth of that Van Gogh painting, it's likely that you and your clients will begin with divergent perspectives on the right price for your services.

Instead of focusing on the monetary or other benefits they stand to gain from consulting work, clients tend to evaluate price by scrutinizing how many hours consultants put into projects.

One client objected to a proposal to improve sales force productivity that included 10 consultants, billed at a substantial hourly rate, for 12 weeks. By focusing on the number of hours and the hourly rate, the client was ready to cancel the project as too pricey. Once the client and consultant worked together to calculate the estimated value of the project outcome, the proposed fees were found to be less than 2 percent of the conservatively estimated benefit the client would achieve.

Whatever pricing approach you ultimately choose for a project, your first objective is to help clients get a realistic understanding of a project's benefits and what those benefits are worth. Then the consultant's fees can be assessed in the context of that value.

Even when clients factor in the value of benefits, most will still push for the best possible deal. For decades, consultants have trained clients to expect negotiable prices, so anticipate some pushback on price. No matter how compelling the cost benefit, clients will always want to pay less.

➤ **Dilemma 2: You Can Never Know Everything**

When clients and consultants evaluate price, both are influenced by gaps in their respective information. Both sides have unresolved risk, making it difficult to evaluate proposed fees. Clients know that it's impossible to judge the true quality of consulting work until projects have been completed, so they try to mitigate the risk of imperfect information. Clients usually insist that:

➤ Price be fixed and predictable before the project begins.

➤ Terms of payment will stretch out until the project is completed.

➤ They get to interview and select the consulting team members.

➤ The client is the final arbiter of what defines project completion.

Conversely, consultants know that even after the most detailed, up-front discovery process and analysis, surprises can cause their profits to evaporate. Therefore, pricing must take into consideration whether project success is achievable in the client's environment.

Consultants must assess whether the client's team can pull off the job and the client's organization is prepared to accept the changes the project will bring. More important, consultants must be sure that the project scope and schedule are not so aggressive that they overrun fees. Consultants must account for these risks in determining price. To protect themselves, consultants should look for pricing strategies that provide:

➤ A variable and flexible pricing structure

➤ Some payment up front

➤ A fixed, achievable schedule

➤ Commitment to additional fees if extraordinary circumstances arise

Even when there's a track record of past performance, what the client and consultant don't know about their risks creates a fundamental conflict between them, which can result in lengthy fee negotiations. What's called for is open, frank discussion of the risks on both sides that will lead to price agreement and allow the project to be launched.

➤ Dilemma 3: What's the Question?

Consumers buy in a certain fashion, whether it's a major appliance, a vehicle, or home furnishings. They gather information about the product from the Web, magazines, print and television ads, and their friends. Then they comparison shop: They compare prices, options, features, colors, availability, delivery schedules, installation charges, warranty, and vendor and manufacturers' track records.

Then the analysis begins. Consumers ask, "Can I afford it?" "Are there less expensive, comparable alternatives?" "Can I get the model I really want for less money elsewhere?"

If buyers of consulting services could ask essentially the same questions, their task would be far less complex. But consulting services are customized for each project, so it's tough to use the same rules as for buying a dishwasher or a television.

Another complication is that, despite a client's effort to specify project needs, each consultant will respond with a different proposal, approach, and price. It's not unusual to hear a client say that one firm's proposed price is twice as high as a competing firm's bid.

Sorting out differences in price and options can be time consuming and unpleasant for clients. Consultants can simplify matters by describing, in quantifiable terms, a realistic estimate of the project benefits. With that information, clients have a solid basis for comparing your price with your worth.

The secret to winning projects is not having the lowest price, but the highest perceived value. Spend as much time calculating a realistic contribution to client value as you do figuring out your fee, and make sure the client understands both. You'll make your client's decision process simpler and tip the scales in your favor. So the right question is not "How much does it cost?" but "How much is it worth to the client?"

■ GUERRILLA PRICING

Guerrilla pricing is about understanding the client and the project, but it's also about flexibility and creativity. Your approach to pricing must be as varied as the clients you serve. To avoid lengthy fee negotiations, make sure your fees reflect four criteria:

1. Agreed-on value for fees
2. Profitability for your practice
3. Simplicity of understanding
4. Fairness to both the consultant and the client

The first step in determining the price of a project is to reach agreement with the client on value for fees. If you propose to help a client reduce indirect expenses by 2 percent, then you must quantify that cost reduction and provide a way to measure it.

Some consultants argue that it's too difficult to quantify the value of a consulting project in advance. But those who take the time to nail down that value will find less price resistance, especially if the value-to-fee ratio is high.

Every project has potential measurable benefits. Of course, some values are easier to measure than others. Here is a simplified example: If a client wants to increase annual net sales by 3 percent, multiply current net sales by 3 percent to figure out the monetary gain the client will receive.

To orient clients in the discussion of what your services are worth, consider the possible drivers of consulting value listed in Table 17.1.

➤ **What Is It Worth?**

Once you have articulated project benefits, figure out, in conjunction with clients, what the proposed changes are worth. Reducing employee turnover by 20 percent might reduce recruiting, hiring, and training costs by that same percentage. The higher cost of employee benefits for longer-term workers might offset that gain by a small

Table 17.1 Drivers of Consulting Value

Consultants Can Help Clients . . .			
Increase	Reduce	Improve	Create
Revenue	Costs	Productivity	Strategy
Profit	Time/effort	Business process	System
Growth/market share	Complaints	Service	Process
Shareholder value	Risk	Information	Business
Employee retention	Turnover	Morale	Product
Return on assets/investment	Conflict	Image/reputation	Service
Efficiency	Paperwork	Skills	Brand
Visibility		Quality	
		Customer loyalty	

percentage, but the client will still realize a net gain. Find out what that would be.

If you help clients improve the quality of their products, that should result in fewer complaints and returns and a lower cost of stocking merchandise. If you improve morale among a client's staff, managers could spend less time in meetings and more time running the business. What is it worth to have motivated workers instead of absences and poor work habits due to low morale?

Quantify all benefits that are relevant to a project and confirm those numbers with the client. That information provides the crucial context in which clients can assess your fees.

➤ Project Profitability

The heart of guerrilla pricing decisions is project profitability—the profit you must earn on a project to stay in business. Begin with an estimate of your costs for completing the project so that you can understand your financial commitment. If you don't have a true picture of your costs, you can easily end up losing money on a project.

Assess the salaries, benefits, and overhead expenses you'll incur. Include an estimate for other expenses, such as travel, interest on working capital loans, preparation time, and other business development expenses associated with the project. You don't need a fancy financial model to calculate these costs, but don't price a project without isolating these numbers. Without them, you're flying blind.

According to one consultant, "It's like the meterless cab rides I took in New Jersey. Unless I pressed the driver for the cost ahead of time, I never knew what the ride would cost until I got there."

In many cases, consultants choose not to pass all project costs along to the client. For example, only a few firms will even try to charge a client for creating a proposal. Whether you recoup them or not, you need to understand all project costs. Then, the next step is to decide the profit margin—the amount of profit—you need for the project, which will vary from firm to firm and client to client.

You can use many formulas to determine profit margin. And you may find that the same formula is not suitable for every project. The point is that a clear understanding of your costs gives you the flexibility to customize pricing to meet the client's needs while ensuring project profitability for you.

➤ It Costs How Much?

Creativity and flexibility are critical in pricing. Of the numerous pricing alternatives available, choose one that best fits the competitive

---

GUERRILLA INTELLIGENCE: INTANGIBLE BENEFITS

As you calculate your fees and forecast profit, remember to include the intangible benefits you receive from projects. In the consulting business, not all profit is purely financial.

While working on projects, you increase the knowledge base of your firm and its consultants. You build new skills and forge new relationships, which can lead to future work. You also generate materials for future marketing, such as references and case studies. These benefits are elements of profit that you should consider when calculating your project fees.

---

situation. If clients say they will only accept fixed-fee proposals, obviously you have to work within those parameters. But that doesn't mean you can't be creative and offer options.

In presenting fees, make it clear and easy for clients to understand how you arrived at your fees. Some consultants build elaborate spreadsheets to calculate their fees, which can cause clients to focus on the accuracy and detail of the spreadsheet instead of the fees. Remember, the client will likely be sharing your proposal with others who may not have the benefit of hearing your presentation directly. So make the pricing method clear.

■ SO MANY PRICES

Clients usually say they don't buy consulting services on price. They'd be foolhardy to choose the lowest price consultant to handle work they consider important—or so the reasoning goes. Nevertheless, when one competitor discounts price, clients often use that leverage to drive all prices lower, creating a price war.

While you may be constrained by what clients want, many pricing options are available. Understand how they work so that you can offer creative combinations. Here's a quick rundown on the most common pricing strategies.

➤ Hourly Rate (Time and Materials)

Fee for service is a standard pricing format used by most service providers, including consultants, lawyers, accountants, and plumbers. It's simply a specified dollar amount for each hour, day, or week you put in on the job. For decades, service providers have trained clients to think that the "hourly rate" is the gold standard of pricing. It is easy to understand and gives clients a simple way to compare rates between competitors. It isn't usually too long after clients see hourly rates, however, before they pressure consultants for discounts.

Clients will also quickly see an advantage for them to cap or limit the total hours that providers can charge for projects. With such limitations, clients must preapprove any work that exceeds the hourly ceiling. With hourly caps, project fees are fixed and clients get some price security. But if the project schedule slips because of an unforeseen event or because the client fails to complete a task on time, consultants can find themselves working for free and losing money.

How to Use Hourly Rates

Hourly pricing limits consultants' opportunities to share in the benefits they're helping to produce for clients, so some consultants try to avoid this strategy. However, many clients demand hourly rate agreements, so they are difficult to avoid. The following guidelines are useful when using this approach:

➤ Establish an hourly or daily rate that will ensure project profitability.

➤ Avoid caps on hours per day or per project.

➤ Provide an hourly or daily rate for each consultant level (for example, partner, senior manager, manager, and consultant). Don't quote a composite rate for all consultants on the project because any change in the consultant mix will impact the project's profit.

➤ Confirm that rates apply only to this project and that other projects can be billed at different rates.

➤ Establish a firm time frame for rates to remain in effect; if a project extends beyond your fiscal year, include any planned rate increases for your practice.

GUERRILLA INTELLIGENCE: THE DOWNSIDE OF FEE CAPS

The biggest drawback to fee caps is that they take the client's focus off the primary objective: achieving the project results. Clients who continually monitor consultants' hours would be better served by focusing on how well the consultants are progressing toward achieving project goals.

➤ Plan how to respond if the client pressures you to discount hourly rates. Be prepared to offer a different consulting team or reduced scope that would fit a lower rate.

➤ Understand how much profit you need for each level of consultants assigned to the project. Know in your own mind the lowest possible rate that you could accept before you would walk away from the project.

➤ Ask for an additional incentive payment if the project results are met or exceeded.

Though not ideal, with proper planning, hourly or daily pricing can lead to acceptable profit margins, especially for larger consulting assignments. Consultants who work alone on projects, however, should be wary of this kind of pricing.

A single practitioner doesn't have the financial leverage of a larger consulting team. With a team, overhead and profit can be spread out among the consultants. To make a reasonable profit, a consultant working alone on an hourly basis might have to charge the client a noncompetitive rate or bill for many more hours.

Even though many consultants would prefer not to use fee-for-service pricing, don't count on it going away anytime soon. We trained clients to think this way, and it will take some time to change their perspective.

➤ Fixed Fees

You've probably heard it said that you can tell how housepainters are being paid by watching them work. If they're going slowly and deliberately, they're being getting paid by the hour. If they're painting fast and furiously, they're getting a fixed fee for the job.

GUERRILLA TACTIC: SHOULD YOU DISCOUNT YOUR RATE?

Discounting hourly or daily rates is a slippery slope. Some consultants believe that quoting a low rate initially will help sell the work and that, at a later date, they can raise their rates. Don't be so sure. Unless you've done something truly remarkable, you'll find clients stubbornly resistant to raising rates as quickly as you'd like, if ever. If clients press for lower rates because they want projects to cost less, suggest reductions in the scope of projects to bring the overall costs down.

| |
GUERRILLA TACTIC: PUT PRICE TO REST

Once pricing is decided for a project and the contract signed, it's best for all concerned if the issue of price can be put aside and not revisited. Your goal should be to agree with the client on a price that will not need to be renegotiated down the line. Your relationship with the client can't develop if you are in a continuing tug-of-war about money.

Under a fixed-fee arrangement, the client pays the consultant a set price for a project. Often, a fixed fee is calculated by multiplying the consultant's hourly or daily rate by the length of time the client expects the project to last, but other formulas are also used. The critical point is that the fee amount is fixed no matter what happens or how long the project takes.

Clients love fixed-fee projects. Their costs are predictable, and the financial risks are shifted to the consultant. If a project schedule is delayed or the objectives change in the middle of the project, the consultant may have to perform more work than originally budgeted, at the fixed price. Most clients will recognize the need to renegotiate fees in this situation, but they have also been known to refuse to pay more.

The most effective way to use fixed-fee pricing is for small, discrete projects or for short phases of large projects for trusted clients. You can't eliminate the impact of unforeseen risk, but limiting the scope of a fixed-fee project will reduce your exposure. Make sure fixed-fee agreements include precisely defined objectives and measures of success that are agreeable to both the consultant and client.

It's also essential to define the role of the client's team in meeting the project schedule. In one case, a client's team members were pulled off a fixed-fee project after the first two weeks because the client needed them to analyze a potential company acquisition. The assignment of the new client team slowed the project down so much that it took several weeks longer to complete the work. The consultant and the client ended up in heated argument about the additional costs that the consultant incurred shuffling the team and orienting the new team members.

► **Contingency Pricing**

Consultants have torn a page from the personal injury lawyers' handbook by adopting contingency pricing methods. Under these

> ## GUERRILLA TACTIC: RISK PREMIUM
>
> Add a risk premium to fixed-fee projects because it is easy to run into problems. When you're receiving a fixed fee, clients can enlarge scope unintentionally or create delays. Manage the scope of the project tightly. Work collaboratively with the client to reach an unambiguous understanding of scope, and set up a process in advance to discuss changes that might occur. If a problem arises, address it immediately.
>
> In fixed-fee projects, ask for a substantial payment before the project begins. It's not uncommon to request 50 percent of the fee at the outset, 25 percent at the halfway point, and 25 percent on completion.

arrangements, a consultant's fee is based on achieving an agreed-on project result. Usually, the consultant receives a specified percentage of the gain resulting from the project.

Contingent fees seem to work well for revenue enhancement, cost reduction, litigation support, and other projects where a monetary impact can be measured with relative ease. Contingent pricing is simple to understand and administer as long as the measurement standards have been specified.

But if the measures of success are not crystal clear, it's easy to get into arguments with clients over this pricing approach. Suppose a client wants you to reduce costs by renegotiating telecommunications equipment leases, and you propose that your fee be 30 percent of the cost reduction achieved. That's a clear measure of success. Measuring precise project results can be both difficult and costly, so be careful to define the measures before the work begins.

Watch out though—contingency pricing can leave the consultant with nothing at all. What if, for some reason, you can't renegotiate those equipment leases to the agreed-on level? You've worked for free and probably alienated the client for failing to perform.

Contingency pricing calls for precautionary measures. To motivate the client to achieve target results and to help your short-term cash flow, ask for a partial up-front, good faith payment against the ultimate fee, and suggest progress payments if the project stays on course. Avoid waiting until the end of the project to receive your fee.

To reduce risk further, ask for an escape clause that kicks in if unforeseen external events make achieving the project results impossible.

Include in that escape clause a provision that you will be paid some portion of your fee for work you perform to the point when the unforeseen events occur.

Consider using contingency pricing in a limited way with trusted clients. If you are sure you can deliver the projected benefits to the client and are willing to take a set percentage of the benefits as your fee, contingency pricing might be your best bet.

➤ "Success" Fees

A variation on contingency pricing is to tie fees to an all-out guarantee: The consultant does not get paid if the client does not deem the project a success. As clients have become more skeptical of the value that consultants provide, they want to base payment on the success achieved. The sentiment seems to be that if consultants are as good as they claim, they should be willing to put their fees on the line.

Under some formulas, only part of a consultant's fees is tied to success, and the rest is paid through a more standard pricing method. Another possibility is that consultants can agree to allow clients to hold back partial fees. For example, if a project calls for $500,000 in fees, the consultant might bill the client for $450,000 and let the client decide whether to pay the final $50,000.

Some clients want to fund projects from the eventual project benefits. Consultants have been known to bankroll projects provided the clients pay the deferred fees later when increased revenue or savings are realized from projects. Such "self-funding" projects allow clients to hire consultants without increasing their budgets.

Clients appreciate the flexibility of consultants who are willing to put their fees at risk, and that may help you win more projects. But to offset the added risk in such contracts, consultants should always ask for bonuses that are to be paid if they exceed expectations.

Contingency pricing is currently used on a limited number of consulting engagements. As clients become more sophisticated in the pricing of consulting services, that percentage may increase.

➤ Value-Based Pricing: The Consultant's Dream

Value-based billing is getting press these days because it represents a path away from the hourly rate model that is so prevalent in the consulting industry. In a value-based fee arrangement, the consultant's fees are tied to the value the project generates.

You share in the benefits but, unlike contingent price arrangements, your fees are not limited to a one-time percentage of the results.

For example, if you were to undertake a project to reduce annual corporate overhead expenses, you could be paid a part of those savings, regardless of how large they might become. So, if you negotiated a 15-to-1 value ratio and the client saved $1,500,000 in corporate overhead, your fee would be $100,000. If those savings reached, say $6,000,000, your fee would be $400,000.

Though clients haven't fully embraced the concept, value-based pricing can provide substantially higher fees for consultants because the higher the value received, the higher the fee. If the project to reduce corporate overhead was priced using either an hourly billing rate or a fixed fee, the consultant's fee would likely be substantially lower than when calculated on a value-based billing strategy.

Pegging fees to value helps clients to see consultants' fees in the context of the benefits they receive from their projects. When the consultants' fees are placed in the larger context of value, larger fees seem more reasonable.

Value-based pricing has been slow to gain acceptance in the consulting business because of difficulties in agreeing on estimates of value and finding methods to measure it. Clients are also unsure how much value they are willing to share with consultants. Some clients feel that the effort required for an equitable value-based pricing program is not worth it, especially since legions of consultants are willing to provide easier to manage, fee-for-service pricing.

How to Use Value-Based Pricing

The rewards for consultants using the value-based approach can be substantial, but the financial risks can also be great. Many events can conspire to create an unhappy ending, ranging from executive turnover to unforeseen business or economic conditions. They can affect the value of a project, and as a result, the consultant's fee.

GUERRILLA INTELLIGENCE: VALUE-BASED PRICING

Value pricing can be hard for clients to grasp because it's unlike other pricing methods they use in business or their personal lives. If value-based pricing was applied to health care, a doctor treating a patient for a broken leg would be paid more if the patient fully recovered, and less if the patient ended up with a slight limp. To complicate matters, before treatment, the doctor and patient would have to agree on a payment scale linked to how well the patient ended up being able to walk.

Use this approach only when you're certain that you can success-fully complete the project and that it will provide profits greater than other pricing methods. To protect against undue financial risks, only agree to value-based fees for existing clients with whom you have a strong track record and relationship. You must know the organiza-tion and culture, including where the bones are buried, and that you can operate effectively in the client's environment. Unless you are confident about these factors, building in the necessary definitions, measures, and controls can become complicated.

Most consulting project teams are a combination of consultants and the clients' personnel, and the teams that actually perform the work drive project outcomes. So, insist on control over the team, its composition, member selection, and their assignments. Teams must have the skills to get the job done. If a client decides to change one or two team members, it can spell trouble.

Eliminate some financial risk by asking for a good-faith payment at the beginning of the project and by setting checkpoints to measure progress against goals. You should also request interim payments. Don't wait for a big bang finish at the end of the project to collect your fee.

Include a rip-cord provision in the project agreement. If condi-tions emerge—such as executive turnover, client team changes, or unforeseen external circumstances—agree on terms for ending the project and on the amount the client will pay you.

➤ Retainers

Two types of retainers exist: prepaid service and unlimited access agreements. Prepaid service agreements are standard in the legal profession. For a set amount paid in advance, a lawyer's clients are entitled to a specified number of hours of legal advice. Most of these retainers are simply prepaid, hourly rate arrangements. As soon as the client has exhausted the allotted number of hours, the retainer must be renewed.

An unlimited access agreement, which is more common in con-sulting, gives a client access to a consultant for a fixed period for a fixed fee. Such retainers assure clients that they will have access to their consultants of choice for advice, coaching, and counseling for a fixed monthly or annual fee. Generally, retainers are used for advi-sory services instead of for completing specific projects.

The value of a retainer to the client is in being able to access the consultant's knowledge and experience, not the consultant's ability to complete projects. A retainer agreement usually limits the number of people in the client's organization who can use the consultant's services. Often, only one client representative has a retainer agreement with the consultant.

Retainers are advantageous to consultants because they provide a known flow of income for a specific period. Top consultants usually have several retainer relationships in their practices.

How to Use Retainers

Retainer agreements work best with trusted clients who need advice on high-priority topics. Try to limit the term of the agreement to 60 to 90 days and include frequent checkpoints to measure success. The retainer agreement should identify who in the client organization has access to the consultant and for what purposes. It should also include a provision to create renewal periods and provide separation between advisory work and project work. If the retained consultant is asked to complete a project, the fee for that work is not deducted from the retainer, but is submitted in a separate proposal.

➤ Equity-Based Pricing

In some circumstances, consultants elect to be paid for their service in the form of stock ownership or options for stock in the client's company instead of cash payment. Some clients, mainly start-ups, may prefer equity payments because they want to preserve their cash. Although consultants can do well if the equity they receive appreciates, the risk of business failure is so high that most consultants prefer to receive some cash along with equity.

How to Use Equity Pricing

Ask for payment in both cash and equity and charge a premium for your services to cover the downside risk. Proceed cautiously with equity pricing, particularly with start-ups. One firm substituted fees for equity in an established Russian truck manufacturer. The potential payout for the consultant was several times the value of hourly rates. But the company went belly-up after several months and the client had no way to pay the consultant except with partially completed truck engines.

Examine the company as if you were a potential investor: Analyze the company's business plan, financial situation, and management before you agree to equity-based pricing.

➤ Composite Pricing

Pricing services is a creative endeavor that works best as a joint effort with your clients. Any of the preceding pricing approaches can be used alone or in combination with one or more of the others. Frequently, a creative combination can be the turning point that helps you win a project.

Composite arrangements can take as many forms as you can imagine. Perhaps you would charge a fixed fee for the first phase of a project with a performance-based bonus if your work exceeded expectations. Building on that success, you might propose value-based pricing for the second phase. For the right client, you could combine fee-for-service fees with an equity arrangement. Some consultants barter their services for clients' products; others help their clients build their businesses by promoting the clients' products. The possibilities for composite pricing strategies are endless. The only real constraint is the creativity of consultants and clients in devising pricing schemes that meet the needs of all concerned.

■ THE SPIRIT OF FAIR PLAY

The pricing of consulting services ultimately comes down to an exchange of money for value provided. But establishing a common vision of value is often tough, given client skepticism about consultants and the high fees most consultants charge.

Clients need consultants, but find it increasingly difficult to evaluate their fees. And because a firm's brand name is no longer so important, it's harder than ever for them to price consulting services. So it's easy to understand why the subject of fees can be difficult for clients and consultants alike.

Emphasize the spirit of fair play by setting fees that strike a balance between the client's perception of value and your need to make a reasonable profit. Strive to reduce risk for both sides and bring predictability to the process. Just because you think you can get higher fees from a client, don't necessarily demand them. Seek the rewards of a long-term relationship instead of a short-term gain. Communicate openly when projects are going well and when problems arise. Always aim to bring projects to completion without any fee surprises.

Chapter 18

The Guerrilla's Competitive Edge

Rainmakers never wing it on sales calls.

—Jeffrey Fox[1]

Browse in your favorite bookstore and you'll find scores of books telling you how to peddle whatever you're selling with integrity, spin, vision, or just with persuasion. You are exhorted to be customer-focused, pursue "premium" leads, use appropriate body language, leave gifts for the receptionist, and handle objections with ease.

With all the weaponry arrayed against them, you'd think clients wouldn't stand a chance. But guerrilla clients see through these tactics from a mile away. In the age of hype, most sales pitches can be summed up by a popular bumper sticker that reads, "They're Lying."

Guerrillas know that the yawning credibility gap in business today has made trust elusive. They focus on the basics and earn clients' trust the tried-and-true way—through attention to detail, innovation, great service, and personal rapport.

■ WHAT SELLING PROGRAMS WON'T TEACH YOU

Selling situations in consulting are as varied as pricing options for projects, and slick sales techniques aren't much use in any of them.

227

But for all selling circumstances, guerrillas have secrets for gaining the competitive edge, including how to:

➤ Prevail over incumbent consultants.

➤ Fend off new competitors.

➤ Compete with low-priced contenders.

➤ Sell in a cattle call.

➤ Proceed when there's no money.

➤ Trump a small firm.

➤ Win against a big firm.

➤ Handle the client as a competitor.

➤ Respond when you're late to the game.

➤ Sell in an unfamiliar industry.

➤ Prevailing over Incumbent Consultants

When a client contacts you about a consulting project, an incumbent consultant may already be entrenched in the client's organization. Clients call in new consultants for any number of reasons. Perhaps they don't know whether incumbents are qualified to complete a project, or they may want fresh perspectives on continuing problems. Sometimes they just think it's time for a change. Whatever the client's reason, incumbents often have the inside track, and you should expect vigorous competition. However, unseating an incumbent can be easier than it seems.

Clients, especially those you don't know, may not be totally candid about why they call in new consultants. It's unlikely that clients will say, "Look, the consultants we have now are doing a fine job, but we want someone to keep them at the top of their game, so we'd like you to come here and mess with their heads." But there are ways to figure out clients' motives.

The client and project qualification process described in Chapter 15 will help you. Ask why, out of all the consultants available, the client called you. The answer you want to hear is that the client called you because of a great referral or your expertise and ability to do the proposed work. Prequalify every lead before investing your time and energy. That analysis is crucial when incumbents are there ahead of you.

In such situations, the discovery process involves more than an evaluation of the client and the project. You must also assess the strength of the incumbent competitor. You want to learn what work the incumbents are performing for the client, what they have completed in the past, who their supporters are in the client's organization, and how successful their work has been.

Some might advise you to ignore the competition and stick to your own game because you may have been contacted to keep the incumbent honest.

After you have prequalified the project and completed your preliminary research on the incumbent, visit the client's site to conduct discovery. If you want to pursue the project, look for ways to change the client's thinking about how to approach the work. You are, after all, the expert.

Clients, anticipating that their customer satisfaction project would take three months, asked the incumbent and two other consultants for proposals. The incumbent and one of the challengers put together solid proposals that would generate the results the clients requested within the three-month period. But the clients awarded the project to the third competitor, who proposed to deliver results every thirty days so that the clients would not have to wait three months to receive the benefits. The winner's new approach was the decisive factor in the award.

The most important objective of your discovery investigation is to determine incumbents' strengths and weaknesses. Identify incumbents' weaknesses, but don't talk about them. Instead, focus on your strengths in areas where incumbents are vulnerable. Beat incumbents on quality and substance, not fees.

In another case, a client asked for consulting help with a manufacturing strategy project that spanned the company's six global divisions. The incumbent consultants were well qualified, but the new consultants learned that the incumbents did not have consultants in all the client's locations. The new consultants, who had people on the ground, ready to go in all the client's locations, won the project because they highlighted that strength in their proposal.

GUERRILLA INTELLIGENCE: DON'T BAD-MOUTH THE COMPETITION

Don't criticize competitors. Clients will likely see your comments as unprofessional, and they may interpret your criticism as disparaging their judgment in selecting a consultant in the first place. When you attack others, you run the risk of undermining your credibility. Be quick to praise when it's deserved and slow to criticize when you perceive faults.

To compete effectively against an incumbent, your project strategy must be distinguishable from that of the incumbent. If it's not, the client probably won't be willing to incur the costs and endure the headaches of bringing in a new consultant.

Call on reinforcements to advance your case. Arrange for past clients to speak directly to the current client. Don't rely exclusively on written testimonials—personal contacts are more powerful in such situations.

Even though the client may be familiar with your white papers, reports, and articles, use them to reinforce and demonstrate your knowledge, experience, and perspectives. Once again, your task is to differentiate yourself from the competition. But that task is more focused and directed when you know exactly who the competition is— in this case, the incumbent.

➤ Fending Off New Competitors

You're working at a client's site, and you look up to see your client giving the grand tour to two people you know—rival consultants. Uh oh, what are they doing here? Sometimes the tables are reversed, and you are the incumbent when the client calls in new consultants. Consider yourself lucky if you learn about it in advance. Business with clients is never secure, so always expect to be challenged.

Don't jump to conclusions when you find out that you have a challenger. Quietly give your team the intruder alert: Stay cool, be cooperative, and remain focused on the project. But circle the wagons. Guard your tongues and your work papers.

When competing for a business process improvement project, a careless consultant left multiple copies of the team's entire proposal on a table in the client's copier room. Unknowingly, the client's mail clerk put the copies in a manila envelope and delivered them to the competition. The careless consultant's firm narrowly won the project, but his lapse nearly cost the firm the engagement.

Competitors may surface because clients ask for their help. In other instances, rival consultants may appear because they are investing in a new line of service and trying to sell it your client. Whatever the reason, the best time to plan your response to competitors is before they arrive.

When your clients are pleased with your work, incumbency provides an advantage against challengers. That advantage can quickly vanish, however, if you neglect client relationships. Your first and best defense is to develop client-level marketing plans for the clients you want to keep. We discuss such plans in detail in Chapter 19, but

GUERRILLA TACTIC: USE PERSONALIZED ATTENTION TO KEEP CLIENTS

If you haven't already done so, consider adding personalized microsites to your Web site for specific clients. You can create a microsite using material customized for a client, and then provide the client with a unique URL to access the site. An alternative is to ask clients for space on their internal sites, or intranets, for posting that material.

Regularly update and add new information to these postings, such as recent data and reports on industry trends. Help your clients stay on top of recent industry developments by filtering and interpreting information and its relevance to their businesses.

the gist is to build strong relationships with key members of your clients' organizations and continuously provide outstanding results.

Anticipate that challengers will probe your strengths and weaknesses, and return the favor. Find out about them from your sources. Use your relationships and lines of communication within the client's organization to clarify why you have competitors and what they're up to.

In recent years, Master Service Agreements (MSAs) between incumbent consultants and their clients have become more common. In an MSA, a consultant agrees that specific terms and conditions will apply to all of a client's consulting projects; the client, in turn, designates the consultant as the "preferred provider" of services. The MSA takes a lot of pain out of the selling process for both client and consultant because the project rates, terms, and conditions are prenegotiated. With that out of the way, it takes only agreement between the client and the consultant on objectives, scope, staffing, and timing for a new project to begin.

Don't rely on MSAs to block competition. If clients believe that a competitor has a better solution to offer, such agreements can't stem the tide. When competing for a project, a challenger submitted a proposal for the work and a favorable MSA. The client accepted both, and the challenger is now in the hunt for every new project. Clients will switch to another consultant in a flash if they think a competitor can deliver better results, regardless of an MSA with the incumbent.

Know your client's business inside and out. Learn who in the company might want to hire consultants and what they are trying to

---

GUERRILLA INTELLIGENCE: THE INCUMBENT'S ADVANTAGE

Your best defense against competitive threats is the excellence of your performance and the strength of your relationships. Your clients know they can count on you. They may expect more from you than they do of a challenger, but usually they will perceive less risk in sticking with the known.

When facing stiff competition, subtly remind clients of the cumulative value they've received from the projects you've handled for them. When clients are immersed in current problems, their memories may fade. A reminder in the form of a brief history of your consultant-client successes can't hurt.

---

accomplish. A strong network of client contacts will keep you up on internal company developments and arm you to fend off invaders.

➤ Competing with Low-Priced Contenders

In competitive situations, most clients compare proposals by focusing on the results they would receive from each bidder. Ironically, by the time all the competitors have conducted discovery and the proposal process is complete, most promised results look basically the same. So clients negotiate to get the lowest fees, and price can be the critical factor in securing the engagement.

To land projects, some consulting firms use low-fee strategies as an operating principle, while others may have low-cost structures that permit them to work for lower fees. Still others may reduce their fees to "buy" work, begin new relationships, or build new lines of business that they roll out to other clients for higher fees.

To control costs for discretionary consulting services, some clients employ procurement specialists who are seasoned negotiators. Often, they keep low-priced bidders in the competition solely to pressure other bidders to cut their fees. They may have no intention of accepting the low bidder, but want to keep everyone else's feet to the fire.

Instead of reducing fees, suggest alternative project approaches that will result in different levels of price. But don't try to counter low-priced competition by offering additional services at the original price. This reduces your effective rate of return on the project, and clients question why the extra services were not part of the original proposal. If they award you the project, they will continue to wonder

---

GUERRILLA TACTIC: STAND FIRM ON FEES

When bidding against a low-priced competitor, don't lower your fees. Price slashing can backfire because clients wonder why your rates were initially so high. It also signals that additional price negotiations are possible. If you cut your fees, clients may infer that you were trying to gouge them earlier or that you were seeking higher profits than were warranted. Stand firm on your fees, or you will lose credibility you can't recover and you'll face tough price negotiations every time you propose work for the client in the future.

---

what else they left on the table, which plants a seed of distrust that can cause problems later.

Hold firm when you're up against competitors who quote lower prices. Make sure that you can easily justify your fees based on the costs-to-value ratio in your project proposal. When the competitive process turns into a price war, your services become a commodity. That undermines your value in the minds of price-conscious clients and every invoice you submit will turn into a battle.

Instead of caving in on price or the extent of services you will provide, focus your marketing efforts on the issue of risk. Consider the following analogy.

When you need to replace the roof of your house, it's natural to seek price comparisons and easy to pick the lowest-priced bidder. But is that the best value? Will your new, inexpensive roof leak or blow off in a storm? How quickly will it wear out? Does it have the most efficient insulation and design to save you money in other ways like gutter cleaning and energy costs?

To counter low-priced competitors, stress your established record of success and the ways that your talents will decrease clients' risks. Your competitors may promise similar results, so show clients why they can count on you to keep your promises.

When a competing firm offered to complete a client's customer billing project for 50 percent of the price proposed by the nearest competitor, it was an offer the client couldn't refuse. The client hired the low-priced firm, even though the other consultant had demonstrated a better track record on similar projects.

The client took a risk and paid for it: The project was eventually completed, but it ended up costing the client more than any of the other competitors' proposed fees. The firm that completed the work is no longer considered for projects with that client.

In every negotiation, don't forget the personal risk sponsoring executives take when hiring consultants. Projects may be strategic initiatives that position those executives for promotion. The last thing they want is for consultant-caused failure to derail their career plans.

Since most clients really don't want consultants around, emphasize in your proposal the speed and value you'll provide. Your promise to deliver exceptional work, quickly, and at low client risk can displace lower-priced bids.

Clients seldom hire consultants to perform their most important work solely because they propose the lowest fees. If that is what a client wants, don't waste your time.

➤ Selling in a Cattle Call

A cattle call, also known as a beauty contest, is a selection process run by a task force that sends requests for proposals (RFPs) to numerous consultants at once. Consultants who participate answer an endless series of questions about their qualifications. It's not uncommon to see a three-pound RFP for one of these competitions. If you receive an RFP with a serial number on the cover page, you'll know you've been invited to a cattle call.

Many consultants specialize in and excel at responding to RFPs. Government agencies, large corporations, and nonprofit groups routinely issue RFPs in accordance with their competitive bidding requirements. A task force is often charged with conducting a fair and unbiased process to find the ideal consultant. Before awarding a project, the task force members must provide assurance that they "reviewed the entire market."

The rules for cattle calls are precise, schedules are fixed, and the RFP spells out project specifications. Normally, consultants don't meet the real buyers. Any questions that arise are addressed in bidders' conferences that are open to all interested parties. Answers to questions are shared with all bidders.

Consultants usually attend these meetings just to find out who else is competing. Substantive discussions rarely occur at bidders' conferences, as consultants are reluctant to reveal their sales strategies through their questions.

Despite numerous safeguards, buyers usually have identified the consultants they prefer long before the sales process begins. If that's the case, consultants who have not established a relationship with the buyer or the buying agency are at a disadvantage.

Responding to a cattle call is expensive. It takes time and effort to supply the laundry lists of detailed project specifications and consultant qualifications that most RFPs require. And, if you make the first cut, you usually have to get through a labyrinth of additional qualifying steps before the final decision is made. If you do win the project, a formal protest by a defeated consultant could delay the project and add to your costs.

Some consultants don't respond to any voluminous RFPs. Others submit generic letters about their qualifications and offer to discuss the project requirements with the decision makers. This tactic rarely works, so make a decision: Either jump into the RFP process with both feet or let those projects pass.

Since RFPs are usually issued for actual, funded projects, it can be foolish to walk away when you're qualified to deliver what the buyers need. But before you respond to a cattle call, carefully evaluate the investment you will surely have to make.

If you don't have any higher priority opportunities, respond to the RFP. Then advance through the process step by step and demonstrate why you are the safe and solid choice. Unless you know influential task force members, you probably will not be the preferred choice. In most cases, your RFP response will be scored mechanically on a spreadsheet that ranks you with other bidders. Understand the evaluation criteria and the scoring system so you can tailor your responses accordingly.

The following three rules will help you stay in the running:

1. Answer each question precisely as requested in the RFP. Make all your responses concise, easy to read, and relevant.

2. Keep your answers brief, but responsive. Make sure you meet every requirement set forth in the RFP.

3. Load up on references, testimonials, and pertinent case studies.

Cattle calls are hard to win, and negotiating fees for such projects can be just as difficult. Guerrillas prefer to use their resources for more likely wins. But if a cattle call project is directly in your area of expertise and you don't have any other leads to pursue, it's at least worth a try.

➤ Proceeding When There's No Money

In their work with clients, observant consultants often spot ways to help with other projects. In some instances, a project is identified, the client wants to do the work, and you are qualified, but there is no budget for the work. It may seem like a long shot.

Even when no funds have been earmarked for consultants, money can appear like magic if you have a good idea and a strong relationship with the decision maker. To secure funds for a project, work with your client to build an airtight case for how the project benefits outweigh the completion costs. Don't hard-sell the project; let the ratio of benefits to costs speak for itself.

When a project is their idea, some consultants agree to do the work and defer payment until a later budget cycle. That is not a good plan. Instead, ask to be the sole source provider of the service once the project is approved and funded. If the relationship is solid, many clients will agree.

A CEO asked a consultant for an organizational assessment of the planned restructuring of a company business unit. The consultant agreed to do the work "on spec," with payment to be made in the subsequent fiscal quarter. After six consultants worked on the project for two months, the company's board of directors sacked the CEO. Despite valiant efforts, the consulting firm was unable to recover any fees for its work.

Too many unknowns exist to work without payment. Your key contact, the executive sponsor, or other essential personnel, could relocate, leave the company, or be fired. A new management team could decide to take the company in another direction, its stock might dramatically slump, or a huge deal might fall through.

By helping the client build a strong case for the project, you can strengthen your relationship, generate goodwill, and position yourself for the future award of a project that you helped design.

➤ Trumping a Small Firm

Competing against a smaller firm is not a slam dunk. Many small firms have highly specialized senior practitioners who have built close personal relationships with clients—giving them the inside scoop on projects. Often, smaller firms have lower overhead costs so their fees can be measurably less, yet they can deliver quality comparable to or better than that of large firms. And clients often feel that they get more attention from smaller firms.

If you are part of a large firm, ignore smaller firms at your peril. For some projects, it may make sense for big firms to collaborate with smaller competitors on proposals. Joint efforts can fill service gaps for both firms and give clients better results. Consulting industry expert Fiona Czerniawska says, "I see a growing trend amongst clients to switch away from the mega-deal with one consultancy, and pressure to get multiple firms to collaborate on projects. The message is that clients . . . don't expect one firm to supply everything."[2]

If you choose to compete with smaller firms, you'll face two obstacles: price and senior-level practitioners. Don't compete on price. Consider, instead, how to use the broader resources of your firm to get answers faster, and focus on your implementation capabilities, which many small firms lack.

Create a competitive advantage by giving clients access to your networks, which are usually more extensive than those of smaller competitors. Clients can benefit from interacting with your other clients and network members. They can discuss shared issues and will realize that the competition does not have the same breadth and depth of client experiences. Use your more extensive list of qualifications to help clients see how selecting your firm will reduce their risks.

A client asked a large firm and a small firm to bid on a project to improve sales-force effectiveness. The smaller firm had successfully completed numerous, similar projects across a range of industries. In this, their niche, the small firm's qualifications were impeccable and their rates favorable.

The large firm had comparable qualifications, but had a higher price tag. The larger firm won the work for three reasons: (1) It committed more consultants to the discovery process to develop the client relationship and produce an outstanding proposal; (2) before the proposal was written, the firm assembled a group of other clients to discuss how similar projects had gone for them; and (3) the firm demonstrated an impressive record of implementing effective solutions for 75 clients.

➤ **Winning against a Big Firm**

Large consulting firms offer more diverse services, employ more people, and invest more in promotion than smaller competitors. Larger firms can also spend more to compete for work and will often do so when important long-term projects or relationships are at stake. But they have serious competitive weaknesses.

When a retail client asked for bids on a brand management project, a small firm went up against one of the big guys and won. The large firm proposed a comprehensive approach to the project that included project management and implementation in addition to the necessary strategic planning. The small firm had more depth of expertise on branding than the big firm, but less ability to manage the entire project. So the small firm proposed that its experts would complete the strategy work and the client would manage the project.

In addition to providing such creative solutions, small firms must claim the high ground early in the sales process. Large firms are often lumbering and slow to return calls or respond to new client requests. If you're in a small firm, speed and responsiveness can give you an edge. Any initial advantage is important because when large firms finally gear up, they can be formidable rivals.

Stay close to clients throughout the sales process because the big guys often don't. They may be too busy looking for the next sales lead and spend only limited time with the client early in the sales process. Move quickly to create strong impressions before the Goliaths get in the game.

Remove any doubts in the client's mind about whether your small firm can provide the desired results by quickly demonstrating a thorough understanding of the client's problem. Arrange for calls from your firm's well-pleased clients to help eliminate the new client's fears.

Resist the temptation to emphasize selling points that sophisticated buyers already know. In most cases your fees will be less than

GUERRILLA INTELLIGENCE: WHAT DOES THE CLIENT WANT?

Some clients want advice and counsel from a senior practitioner, which small firms are more likely to provide. In the big firms, the senior practitioners—the partners—tend to be revenue generators who help sell services, but rely on project managers to work directly with clients. The project managers are knowledgeable and skilled, but often their experience can't match that of small firm senior practitioners. Small firms can level the playing field by providing access to their experienced senior practitioners.

those of a larger firm. However, large firms may cut rates to beat the competition. When smaller firms focus on their lower rates, they risk starting price wars. They might win, but ultimately regret it because of eroded profit margins.

Even if you think it's true, don't suggest that a large firm will "back up the bus" to train a legion of inexperienced youngsters on the project at the client's expense. Also don't point out that a larger firm's fees are bloated because of its huge overhead. Experienced buyers know the score and will factor that information into their decisions. Again, emphasize your strengths, not the competition's weaknesses.

➤ Handling the Client as a Competitor

Many consultants forget that their most formidable—and invisible— competitor in the sales process may be the client. In every consulting opportunity, clients have two choices that don't include consultants: They can decide not to do the project; or they can do the project themselves, without outside help.

Competing against an undeclared rival is the most complicated selling situation you can face because it involves so much you don't know. You don't know what will kill the project or what will keep it alive. You also don't know what criteria will drive the project to the client's team. The only certainty is that if clients believe they can complete a project without consultants, you won't get the job—regardless of your qualifications.

Your best approach is to stress your firm's ability to deliver the proposed benefits (1) fully, (2) quickly, and (3) with little or no disruption, while (4) giving the prospective client a significant role in all phases of the project. Describe every instance where you've worked this way and back it up with calls from past clients.

Stress your intention to share the knowledge gained from the project with the clients and to work collaboratively with them. Some clients are motivated to run projects themselves because they want to keep control of the process. Be sensitive to this need and make it possible for clients to retain the control they want. Never claim that you have a "superior" plan for completing a project; it could alienate clients who think they have a better approach.

If the client decides to go it alone, position yourself for the future. Offer to provide advice, guidance, or assistance during the project if needed. Clients often reverse themselves or change direction in midstream, especially when they encounter roadblocks. When and if they do, you want to be the first one they remember and turn to for help.

➤ Responding When You're Late to the Game

You are excited to get the call from a client who wants you to submit a proposal on an interesting project, and your brain goes into overdrive thinking about all the questions you want to ask. Then the client adds, "The proposal is due in one week, and we've already received two from other consultants." The line has formed, and you are bringing up the rear.

The client has probably had extensive interviews with your competitors, heard their ideas, and helped with their proposals. By the time you enter the competition, a front-runner may already exist. The client's team may be tired of answering questions from other consultants, and the last thing they want is more of the same from a latecomer.

On the other hand, it's possible that the client is unhappy with the current choices and is still shopping. Even though time is short, don't budge until you complete the prequalification step in Chapter 15. Your hope is that you are not LIFO—last in, first out.

If everything checks out, take your best shot: Show how fast your team can get up to speed. Call in all your chips to connect with people who know the client and who can help you with the proposal. Bring the A team to the assignment. When playing catch-up, you need the creativity, insights, and experience of your best people to promptly clarify the problem, develop a solution, and prepare a proposal.

At the risk of sounding cliché, others win when you're playing catch-up. If you pursue a lead in this situation, be prepared to log long days and nights to meet the deadline. Without that commitment, you'll surely lose. Remember—to come from behind and win, you must be moving faster than the current leader.

➤ Selling in an Unfamiliar Industry

The services of some consultants cut across many industries. For example, human resources consultants can be as useful to hospitals as they are to consumer products companies. But many clients want "industry experts" and won't hire consultants who lack specific industry expertise. It can be tricky to compete for projects in industries in which you haven't worked, but it can be done. Apply a two-part strategy.

First, study the client's company and industry. Find out about the issues the client is facing. Discuss the company with your network contacts. If possible, talk to the client's customers. Develop insights into the company and industry.

> ### GUERRILLA INTELLIGENCE: ALL CLIENTS ARE UNIQUE
>
> Some consultants make the mistake of telling a client that in-dustry-specific experience is not important in their area of service. They tell clients about their extensive background in serving others with similar issues, and assure clients that they can easily learn whatever is needed to produce the desired results. A consultant told a client, "Accounts payable are accounts payable. It doesn't matter what industry you're in, the problems are the same."
>
> Telling clients that their issues are not special is dangerous. All clients believe their situations are unique, and they're right. Failure to recognize that truth will put you on a fast track out of the consulting business.

Second, impress on the client that "best practices"—the approaches that one company invents and everyone else follows—don't solve all problems. Industry experts tend to rely heavily on best practices, even though they often don't work. Forget best practices and use the insights, knowledge, and inventiveness gleaned from your experience in other industries. Help the client understand why group-think leads to the same old industry answers, not innovative solutions.

■ FINAL THOUGHTS

There are many permutations of the preceding selling situations. If there's one rule about the sales process for consulting services, it's that each circumstance presents its own challenges. If you really want a project, there's always a way to win it, whether you're the incumbent or challenger. Just keep in mind that clients no longer buy just on brand or size, but on results. If your firm can bring clients the result they need, you'll win—every time.

Chapter 19

After the Sale

Selling While Serving

Watch your relationship balance sheet; assume it is worse than it appears, and fix it.

—HARRY BECKWITH[1]

A client has agreed to hire you and congratulations are in order for the successful sale. Now the real marketing work begins—*after* you have landed the client engagement. As stressed earlier, your goal should be to obtain 60 percent of your new business from current clients or from their networks.

Many consultants fail to build the client relationships necessary to achieve that goal. If you find yourself in the following situation, it's a warning sign that you are on the wrong track.

You're just finishing up a productive meeting with a long-term client discussing the details of an ongoing project. The conversation shifts to other topics, and the client asks how you are faring in the race for a new project that another executive in the organization is sponsoring. You are stunned because you weren't aware of this important opportunity. Your firm is well qualified for the new project, but now you would have to play catch-up to be considered for the work.

Although the best consultants can recapture lost ground, learning about a project late or secondhand signals that you need to devote more effort to cultivating relationships within the client's organization. You

---

GUERRILLA INTELLIGENCE: ARE YOU IN THE LOOP?

You won't win every project from existing clients, nor will you be qualified to submit proposals on all work. It may seem obvious, but many consultants don't strive to build the relationships with clients that keep them informed about:

➤ What's going on in the client's organization.

➤ The people involved.

➤ What you can do to help, even if that means steering the client to a competing firm to handle the work.

If you find yourself out of the loop, your client relationship balance sheet needs fixing.

---

want decision makers to know the extent of your firm's capabilities and to call you whenever a new need arises. Or at least, ask your opinion about the consultants they should consider if the project is outside your area of expertise.

■ THE SMALLEST TARGET IS THE BIGGEST

Your clients should be your most important target market. Although they are your smallest market in size, they represent the highest potential for profits. Not only should the bulk of your new business come from existing clients, but 60 percent of your marketing budget and effort should be devoted to enhancing the value of those relationships.

It's more efficient to use your resources to win new business from or through existing clients. It is far less costly to sell to an existing client than to a prospect, so the return on your marketing investment is much higher. You can deliver services more easily, and you don't have to dig out every new lead from square one.

Some consultants may argue that such a high degree of client concentration is risky for a practice. But consider the case where three clients account for 40 percent of a firm's gross revenue. Each client has worked steadily with the firm for 10 years, and they are the firm's most profitable accounts.

In good years and bad, these three clients seek help and pay handsomely for the firm's assistance. Most projects they undertake are not competitive, but are awarded directly to the firm. In rare cases when RFPs are issued, the firm still wins far more than it loses.

Many competitors hawk their wares to these three clients, some with minor successes. But not a single competitor has established a strong enough relationship to unseat the incumbent for anything but the smallest projects. Build the right relationships, and existing clients will be your best source of ongoing business.

■ CLIENT-LEVEL MARKETING

Part of effective marketing to existing clients is simply your mind-set; you must think about them as prospective clients. That doesn't mean taking advantage of your position to sell them what they don't need, and it doesn't mean always being in a smarmy sales mode. What it does call for is a proactive, client-level marketing plan tailored to each client.

Adapt the marketing plan described in Chapter 4 to create a client-level marketing plan for each client organization. Identify your purpose with each client, how you will achieve it, the specific people in the organization you plan to approach, and how you will differentiate your services for each. Outline the tactics you'll use and how much time, money, and effort you will spend on the plan.

Assuming you have properly qualified each client and project, you should want long-term relationships with most of your existing clients. Some clients will be more important to your practice than others, but plan some client-level marketing for all your clients.

In true guerrilla fashion, your client-level marketing must be flexible and creative. One of the guerrilla's greatest strengths is the ability to swiftly adapt to changing situations. Nowhere will that skill serve you better than in the give-and-take of developing quality relationships. To that end, client-level marketing must be unobtrusive and collaborative; it must help clients in meaningful ways and target their issues. Your plan should be based on helping clients first and selling second.

■ THE SEVEN RULES OF ENGAGEMENT

Relationships with clients are getting harder to establish because of increased competition and clients' skepticism about consultants' credibility. Plus, nearly all consultants try some form of marketing to existing clients, whether they call it account management or project add-on strategy. Follow the guerrilla rules of engagement to get and keep your edge.

➤ Rule 1: Make It Real—Real Fast

After a project agreement is signed, clients often have conflicting emotions. They're optimistic about your selection, but also feel a sense of uncertainty about what's to come. They can be nervous, fearful, and skeptical about whether you can achieve the project objectives and even may wonder whether proceeding with the project was a good idea. Clients are also concerned about the impact projects will have on their organizations and staffs. They may be reluctant to cede control to you, or may worry about the career and political implications of your selection.

Theodore Levitt, author of *The Marketing Imagination,* warns us that with intangible products like consulting services, the client *". . . usually doesn't know what he's getting until he doesn't.* Only when he doesn't get what he bargained for does he become aware of *what he bargained for."*[2] Levitt rightly points out that clients often can't articulate what they want, but they always know when they are dissatisfied.

With less than one third of a multimillion-dollar project completed, a highly skilled technology firm lost the project. The client was dissatisfied with the work and with team communication, so they booted the firm and started over with a new consultant, wasting several million dollars. If the unlucky firm had done a better job early in the project, it could have avoided the ax and the financial battle that followed.

As soon as a project moves from the sales phase to the delivery phase, clients form lasting impressions about your team and its performance. Move quickly to make results real for clients so they know they are getting what they bargained for—even if they're not quite sure what that is. Get the project off to a quick, organized start and let clients see that the team will achieve results. Here are a few practical ways to proceed:

Demystify Project Administrivia

One or two meetings with the client team early in the process can steer emerging relationships in the right direction. Don't assume clients know all your internal processes, even if you spelled them out in your proposal. And don't assume you know theirs. It may seem like a waste of time at the outset of a project when everyone is itching to get to the task, but an early meeting of the minds on administrative details prevents subsequent confusion, acrimony, and lost productivity. Review billing rates, payment terms, and who will be responsible for completing paperwork.

Clarify Roles and Lines of Communication
Put in writing how you would like to do business. Provide contact information for your firm and the telephone numbers and e-mail addresses of project team members. Go over the roles and responsibilities of the consulting and client teams. Create a clear set of guidelines for communicating problems and resolving open issues. Set up a regular schedule to talk, review project progress, and plan. Make sure that every meeting has a purpose and is worth the time spent. If you engage in early dialogues, you'll uncover incorrect assumptions, potential scope changes, and easier ways to work together.

Revisit the Work Plan
Often, subtle changes take place in the interval between the submission of a proposal and the project's start date. Reduce the client's natural anxiety by reviewing, in detail, the work plan for the project and how each task relates to the ultimate result the client wants to achieve. It's important for all team members to see how their small pieces of the project fit into the big picture. Review resources and schedules carefully to minimize surprises. Don't let clients think, even for a second, that they made a bad decision in selecting you for their projects.

GUERRILLA TIP: SEND A WELCOME PACKAGE

It may sound old school, but some consultants send clients a welcome package at the beginning of projects. The package includes some details previously described, such as the names and contact information for the consulting team members, but it can also include invitations to upcoming events, new research the firm has published, and a letter thanking clients for their business.

Building consultant-client relationships is a mutual process. All parties must understand one another's personalities, approaches, skills, strengths, and weaknesses. Some relationships immediately move forward, whereas others never get off the starting block. Sprint to make the intangible tangible for your clients.

➤ Rule 2: Results Rule

In his *Harvard Business Review* article, "How to Buy/Sell Professional Services," Warren J. Wittreich points out, "Any selling involved in a professional service has just begun when the contract is signed. All that has been sold up to that time is a promise. *The major 'sale' comes in delivering on that promise."*[3]

Clients seek relationships with consultants for one reason: results. As repeatedly stressed in this book, the prerequisite for long-term, profitable client relationships is flawless delivery of every benefit and value you promise in your proposals or confirmation letters. Clients place great trust in consultants, and the fastest way to lose that trust is to perform poorly on a project.

Flawless delivery means that you:

➤ Start and end the project on time.

➤ Respect the budget.

➤ Keep disruption to the client's organization to an agreed-on minimum.

➤ Avoid surprises (if the proposal states that you need five people to complete the work, don't request five more people two weeks later).

➤ Ensure success by helping the client use what the project develops. Seek clients' advice on how project results can be made most valuable to them.

Use the project work as a hands-on opportunity to show clients what you and your firm can do, prove that you are always thinking about their problems, and demonstrate how you work closely with their team. Producing results is not just about achievements at the end of the project, but also about each day's incremental accomplishments.

Delivering excellent results provides value that clients can quantify and exponentially increases the potential for your client relationships to bring more work your way.

➤ Rule 3: Expect a Cast of Characters

Walking into a client environment can be like landing on an alien planet. You don't speak the language, and often you can't interpret what you see and hear. Attempting to build rapport with clients you encounter is delicate work. It requires well-developed interpersonal skills to identify the roles, influence, and characteristics of people in the organization and to figure out their needs.

It's dangerous to generalize about people because their motivations are complex, but here are a few examples of characters you might identify from their behavior: supporters, detractors, and the disengaged.

For the most part, it's unlikely that a client will walk up to you and say, "Hi, I'm your worst enemy here." Listen and think about what you observe. If someone says, "I don't care what the team decides, just tell me what you want me to do," there's probably a good reason that person is disengaged. Try to discover what it is.

Consultants who are conducting client-level marketing should be wary of clients who are takers—they can milk relationships dry. They may feel entitled to and press for discounted services just because of the volume of work they've given you. These requests can be costly, so carefully evaluate what you stand to gain or lose on each client request. Think about surprising them before they ask by providing them with occasional free extras. Just be sure you understand that they may continually demand or feel entitled to such bonuses.

Long-term clients can be suspicious of your motives. When you bring them something valuable, they may think you're angling to sell—even if what you offer is free. Don't let it dissuade you. Keep offering clients ideas, understand their sensitivity, and try not to blatantly sell. Clear thinkers will recognize and appreciate the perspectives you consistently offer.

GUERRILLA INTELLIGENCE: ALLY OR FOE?

The cruelest foe is a masked benefactor.
—Ralph Waldo Emerson*

Consulting projects are often controversial, creating both supporters and foes in client organizations. You will always have detractors—people who were against hiring you in the first place and never seem satisfied with your work. We'd all rather bask in the approval of supporters and avoid contact with detractors, but that's not realistic.

While client relationships should be cordial, clients don't have to be your friends to help you succeed. With some detractors, you may not get any further than a grudging acknowledgment that the project was not as big a disaster as they thought it would be. You never know, though—those in your detractors' networks who understand their negativity may perceive their opinions about you in a positive way.

*Ralph Waldo Emerson's quote is from his article, "The Sovereignty of Ethics," *Lectures and Biographical Sketches* (1883). Reprint: Leonard Roy Frank, ed., *Random House Webster's Quotationary* (New York: Random House, 1999), p. 239.

GUERRILLA TIP: FEE FATIGUE

Long-term clients can get fee fatigue: They simply get tired of paying consultants. In most cases, it's not triggered by poor service on your part, nor can it be prevented. Usually, they just need a break from working with outsiders. Learn to recognize the symptoms of fee fatigue and openly discuss this with the client.

Don't plan to settle in permanently with any client—get a project done and clear out. Your goal should be to return for another project in the future. You may well find that absence does make the client's heart grow fonder.

Some clients want to improve their industry visibility to promote their companies and their careers. Help them achieve their goals: Facilitate their participation in panel discussions at industry forums, publish jointly developed case studies and articles, or arrange for them to speak at conferences.

You can also help clients who want to extend their personal networks. Introduce clients to one another to share ideas and approaches. Clients love to discuss industry issues with their peers and with experts both in and out of their industries.

The clients with whom you will build the most rewarding relationships are those who take you into their confidence and include you as a trusted advisor. But you can also have profitable short-term relationships with any clients who respect your work and get along with you.

GUERRILLA INTELLIGENCE: THE RELATIONSHIP CHALLENGE

Consultants must remain objective to be effective, which requires that they keep a certain professional distance from clients. On the other hand, they have to get close enough to clients to become known and trusted. How do you do that? Tell the truth to your clients, even when it's unwelcome. That will earn you "objectivity points," which are better than style points or brownie points from the consultant's point of view.

Obviously, you want to sell clients more work. You know that and so do they. But telling them the truth about what they need always takes precedence over selling more work.

Always act in the best interests of the people in your clients' organizations, even if their actions seem to conflict with your short-term interests. Some consultants, to make more money, will push for work that is not in their clients' interests by suggesting a more complex and costly solution to a problem than necessary. Such actions are shortsighted and eventually will come back to haunt you. Sooner or later, they will tarnish your reputation with the client, and you'll be gone.

Every member of your client's organization is your client. Every interaction is a chance to influence each person's network by creating an advocate for you and your firm. Never underestimate how far an impression can travel, especially in the Internet age. Keep in mind that the staff member you speak with today could be the CEO tomorrow. People often change companies and even careers, so all relationships are important.

➤ Rule 4: Draw Yourself a Diagram

For every client organization, develop the influence map mentioned in Chapter 3 to help you quickly figure out who's who and who might need your help. Plan how you will meet the key executives in the client's organization. Determine if they are buyers of consulting services and if they will be your advocates, maintain neutrality, or be adverse to you.

Continually seek new relationships within the client's organization. Know about the industry players, your clients' competitors, and all those who influence the business. Regularly assess your relationships and target individuals who are important in reaching your goals.

If you find that 80 percent of a client's buyers don't like your firm, save your resources and put your efforts into getting business from other clients.

➤ Rule 5: Invest in Strategic Clients

All client relationships have potential value, but some clients have more strategic importance to your practice than others. And strategic clients warrant special investments.

Take a lesson from the airline industry's marketing. Airlines have frequent-flier programs to provide additional services to valued customers on the basis of the miles they fly or money they spend. In exchange for their repeat business, frequent fliers receive preferential seating, expedited check-in, upgrades, advance notice of special fares and packages, lounge use, and other bonuses. The airlines have

GUERRILLA TIP: EXTEND YOUR REACH WITH SOCIAL NETWORK SOFTWARE

Dubbed the Technology of the Year 2003 by *Business 2.0*, Social Network Applications analyze networks of people and their contacts to extend your personal and professional network faster and further. These software programs use social network theory to do everything from matching people with others in their own organizations to generating sales leads.

Vendors claim their programs can provide access to and insights about decision makers and get you business introductions that might not otherwise happen. They also say the software increases sales leads and shortens the sales cycle.

Some critics of these programs assert that social network software is another dot-com bomb waiting to happen. In the meantime, some consultants have had success with these tools so you may want to take a look at a few, like Spoke, Ryze, Visible Path, and ZeroDegrees.

created strategic relationships with their best customers scaled to the amount of business they conduct with them.

Before you invest in a strategic client, consider the following criteria.

Practice Building

Identify the practice-building benefits that justify investing in the client beyond the current project. Will an added investment generate new services you can market, an expanded industry presence, or new members for your network? If so, are they worth the investment required? Additional investment may be worthwhile if a client has the potential to refer business to you. The client may offer you long-term projects or the opportunity to move in interesting new directions. In addition, if the client is a prestigious industry or thought leader, examine whether your added investment could increase your standing in the industry or produce important referrals.

Chemistry and Culture

Consulting is a high-contact business and the success of projects hinges on the consultants' energy and motivation. A client's organizational culture strongly influences consultants' energy. Consultants thrive in an open, cordial, responsive setting, but may be discouraged when treated poorly, have their invoices held unreasonably, have no access to authority, face endless red tape, and receive knee-jerk reactions in response to their recommendations.

During a project to help a retail client decide how best to survive bankruptcy, consultants found themselves in the project from hell. The client's site was like a ghost town—eerily silent with empty cubicles everywhere. What was worse, the organization's remaining employees deeply resented the consultants' presence. They felt the consultants were high-priced replacements for their former colleagues, and so they were sullen and uncooperative at every turn.

If a client's staff mixes well with the consulting team, it is easier to justify more marketing investment to retain that client's business. Some clients deliberately keep consultants at arm's length and resist efforts to build relationships. Although these situations can be awkward, they are workable. Clients are undesirable if they are not open to your ideas and are unwilling to see you as a potential advisor on a broader range of topics or future projects.

Will It Work?

Unless you're financially desperate, it makes little sense to pursue projects that you feel can't produce the desired result. In some cases, you may not have the right qualifications or experience, or the client may appear to be unreasonable or unresponsive.

Trust your instincts. Certain projects and clients were never meant to be. Committing ongoing marketing efforts to a client that has all the signs of trouble can wreck your reputation, kill your staff's morale, and spike employee turnover. Help the client find another firm instead. You'll earn gratitude from the client for your help and from the new consultant for the referral.

Profit

Again, profit is imperative for long-term relationships. Can you profit from working with this client, and if so, how much? Volume of fees is usually a false indicator of profit because large-fee projects can lock you into low margins for years. Look at forecasted profit to decide whether the client warrants additional marketing attention.

Sometimes clients tempt you with promises to provide new business referrals, expand your network, or put you in the project opportunity lead stream. Discount all such promises and evaluate whether the relationship can actually produce the benefits necessary for an additional investment.

Ask yourself whether the client will require sufficient consulting services for you to profit long-term, both financially and otherwise.

Location

Every consultant has a different perspective on travel. Most are resigned to travel being a part of the business. Think about where your clients are located and decide whether the investment in travel is worth it. And don't forget to evaluate the impact of traveling on your other client commitments and on your life: Travel can exact a severe physical toll.

Clients whose locations are close to yours may be preferable for long-term relationships. In *The Art of War,* Sun Tzu calls this the "facile," or easy ground.[4] While certainly not the only factor in your decision, location should be a consideration.

Identifying a strategic client comes down to one question: Will it be mutually beneficial for you and the client to invest in each other? If the answer is yes, that client goes to the top of your list. Then, you must decide how much of your profit or time you are willing to invest in the client to win more work or referrals. That will vary with the size and profitability of your practice. To return to the airline analogy, some frequent fliers receive more preferential treatment than others based on how much business they do with the airlines. You can also apply that approach to your best clients.

➤ Rule 6: Loyalty Is a Two-Way Street

Client loyalty is tough to come by. Clients who think another consultant can provide greater value may be quick to forget about the past miracles you've pulled off for them and switch firms. Managing client relationships is about mutual long-term gain. No loyalty should be expected on either side without that.

Some consultants are easily drawn to the next sales opportunity with a different client instead of building on established client relationships to generate new projects. Perhaps it's the lure of the chase or the excitement of new clients, but it's often a mistake to abandon a strategic client for an unknown entity.

Be patient and understand the realities clients face. Don't throw in the towel when things don't go your way or you think clients don't show appropriate appreciation for you. Clients have an obligation to check out alternatives and consider every option that might help them achieve their goals. And your firm may not be the one they need at the time.

Even though your clients may not seem loyal to you, be loyal to them. Despite their inconsistency and explorations with other consultants, always provide them with consistently great service. Give them focused, useful points of view as promptly as possible. Keep in mind that you can offer existing clients higher quality work, with similar or less effort, at higher profit margins than your competitors.

➤ Rule 7: Know When to Fold 'Em

Know when to walk away from a client relationship. Not all clients are worth the investment necessary to get more business from them. Although most clients add to your practice, some subtract. Try to continue working with clients who share your interest in long-term relationships. Consider pulling the plug on client relationships in the following circumstances:

➤ *They are only transaction-oriented.* Clients that only care about one project at a time and are unmoved by the wonders you have worked for them in the past are usually poor investments. If they treat you like a vendor instead of like a professional advisor, look elsewhere.

➤ *They are openly opportunistic.* Some clients will switch consultants in a heartbeat. Often for small decreases in consulting fees, these clients change consultants faster than you can say Benedict Arnold. Don't waste your time with them unless you are prepared to play an endless game of fee negotiation.

➤ *Every interaction is adversarial.* If you love to fight, then this may be your ideal client. For the rest of us, dealing with contentious people is a drag. Let them find other victims to torture.

➤ *They don't reciprocate.* Some clients ask consultants for unpaid extras like conducting research and making presentations. After the extras are provided, they turn around and hire your competitor, even though you are well qualified to complete the work. Reciprocity shouldn't be expected in every case, but consultants should expect some consideration for past efforts.

➤ *You become isolated from decision makers.* As pointed out earlier, you shouldn't take on a project if you don't have access to decision makers. But if, as a project unfolds, you are shunted off to gatekeepers who can only say "no" and thwart your attempts to reach those who can say "yes"—it's time to think about throwing down your cards and getting out of the game.

It is critical to your long-term success to know when to pull back from, or even drop out of, a client relationship. Don't remain engaged in an unproductive situation—it's not good for you or for your practice.

Carefully select the clients with whom you want to build long-term relationships; they are the backbone of your consulting practice. The objective of your client-level marketing should be to create partnerships with your most profitable clients so that you can help plan and participate in their future consulting needs. Although consultants provide services to clients, ultimately consulting is a people business, and it will only be as successful as the relationships you forge with the people in your clients' organizations.

Part
IV

Pulling It All Together

Chapter 20

Put Your Plan into Action

In the field of opportunity, it's plowin' time again.

—Neil Young[1]

Although the standard warning on a car's side-view mirror—Objects in mirror are closer than they appear—refers to traffic hazards, it also applies to the dynamics of the consulting industry. No matter how secure consultants feel about their clients or niches in the industry, competitors can overtake them from behind in a flash. Guerrilla marketing is a consultant's insurance against being run off the road.

Although competition for clients has never been more intense, now is *the* time to be a consultant. Change has become a constant, and consultants flourish in times of change. Clients are rethinking every aspect of their businesses as suppliers, competitors, and customers push them to do everything better, faster, and cheaper. Clients now need more help than ever, and that's not going to change anytime soon.

What is changing, however, is how consultants market their businesses. Some of the marketing tactics in this book are time-proven methods. For decades, consultants have written articles and conducted surveys—and they work. But today, consulting begins and ends with marketing, and if you don't continually market your services, you risk ending up in a corporate gig or the unemployment line. If the market doesn't know you and what you do, it won't matter how good you are.

> ### GUERRILLA INTELLIGENCE: MARKETING IS EVERYTHING
>
> Every action you take has a marketing implication. Each inter-action, from the briefest telephone call or unexpected encounter to the most prestigious keynote speech, affects how clients view you and your firm. Whatever you and your staff say and do influences clients' views of your firm. Sensitize everyone in your firm to the importance of personal marketing by emphasizing that their behavior shapes clients' impressions of your firm. As a consultant once remarked, "A black mark from a negative client interaction takes a lot of white paint to cover."

■ IT *IS* PERSONAL

Your marketing tools—such as speeches, articles, and your Web site— are just the first step. Marketing weapons get you into a prospective client's conference room, but your professional competence, communication, selling skills, and follow-up will determine whether you land the job. If you pass the initial hurdle, you'll rely on your network of satisfied clients to help you along.

Consulting is built on personal and working relationships. Referrals from a strong network of satisfied clients will eventually account for the lion's share of your business. No matter how strong those referrals may be, prospective clients will always check your references. And when you get great references from great people, you're more apt to get great jobs. Remember, clients will also check with their own networks of colleagues to get an independent sense of you and your firm.

Concentrate on developing and strengthening relationships:

➤ Build networks of supporters, clients, and collaborators who will help you.

➤ Rely on a diverse array of other professionals and consultants who complement your skills and fill in your weaknesses.

➤ Keep in contact with past clients. Position yourself as a resource for them.

It's a common myth in consulting that the larger your network is, the more effective your marketing efforts will be. The conventional wisdom says that the result of a huge network will always be more referrals, broader visibility, and more lucrative business.

But, in consulting, size doesn't matter. One highly successful consultant has only seven members in his business network. He is successful because all his contacts are influential in their organizations, are substantial buyers of consulting services, and are eager sources of referrals.

As you build your network, follow guerrilla wisdom: Strive for quality, not quantity. Remember, relationships take precious time to build and nurture. Make sure you're aiming at the right targets.

■ ALL DETAILS ARE MAJOR

Clients abhor small screwups like incorrect invoices, spelling errors, and unclear communication. Sweat every detail of every task. Leave nothing to chance. Check all documents to ensure they're error-free, including proposals, invoices, reports, contracts, and all written materials and communications. Never sign or indicate your approval of anything that you haven't carefully reviewed. Your clients may never mention your attention to detail, but they will respect and reward you for it.

■ PROMPTLY FOLLOW UP ON EVERY COMMITMENT

By letting commitments languish, you can lose relationship capital. Meet every deadline; don't miss or be late for appointments, meetings, or events. Return telephone calls, e-mail, and other correspondence as promised. Your promptness demonstrates that you respect other people's time.

Make sure your staff knows your clients' names, greets them warmly, and treats them with unfailing courtesy and respect.

■ KNOW YOUR CLIENTS WELL

Understand your client's objectives, needs, culture, politics, problems, and career issues. Some consultants burrow into their current projects and miss the big issues with which their clients are wrestling. Study all facets of your client's operation. The more you know, the more likely you'll be to find new work. Be discreet and don't meddle in client politics.

■ KEEP CLIENTS IN THE LOOP

Client sponsors can easily get swept up by other issues and lose touch with the details of the project. Advise them of developments and solicit their opinions and guidance. Avoid surprises. When you head into a client status meeting, never wing it. If you don't know, admit it and promise to quickly get the answer. When you provide answers, make sure that they're thorough and complete.

■ BE FAIR

Although you may be pushed to generate maximum fees in every situation, don't take today what could cost you tomorrow. Treat your clients, your staff, and everyone you deal with fairly. Don't give away your services, but don't be greedy.

Since your primary objective is to build lasting client relationships, think of the future and potential revenue, not simply what you can squeeze out of a single project now. Be willing to give and take, and charge reasonable fees.

Accept complete responsibility for your role in projects. Admit mistakes and quickly fix them. Find the sources of misunderstandings and clear the air. Never blame clients for project failures, even when they caused the mistakes. Do your best to make assignments work.

■ INVEST IN YOURSELF

Invest in yourself, in your own professional development, and in the development of your staff. Take and sponsor courses; read and subscribe to informative publications; attend seminars, workshops, and events. Meet your peers, experts, and authorities in your areas of interest. Question them and learn from them.

Use your network to be at least one step ahead of the field on industry issues, trends, and the competitive environment. Master your skills and the delivery of your services. Regularly analyze every aspect of your consulting practice from initial prospect contacts and project management through project completion. Then take tangible steps to improve all deficiencies.

Stress creativity, new ideas, and approaches. Periodically step back to gain new perspectives. Take time to regenerate your thinking; brainstorm and develop new ideas and services. Associate with experts in different disciplines and see what you can import to your consulting practice.

■ BE CREATIVE AND PROVOCATIVE

Challenge every given, every accepted fact, rule, and assumption. Always ask does it have to be this way? Is there a better way? Try to adopt different perspectives. Look at situations from many viewpoints, including those of your clients, their clients, customers, employees, suppliers, and outside observers. Always be open. Be willing to explore the value of new and novel approaches. The instant you feel yourself instinctively rejecting any idea or suggestion, stop and reevaluate your reaction.

■ KEEP YOUR EYES AND EARS OPEN

Understand the competitive market. Know the competition thoroughly, both their weaknesses and strengths. Check with your network members, visit your competitors' Web sites and read their newsletters. Summaries of their materials are often free.

Learn what markets and clients your competitors are serving. Identify the issues they're handling, the research they're conducting, and initiatives they're pursuing. See how their work fits with industry trends and where you stand in the competitive mix. Think about and adjust your marketing plan in accordance with your discoveries.

■ TRUST YOUR DECISIONS

Remain patient. Getting results from your marketing can seem to take forever, but hang in there and don't give up. When you feel that you're making headway, don't stop—stay the course. Small successes can create marketing momentum that, over time, will attract more leads and business for your practice. If you give up on marketing, you'll lose your momentum and may have to start from scratch.

■ PUTTING YOUR PLAN INTO ACTION

A plan without action isn't effective; it's simply a plan, not a solution. It's relatively easy to plan, but implementing your plan requires resolute effort. Executing your plan to perfection takes commitment, coordination, patience, and trust—and results may not appear overnight.

Expect to encounter resistance, delays, and setbacks. Don't become discouraged; they're all a part of the process. Trust your plan. A well-conceived plan should be flexible enough to accommodate necessary changes and will eventually produce the desired results.

■ MAKING MARKETING WORK

If you read only one section in this book, let it be this one. Copy it, highlight it, or place a bookmark in it, but come back to it. It's the best refresher on keeping your marketing on course.

➤ Remember Your Values

Periodically compare your practice performance to your original plans. First, identify your ultimate goals, what you hoped to accomplish—for clients and for yourself—financially, professionally, and personally. Do they still hold true? Is what you're now doing a career or an interim step? Will your findings change the potential clients you plan to target and the development of your marketing plan?

Examine your role in the consulting industry; determine the part you want to play. Does it conform to how you want to lead your life? By looking to the future, you can find guidelines that will motivate you to take the steps you need to succeed.

➤ Select Your Targets

Define your market and thoroughly research it from top to bottom. Understand the competitive environment and identify your rivals' strengths and weaknesses. Discover what the market and potential clients need. Find hot-button issues you can address, but don't select too many targets. Choose an industry segment or a group of companies to target even if you specialize in a specific business function, such as finance, fulfillment, or production.

Concentrate your efforts on markets that need your expertise or are underserved. If you enter a crowded market, be prepared to make a marketing splash to overcome the advantage held by incumbent firms.

➤ Distinguish Yourself

Consultants tend to market their services similarly: Their materials look the same, contain the same words, and provide the same charts. Even their Web sites and brochures look alike. However, consulting is a huge industry filled with many highly branded and talent-rich firms. Use their marketing similarity to your advantage; distinguish yourself because most clients are looking for fresh ideas.

Resist temptation and don't look at other consultants' marketing materials until you've developed your own concepts. Create distance, stand out, be provocative, and don't worry about alienating potential clients. Those who may be offended are probably companies you should avoid. Offer something special and different, or you won't get business. It's that simple.

➤ Create Your Marketing Plan

Your marketing plan identifies you and the value and approach you bring to the market. It describes, in direct, simple terms, your firm and your ongoing marketing program. It forces you to boil down your marketing ideas to their essence and to express them so that clients, potential clients, consultants, and collaborators can clearly understand your meaning. Your marketing plan is the centerpiece of your marketing approach and determines how you'll be regarded in the market.

➤ Choose Your Marketing Weapons

Focus on your Web site and identify other sales tactics, such as speaking, writing, publishing, and publicity. Choose weapons that will spread your message through various media outlets. Identify the members of your staff who will be responsible for the various elements of your campaign, including design, execution, and measurement. Determine the order in which you plan to launch each marketing initiative and coordinate it with the rest of your campaign.

Don't kick off all your marketing measures at once. Instead, stagger your initiatives and execute your plan methodically to obtain frequent exposure over an extended period. Don't blow your entire budget all at once or prospective clients will soon forget about you. Keep reminding them and they'll not only notice you, they'll give you credibility and accept you as a viable player in the industry.

➤ Set Up a Marketing Calendar

Identify how and when you would like to launch your program to market your consulting services. Design a precise, step-by-step listing of how you wish to proceed, but make it flexible enough to accommodate change. Build in substantial lead time so that you can prepare and coordinate all items entered on your calendar. Write a separate plan for the preparation and testing of your marketing materials before your campaign begins.

➤ **Launch Your Marketing Program**

Follow your marketing calendar even if it doesn't seem to be producing results. Avoid the temptation to alter it for at least a few months. If you have designed it carefully and thoroughly tested it, the plan should work, so give it time. At some point, your program should begin to create momentum and build, but the process may be gradual and take more time than you expect.

If, after some time has passed, it seems clear that a part of your marketing plan is not working or generating the momentum you need, see what you can add to get it going. If that fails, change course and move in other directions.

➤ **Stay on Track**

Implement all items at the times designated on your marketing calendar. Your clients and prospects will expect—and hopefully look forward to receiving—your zine, articles, and other materials. Meet your deadlines; plan ahead. Anticipate when projects, proposals, or other interruptions could demand your attention and try to stagger them so they won't arise when you're putting out your zine or writing an article.

In marketing, consistency and continuity pay big dividends. If you suspend or delay your program, you risk losing the benefits of the exposure you've worked so hard to get. Keep in mind that your competitors will still be marketing. In fact, in your absence, they may even step up their marketing efforts.

➤ **Measure Performance**

Identify which of your marketing approaches are working and which are not. Also determine how well they're doing. Many consultants don't track the return on investment from each of their marketing efforts. Instead, they assume that when a program creates leads, it's worth the investment.

Monitor how well each marketing initiative is serving to bring in leads. Any efforts that are not producing leads should be reassessed. A consultant who wrote a series of articles for a human resources magazine received responses only from readers who were searching for jobs. When the consultant broadened his focus and published pieces in other industry journals, leads poured in.

➤ Regenerate

Sooner or later, every plan needs revision. Conditions always change and your plan must be flexible enough to address the new order. Review the results of your marketing efforts every quarter and add or subtract weapons from your arsenal accordingly. Also consider changing your order for rolling out various marketing initiatives. On the basis of your review, you may decide to offer new services or employ new market weapons.

Three simple words summarize how consultants succeed with guerrilla marketing:

1. Action
2. Passion
3. Creativity

These three words represent the difference between those who sell a few projects and those who build sustainable, profitable consulting practices. This is a great time to be a consultant. More than ever, clients need help, and they are open to the new ideas and approaches that you can supply. Let guerrilla marketing lead the way and help you finish first.

Notes

■ CHAPTER 1: WHY CONSULTANTS NEED GUERRILLA MARKETING

1. From the book, *True Professionalism: The Courage to Care about Your People, Your Clients, and Your Career* (New York: Free Press, 1997), p. 5.
2. Statistic on the size of the consulting industry is from Kennedy Information, Inc., *The Global Information Technology Management Consulting Marketplace: Key Data, Forecasts and Trends* (2003), p. 15. Some experts may quibble over Kennedy's estimates or forecasts for the size of the industry, but the point is that the numbers are big.
3. Statistic on client satisfaction with consultants is from Kennedy Information, Inc., "Kennedy Information: Client Intelligence Report" (May 2002).
4. From the interview, "How to Satisfy Clients: An Interview with Steve Banis and Mac McManus," *Management Consulting News* (January 6, 2004). Available from www.managementconsultingnews.com/newsletter_jan_04.htm#4.

   In the same interview, Banis noted that "Clients are going to expect consultants to listen better and develop a deeper understanding of the client's business. They are also going to expect new ideas. Clients are saying don't come at us with the same approach anymore. And there is going to be a major backlash against technology being the answer to everything. Dissatisfaction is already evident about big technology projects not living up to their billing."
5. From the *New York Times* (June 30, 2002), Business Section, p. 4.
6. From the interview, "Meet the MasterMinds: A Conversation with Tom Peters," *Management Consulting News* (December 2, 2003). Available from www.managementconsultingnews.com/newsletter_dec_03.htm#2.

   Peters went on to observe that "If IBM is now IBM Global Services and UPS is UPS Logistics instead of a bunch of guys with trucks, all of the value added is going to come from this consulting-like intellectual capital.

"And for the consultants, maybe we are going to find ourselves competing with former departments. The proof of the pudding is IBM buying PwC Consulting. IBM turns itself into a consultancy and what does it do? It buys the consultants. Why wouldn't UPS do the same thing?"

7. References from *The Anatomy of Buzz: How to Create Word-of-Mouth Marketing* (New York: Doubleday, 2000), pp. 13–14.

8. From the *Financial Times* (December 16, 2003).

9. Thomas Watson Sr. is well known for his alleged 1943 statement: "I think there is a world market for maybe five computers," but there is no evidence he ever said that. One author tried to locate the quote and was unable to find any speeches or documents of Watson's that contain this quotation.

■ CHAPTER 2: WHAT IS GUERRILLA MARKETING FOR CONSULTANTS?

1. From the book, *Relationship Marketing: Successful Strategies for the Age of the Customer* (Reading, MA: Perseus, 1993), p. 1.

2. From the book, *Positioning: The Battle for Your Mind* (New York: McGraw-Hill, 2001), p. 5.

3. From the Web page www.quotationspage.com/quotes/howard_aiken.

4. From the book, *What Clients Love: A Field Guide to Growing Your Business* (New York: Warner Books, 2003), p. 5.

■ CHAPTER 3: THIRTEEN GUERRILLA MARKETING SECRETS

1. From the interview, "Meet the MasterMinds: Seven Questions for Seth Godin," *Management Consulting News* (June 3, 2003). Available from http://www.managementconsultingnews.com/newsletter_june_03.htm.

2. From his article, "How to Buy/Sell Professional Services," *Harvard Business Review* (March/April 1966), p. 130.

3. Statistic on how clients choose service providers is from "Marketing Returns: Leadership, Innovation and Results," by the Information Technology Sales and Marketing Association (ITSMA), p. 9. Information was presented in opening session by Dave Munn, CEO of ITSMA, at a conference held in Oakland, California, October 20–22, 2003.

4. Information on how clients find solution providers is from the same ITSMA study as above, p. 22. Information presented in a breakout session by Julie Schwartz, ITSMA analyst, at the same conference.

5. From the book, *Intellectual Capital: The New Wealth of Organizations* (New York: Doubleday, 1998), p. xix.

6. Statistic on client retention presented at "The Annual Conference of the Institute of Management Consultants" held in Houston, Texas, May 2002. Information presented by Wayne Cooper, Kennedy Information, Inc.

■ CHAPTER 4: ANATOMY OF A MARKETING PLAN

1. From Philip Kotler, Thomas Hayes, and Paul N. Bloom, *Marketing Professional Services: Forward-Thinking Strategies for Boosting Your Business, Your Image, and Your Profits* (Upper Saddle River, NJ: Prentice Hall, 2002), p. 6.
2. Advertising copy is from David Ogilvy, *Ogilvy on Advertising* (New York: Vintage, 1985), p. 118.
3. From the book, *Marketing Imagination: New, Expanded Edition* (New York: Free Press, 1986), p. 72.
4. See note 1, p. 155 for study on pricing strategies.
5. See note 1, p. 155 for study on differentiation strategies.
6. Study on reducing client perception of risk is from Doug Hall, *Meaningful Marketing* (Cincinnati, OH: Brain Brew Books, 2003), p. 180.

■ CHAPTER 5: THE GUERRILLA'S MARKETING ROAD MAP

1. From the interview, "Meet the MasterMinds: Al Ries on the Immutable Laws of Branding a Consultancy," *Management Consulting News* (May 6, 2003). Available from http://www.managementconsultingnews.com /newsletter_may_03.htm.

   In the interview, Ries also says, "Whatever you are doing today, your business would be stronger and more profitable in the long run if you concentrated your activities on one industry, one region, one function, or one problem."
2. For additional information on Richard Dawkins and the discovery of memes, see www.world-of-dawkins.com/Dawkins/Biography/bio.shtml.

■ CHAPTER 6: BEYOND WEB SITES: CREATE A CLIENT-CENTERED WEB PRESENCE

1. Statistics on how clients find service providers on the Web is from "Customer Research," by Information Technology Sales and Marketing Association (ITSMA; August 2003).

2. Statistics on Internet users' level of trust in online content is from "A Matter of Trust: What Users Want from Web Sites," by Princeton Survey Research Associates (January 2002), p. 1.

■ CHAPTER 7: BOOST YOUR WEB PRESENCE WITH A ZINE

1. Statistics indicating that businesspeople prefer e-mail over the telephone as a business communication tool is from David Yockelson and Matt Cain, *The Survey Says: E-Mail Beats the Phone: Content & Collaboration Strategies, Web & Collaboration Strategies* (June 12, 2003). Available from www.metagroup.com/us/displayArticle.do?oid=40667.
2. Statistic indicating that e-mail will become a primary source of information is from *50 Tips to Maximize Email Marketing Success* (2002). Available from www.gotmarketing.com.
3. Statistics on e-mail are from Quris, Inc., *How Email Practices Can Win or Lose Long-Term Business* (October 2003), p. 6.
4. Statistic on e-mail marketers is from Quris, Inc., *How Companies Can Enter and Remain in the Customer Email Inner Circle* (September 2003), p. 5.

■ CHAPTER 8: TALKING HEADS: THE COST OF FREE PUBLICITY

1. Jay Conrad Levinson, Rick Frishman, and Jill Lublin, *Guerrilla Publicity: Hundreds of Sure-Fire Tactics to Get Maximum Sales for Minimum Dollars* (Holbrook, MA: Adams Media Corporation, 2002).

■ CHAPTER 9: WHEN IT PAYS TO ADVERTISE

1. From "NO B.S. MARKETING E-LETTER" (July 2002). Available from www.dankennedy.com.

■ CHAPTER 10: WRITE THIS WAY

1. A song lyric from "Words Get in the Way," *Gloria Estefan's Greatest Hits* (Sony label: Original release date, November 3, 1992).
2. William Zinsser, *On Writing Well: The Classic Guide to Writing Nonfiction* (New York: HarperCollins, 2001), 25th ed., p. 7.
3. From Leonard Roy Frank, ed., *Random House Webster's Quotationary* (New York: Random House, 1999), p. 955.

■ CHAPTER 11: FIVE STEPS TO A WINNING SPEECH

1. Opening quote was advice on speechmaking given to Roosevelt's son. From Leonard Roy Frank, ed., *Random House Webster's Quotationary* (New York: Random House, 1999), p. 686.
2. From the book, *Working the Room: How to Move People to Action through Audience-Centered Speaking* (Boston: Harvard Business School Press, 2003), p. 2.
3. The Decker Grid System was created by communications expert, Bert Decker.

    In an interview, "This Month's Featured MasterMind: Bert Decker on Effective Communication," *Management Consulting News* (August 6, 2002), Decker said, "The Grid System is a quick, easy way to create a high-impact presentation, or any communication. Once you have a subject for the communication, you identify the four cornerstones of the communication—the audience, your point of view on the subject, the action you want your audience to take and the benefits to your audience if they take that action." Available from http://www.managementconsultingnews .com/newsletter_aug_02_final.htm.

    Building on that foundation, the Grid System explains, step-by-step, how to compose your communication. Find out more about Decker's method at www.boldassurance.com.
4. From the interview, "Meet the MasterMinds: Nick Morgan on the Secrets of Powerful Speaking," *Management Consulting News* (September 3, 2002). Available from www.managementconsultingnews.com/newsletter_sept _03.htm.

    In the interview, Morgan went on to say that most speakers ". . . don't rehearse at all. CEO's and senior level people will rehearse a big speech once the night before, or read over the notes and think they can wing it. How many times do you see people creating PowerPoint slides on the plane or train on the way to a meeting?"
5. Statistic on speakers is from "Speaker Usage Monitor: Wave 1," a report by the National Speakers Association (June 2003), p. 15.
6. From Grady Jim Robinson, *Did I Ever Tell You About the Time: How to Develop and Deliver a Speech Using Stories That Get Your Message Across* (New York: McGraw-Hill, 2000), p. ix.
7. See note 6, p. 206, for Grady Jim Robinson quote on storytelling.
8. See note 6, p. 211, for Grady Jim Robinson quote on speakers using self-revelation.
9. Statistics on speakers' years of experience are from the "National Speakers Association 2003 Member Survey" (April 2003). Available from http://www.nsaspeaker.org/2003_survey_results.shtml.
10. See note 5, p. 9, for statistic on hiring of industry experts as speakers.
11. Research result on the power of a demonstration is from Doug Hall, *Meaningful Marketing* (Cincinnati, OH: Brain Brew Books, 2003), p. 64.

■ CHAPTER 12: BOOK PUBLISHING: THE GUERRILLA'S 800-POUND GORILLA

1. From the interview, "Meet the MasterMinds: A Conversation with Tom Peters," *Management Consulting News* (December 2, 2003). Available from http://www.managementconsultingnews.com /newsletter_dec_03.htm#2.
2. Michael Hammer and James Champy, *Reengineering the Corporation: A Manifesto for Business Revolution* (New York: HarperCollins, 1993), p. 32.
3. Jeff Herman, *Jeff Herman's Guide to Book Publishers, Editors and Literary Agents 2004: Who They Are! What They Want! and How to Win Them Over!* (2003), 14th ed.
4. Michael Larsen, *Literary Agents: What They Do, How They Do It, and How to Find and Work with the Right One for You* (New York: Wiley, 1996).
5. Seth Godin, *Purple Cow: Transform Your Business by Being Remarkable* (New York: Portfolio Penguin Group, 2003).

■ CHAPTER 13: SURVEY SAID! MAKE SURVEYS AND PROPRIETARY RESEARCH WORK

1. The University of Michigan conducts a survey of consumer confidence each month. The report is widely accepted as representing consumers' outlook on the state of the U.S. economy. For more information, see the Web site, www.sca.isr.umich.edu.

■ CHAPTER 14: THE POWER OF GIVING BACK

1. From "Dejection: An Ode," Leonard Roy Frank, ed., *Random House Webster's Quotationary* (New York: Random House, 1999), p. 311.

■ CHAPTER 15: ALL PROJECTS ARE NOT CREATED EQUAL

1. From *Making Rain: The Secrets of Building Lifelong Client Loyalty* (Hoboken, NJ: Wiley, 2003), p. xiii.

    In an interview in *Management Consulting News*, "This Month's Featured MasterMind: Andrew Sobel on the Secrets of Making Rain," February 4, 2003, Sobel clarified that "in terms of adding value, you have to go beyond the core value of the contract, beyond what the client contracts with you, the consultant, to deliver. Client loyalty increases when you add value in ways that clients don't expect, when you make them aware of problems and issues that perhaps they didn't even know they had. So maybe you are hired to do a cost reduction project, but you end up making some insightful recommendations about organizational structure. You see the big picture and keep your eyes and ears open. You bring clients surprise value and they say, wow, that was really helpful." Available from http://managementconsultingnews.com/newsletter_feb_03.htm#2.

2. Research on client satisfaction is from Ross McManus, *Selling and Satisfying the Fortune 1000 in a Post-Enron World, a Survey of Client Satisfaction* (November 2003). Available from http://ross-mcmanus.com/release111803.html.

According to senior executives, not understanding their business was the number one reason for terminating professional service providers and consultants. According to the study, one in nine top executives said relationships with their professional services providers and consultants were "significantly deteriorating," possibly leading to termination within the next twelve months.

■ CHAPTER 16: "SEND ME A PROPOSAL": CREATE PROPOSALS THAT WIN

1. From the interview, "Meet the MasterMinds: Jeff Thull on Mastering the Complex Sale," *Management Consulting News* (October 7, 2003). Available from http://www.managementconsultingnews.com/newsletter_oct_03.htm.

■ CHAPTER 17: THE PRICE IS RIGHT

1. From Leonard Roy Frank, ed., *The Random House Webster's Wit & Humor Quotationary* (New York: Random House, 2000), p. 9.

■ CHAPTER 18: THE GUERRILLA'S COMPETITIVE EDGE

1. From the interview, "Sales Strategies of a Rainmaker with Jeffrey Fox," *Management Consulting News* (May 6, 2003). Available from http://www.managementconsultingnews.com/newsletter_may_03.htm.

In the interview, Fox goes on to describe how rainmakers sell: "They don't depend on their experience, twenty years in the business or a close relationship with the client. They pre-call plan, and they do it in writing."

2. From the interview, "Meet the MasterMinds: Fiona Czerniawska on Trends in Consulting," *Management Consulting News* (February 3, 2004). Available from http://www.managementconsultingnews.com/newsletter_feb_04.htm.

Czerniawska goes on to say that "clients may feel that no one firm can handle either the scale or complexity of their large projects, and they may want a partnership with five or six firms. Or clients may cut projects down into small pieces that they give to specialist firms."

■ CHAPTER 19: AFTER THE SALE: SELLING WHILE SERVING

1. From the book, *Selling the Invisible: A Field Guide to Modern Marketing* (New York: Warner Books, 1997), p. 219.

   In an interview in *Management Consulting News*, "Meet the Master-Minds: Harry Beckwith on What Clients Love" (February 4, 2003), Beckwith stressed that, "Consultants must first recognize that they are selling a relationship rather than competence and advice. You must win the person to win the business, and you must keep winning the person to keep the business." Available from http://www.managementconsultingnews.com /newsletter_feb_03.htm.
2. From the book, *The Marketing Imagination* (New York: Free Press, 1986), p. 105.
3. From the article, "How to Buy/Sell Professional Services," *Harvard Business Review* (March/April 1966), p. 130.
4. Sun Tzu, James Clavell, trans., *The Art of War* (New York: Dell, 1983), p. 56.

■ CHAPTER 20: PUT YOUR PLAN INTO ACTION

1. Song lyric from "Field of Opportunity," *Comes a Time* by Neil Young, Crazy Horse (Warner Brothers label: Original release date, October 1978).

Resource Guide

BOOKS

Client Relationship Building

Capon, Noel. *Key Account Management and Planning: The Comprehensive Handbook for Managing Your Company's Most Important Strategic Asset.* New York: Free Press, 2001.

Carucci, Ron A., William A. Pasmore, and the Colleagues of Mercer Delta. *Relationships That Enable Enterprise Change: Leveraging the Client-Consultant Connection.* San Francisco: Jossey-Bass/Pfeiffer, 2002.

Carucci, Ron A., and Toby J. Tetenbaum. *The Value-Creating Consultant: How to Build and Sustain Lasting Client Relationships.* New York: AMACOM, 2000.

Dawson, Ross. *Developing Knowledge-Based Client Relationships: The Future of Professional Services.* Boston: Butterworth-Heinemann, 2000.

McKenna, Regis. *Relationship Marketing: Successful Strategies for the Age of the Customer.* Reading, MA: Perseus Books, 1991.

Sheth, Jagdish, and Andrew Sobel. *Clients for Life: How Great Professionals Develop Breakthrough Relationships.* New York: Simon & Schuster, 2000.

Sobel, Andrew. *Making Rain: The Secrets of Building Lifelong Client Loyalty.* Hoboken, NJ: John Wiley & Sons, 2003.

Stevenson, Tom, and Sam Barcus. *The Relationship Advantage: Become a Trusted Advisor and Create Clients for Life.* Chicago: Dearborn Trade Publishing, 2003.

The Consulting Process

Ayan, Jordan. *Aha! 10 Ways to Free Your Creative Spirit and Find Your Great Ideas.* New York: Crown Publishers, 1997.

Barcus, Sam W., III, and Joseph W. Wilkinson. *Handbook of Management Consulting Services.* New York: McGraw-Hill, 1995.

Block, Peter. *Flawless Consulting: A Guide to Getting Your Expertise Used.* San Francisco: Jossey-Bass/Pfeiffer, Second Edition, 2000.

Bridges, William. *Managing Transitions: Making the Most of Change*. Cambridge, MA: Perseus Publishing, 2003.

Buzan, Tony, and Barry Buzan. *The Mind Map Book: How to Use Radiant Thinking to Maximize Your Brain's Untapped Potential*. New York: Penguin Books, 1993.

Cope, Nick. *The Seven Cs of Consulting: Your complete blueprint for any consultancy assignment*. London: Financial Times Prentice Hall, 2000.

Czerniawska, Fiona. *Value-Based Consulting*. London: Palgrave, 2002.

Fisher, Roger, William Ury, and Bruce Patton. *Getting to Yes: Negotiating Agreement without Giving In*. New York: Penguin Group, 1991.

Gelb, Michael J. *Discover Your Genius: How to Think Like History's Ten Most Revolutionary Minds*. New York: Harper-Collins Publishers, 2002.

Hall, Doug. *Jump Start Your Business Brain: Win More, Lose Less and Make More Money with Your New Products, Services, Sales and Advertising*. Cincinnati, OH: Brain-Brew Books, 2001.

———. *Jump Start Your Brain*. New York: Warner Books, 1995.

Hoopes, James. *False Prophets: The Gurus Who Created Modern Marketing and Why Their Ideas Are Bad for Business Today*. Cambridge, MA: Perseus Publishing, 2003.

Kotter, John P., and Dan S. Cohen. *The Heart of Change: Real Life Stories of How People Change Their Organizations*. Boston: Harvard Business School Press, 2002.

Leonard, George. *Mastery: The Keys to Success and Long-Term Fulfillment*. New York: Plume/Penguin Group, 1992.

Maister, David H. *True Professionalism: The Courage to Care about Your People, Your Clients, and Your Career*. New York: Free Press, 1997.

———. *Managing the Professional Service Firm*. New York: Free Press, 1993.

Maister, David H., Charles H. Green, and Robert M. Galford. *The Trusted Advisor*. New York: Free Press, 2000.

McKenna, Patrick, and David H. Maister. *First among Equals: How to Manage a Group of Professionals*. New York: Free Press, 2002.

Michalko, Michael. *Cracking Creativity: The Secrets of Creative Genius*. Berkeley, CA: Ten Speed Press, 1998.

Nadler, Gerald, and Shozo Hibino. *Breakthrough Thinking: The Seven Principles of Creative Problem Solving*. Roseville, CA: Prima Publishing, Second Edition, 1998.

Peters, Tom. *Re-imagine! Business Excellence in a Disruptive Age*. London: Dorling Kindersley Limited, 2003.

Phillips, Jack J. *The Consultant's Scorecard: Tracking Results and Bottom-Line Impact of Consulting Projects*. New York: McGraw-Hill, 2000.

Schaffer, Robert H. *High-Impact Consulting: How Clients and Consultants Can Work Together to Achieve Extraordinary Results*. San Francisco: Jossey-Bass, 2002.

Stone, Douglas, Bruce Patton, and Sheila Heen. *Difficult Conversations: How to Discuss What Matters Most*. New York: Penguin Group, 1999.

Von Oech, Roger. *Expect the Unexpected (Or You Won't Find It): A Creativity Tool Based on the Ancient Wisdom of Heraclitus*. New York: Free Press, 2001.

Weinberg, Gerald M. *The Secrets of Consulting: A Guide to Giving & Getting Advice Successfully.* New York: Dorset House Publishing, 1985.
———. *More Secrets of Consulting: The Consultant's Tool Kit.* New York: Dorset House Publishing, 2002.
Weiss, Alan. *Great Consulting Challenges and How to Surmount Them: Powerful Techniques for the Successful Practitioner.* San Francisco: Jossey-Bass/Pfeiffer, 2003.
———. *Process Consulting: How to Launch, Implement, and Conclude Successful Consulting Projects.* San Francisco: Jossey-Bass/Pfeiffer, 2002.
———. *The Ultimate Consultant: Powerful Techniques for the Successful Practitioner.* San Francisco: Jossey-Bass/Pfeiffer, 2001.

Marketing Professional Services

Beckwith, Harry. *What Clients Love: A Field Guide to Growing Your Business.* New York: Warner Books, 2003.
———. *The Invisible Touch: The Four Keys to Modern Marketing.* New York: Warner Books, 2000.
———. *Selling the Invisible: A Field Guide to Modern Marketing.* New York: Warner Books, 1997.
Connor, Dick, and Jeff Davidson. *Marketing Your Consulting and Professional Services.* New York: John Wiley & Sons, 1997.
Dembitz, Alex, and James Essinger. *Breakthrough Consulting: So You Want to be a Consultant? Turn Your Expertise into a Successful Consulting Business.* London: Pearson Education Limited, 2000.
Forsyth, Patrick. *Marketing Professional Services: Practical Approaches to Practice Development.* London: Kogan Page Limited, Second Edition, 1999.
Fox, Jeffrey J. *How to Become a Marketing Superstar: Unexpected Rules That Ring the Cash Register.* New York: Hyperion, 2003.
———. *How to Become a Rainmaker: The People Who Get and Keep Customers.* New York: Hyperion, 2000.
Godin, Seth. *Purple Cow: Transform Your Business by Being Remarkable.* New York: Portfolio Penguin Group, 2003.
———. *Free Prize Inside: The Next Big Marketing Idea.* New York: Portfolio Penguin Group, 2004.
Hall, Doug. *Meaningful Marketing.* Cincinnati, OH: Brain-Brew Books, 2003.
Harding, Ford. *Rain Making: The Professional's Guide to Attracting New Clients.* Holbrook, MA: Adams Media Corporation, 1994.
———. *Cross-Selling Success: A Rainmaker's Guide to Professional Account Development.* Holbrook, MA: Adams Media Corporation, 2002.
———. *Creating Rainmakers: The Manager's Guide to Training Professionals to Attract New Clients.* Holbrook, MA: Adams Media Corporation, 1998.
Kotler, Philip, Thomas Hayes, and Paul N. Bloom. *Marketing Professional Services: Forward-Thinking Strategies for Boosting Your Business, Your Image, and Your Profits.* Upper Saddle River, NJ: Prentice Hall, 2002.
Kunde, Jesper. *Unique Now . . . or Never: The Brand Is the Company Driver in the New Value Economy.* London: Financial Times Prentice Hall, 2002.

Levine, Michael. *Guerrilla P.R. WIRED: Waging a Successful Publicity Campaign Online, Offline, and Everywhere in Between.* Chicago: McGraw-Hill, 2002.

Levinson, Jay Conrad. *The Way of the Guerrilla: Achieving Success and Balance as an Entrepreneur in the 21st Century.* Boston: Houghton Mifflin Company, 1997.

——. *Mastering Guerrilla Marketing: 100 Profit-Producing Insights You Can Take to the Bank.* Boston: Houghton Mifflin Company, 1999.

——. *Guerrilla Marketing: Secrets for Making Big Profits from Your Small Business.* Boston: Houghton Mifflin Company, 1998.

Levinson, Jay Conrad, Rick Frishman, and Jill Lublin. *Guerrilla Publicity: Hundreds of sure-fire tactics to get maximum sales for minimum dollars.* Holbrook, MA: Adams Media Corporation, 2002.

Levitt, Theodore. *The Marketing Imagination,* New, Expanded Edition. New York: Free Press, 1986.

Lowe, Suzanne C. *Marketplace Masters: How Professional Service Firms Compete to Win.* Westport, CT: Praeger Publishers, 2004.

Mills, Harry. *The Rainmaker's Toolkit: Power Strategies for Finding, Keeping, and Growing Profitable Clients.* New York: AMACOM, 2004.

Payne, Adrian. *The Essence of Service Marketing.* Essex, England: Prentice Hall, 1993.

Ries, Al, and Jack Trout. *Positioning: The Battle for Your Mind.* New York: McGraw-Hill, 2001.

Rosen, Emanuel. *The Anatomy of Buzz: How to Create Word-of-Mouth Marketing.* New York: Doubleday, 2000.

Shenson, Howard A., and Jerry R. Wilson. *138 Quick Ideas to Get More Clients.* New York: John Wiley & Sons, 1993.

Stevens, Mark. *Your Marketing Sucks.* New York: Crown Business, 2003.

Treacy, Michael. *Double-Digit Growth: How Great Companies Achieve It—No Matter What.* New York: Portfolio/Penguin Group, 2003

Trout, Jack, and Steve Rivkin. *Differentiate or Die: Survival in Our Era of Killer Competition.* New York: John Wiley & Sons, 2000.

Proposals and Pricing

Hart, Christopher W. L. *Extraordinary Guarantees: A New Way to Build Quality Throughout Your Company & Ensure Satisfaction for Your Customers.* New York: AMACOM, 1993.

Holtz, Herman. *The Consultant's Guide to Proposal Writing: How to Satisfy Your Clients and Double Your Income.* New York: John Wiley & Sons, 1998.

Johnson-Sheehan, Richard. *Writing Proposals: A Rhetoric for Managing Change.* New York: Longman Publishers, 2002.

Sant, Tom. *Persuasive Business Proposals: Writing to Win More Customers, Clients and Contracts.* New York: AMACOM, 2004.

Public Speaking

Morgan, Nick. *Working the Room: How to Move People to Action through Audience-Centered Speaking.* Boston: Harvard Business School Press, 2003.

Weissman, Jerry. *Presenting to Win: The Art of Telling Your Story.* Upper Saddle River, NJ: Financial Times Prentice Hall, 2003.

Publishing

Booth, Wayne C., Gregory G. Colomb, and Joseph M. Williams. *The Craft of Research.* Chicago: University of Chicago Press, 2003.

Flesch, Rudolf, and A. H. Lass. *The Classic Guide to Better Writing: Step-by-Step Techniques and Exercises to Write Simply, Clearly, and Correctly.* New York: HarperResource, 1996.

Herman, Jeff, and Deborah Levine Herman. *Write the Perfect Book Proposal: 10 That Sold and Why.* New York: John Wiley & Sons, 2001.

——. *Jeff Herman's Guide to Book Publishers, Editors and Literary Agents 2004: Who They Are! What They Want! and How to Win Them Over!,* 14th Edition, Self-published, 2003.

Kremer, John. *1001 Ways to Market Your Book.* Fairfield, IA: Open Horizons, 1998.

Larsen, Michael. *How to Write a Book Proposal.* Cincinnati, OH: Writer's Digest Books, 1997.

——. *Literary Agents: What They Do, How They Do It, and How to Find and Work with the Right One for You.* New York: John Wiley & Sons, 1996.

Levinson, Jay Conrad, Rick Frishman, and Michael Larsen. *Guerrilla Marketing for Writers.* Cincinnati, OH: Writer's Digest Books, 2001.

Poynter, Dan. *The Self-Publishing Manual: How to Write, Print and Sell Your Own Book.* Santa Barbara, CA: Para Publishing, 1979.

Rose, M. J., and Angela Adair-Hoy. *How to Publish and Promote Online.* New York: St. Martin's Griffin, 2001.

Selling Services

Burg, Bob. *Endless Referrals: Network Your Everyday Contacts into Sales.* New York: McGraw-Hill, 1999.

Carlson, Richard K. *Personal Selling Strategies for Consultants and Professionals: The Perfect Sales Equation.* New York: John Wiley & Sons, 1993.

Page, Rick. *Hope Is Not a Strategy: The 6 Keys to Winning the Complex Sale.* New York: Nautilus Press, 2002.

Silverman, George. *The Secrets of Word-of-Mouth Marketing: How to Trigger Exponential Sales Through Runaway Word of Mouth.* New York: AMACOM, 2001.

Thull, Jeff. *Mastering the Complex Sale: How to Compete and Win When the Stakes Are High!* Hoboken, NJ: John Wiley & Sons, 2003.

Surveys

Fink, Arlene, and Jacqueline Kosecoff. *How to Conduct Surveys: A Step-by-Step Guide.* Thousand Oaks, CA: Sage Publications, 1998.

Nardi, Peter. *Doing Survey Research: A Guide to Quantitative Methods.* Boston: Pearson Allyn & Bacon, 2003.

Salant, Priscilla, and Don A. Dillman. *How to Conduct Your Own Survey.* New York: John Wiley & Sons, 1994.

Web Site Design and Promotion

Flanders, Vincent, and Michael Willis. *Web Pages That Suck: Learn Good Design by Looking at Bad Design.* San Francisco: Sybex, 1998.

——. *Son of Web Pages That Suck: Learn Good Design by Looking at Bad Design.* San Francisco: Sybex, 2002.

Krug, Steve. *Don't Make Me Think! A Common Sense Approach to Web Usability.* Indianapolis, IN: New Riders Publishing, 2000.

McGovern, Gerry, and Rob Norton. *Content Critical: Gaining Competitive Advantage Through High-Quality Web Content.* London: Financial Times Prentice Hall, 2002.

Williams, Robin. *The Non-Designer's Design Book: Design and Typographic Principles for the Visual Novice.* Berkeley, CA: Peachpit Press, 1994.

Williams, Robin, and John Tollett. *The Non-Designer's Web Book: An Easy Guide to Creating, Designing, and Posting Your Own Web Site.* Berkeley, CA: Peachpit Press, 2000.

Writing

Bryson, Bill. *Bryson's Dictionary of Troublesome Words.* New York: Broadway Books, 2002.

King, Stephen. *On Writing: A Memoir of the Craft.* New York: Pocket Books, 2000.

Lamott, Anne. *Bird by Bird: Some Instructions on Writing and Life.* New York: Anchor Books, 1994.

Levy, Mark. *Accidental Genius: Revolutionize Your Thinking Through Private Writing.* San Francisco: Berrett-Koehler Publishers, 2000.

Lyon, Elizabeth. *A Writer's Guide to Nonfiction.* New York: Berkeley Publishing Group, 2003.

O'Conner, Patricia T. *Woe Is I: The Grammarphobe's Guide to Better English in Plain English.* New York: Riverhead Books, 1996.

——. *Words Fail Me: What Everyone Who Writes Should Know about Writing.* New York: Harcourt Brace & Company, 1999.

Poynter, Dan. *Writing Nonfiction: Turning Thoughts into Books.* Santa Barbara, CA: Para Publishing, 2000.

——. *Successful Nonfiction.* Santa Barbara, CA: Para Publishing, 2000.

Shertzer, Margaret. *The Elements of Grammar.* New York: Macmillan Publishing Company, 1986.

Strunk, William, Jr., and E. B. White. *The Elements of Style.* New York: Longman Publishers, 2000.

Williams, Joseph M. *Style: Toward Clarity and Grace.* Chicago: University of Chicago Press, 1990.

Zinsser, William. *On Writing Well: The Classic Guide to Writing Nonfiction.* New York: HarperCollins Publishers, 25th edition, 2001.

■ SELECTED NEWSLETTERS AND ONLINE RESOURCES

Client Loyalty. Andrew Sobel, a leading authority on client relationships, publishes a monthly newsletter on the skills and strategies needed to build enduring client loyalty: www.andrewsobel.com.

Guerrilla Marketing. Jay Conrad Levinson, founder of guerrilla marketing, provides tips, articles, and a free zine for subscribers: www.gmarketing .com. Also visit www.guerrillamarketingassociation.com, a membership-based support service for enhancing small business profits.

Inside Consulting. Tom Rodenhauser, founder and president of Consulting Information Services, publishes *Inside Consulting,* a weekly e-mail column that comments on events affecting the consulting industry: www.consultinginfo.com.

Michael Katz. Michael J. Katz is founder and Chief Penguin of Blue Penguin Development, a consulting firm that specializes in the creation and management of effective e-newsletters. He publishes *Michael Katz's E-Newsletter on E-Newsletters,* bi-weekly: www.bluepenguindevelopment .com.

David Maister. David Maister is one of the world's leading authorities on the management of professional service firms: www.davidmaister.com.

Management Consulting News. *MCNews,* a free monthly newsletter, features the best of the best from leading thinkers, writers, management consultants, and many others, all focused on ideas and tools you can use: www.managementconsultingnews.com.

WordBiz. The *Word Biz Report,* published twice monthly by Debbie Weil, was the first e-newsletter about online copywriting and the business of words: www.wordbiz.com.

MarketingProfs.com. This online publishing company specializes in providing strategic and tactical marketing know-how to Internet and offline marketing professionals. The *MarketingProfs* newsletter is published twice monthly: www.marketingprofs.com.

Marketing Sherpa. Over 140,000 marketing, advertising, and PR pros get free practical know-how and case studies every week: www.marketingsherpa .com.

SpeakerNet News. *SpeakerNet News* is a weekly newsletter and discussion list that is sent to over 3,500 professional speakers, consultants, trainers, and authors. You'll find tips on sales and marketing, travel, technology, PR, conducting better presentations, and other key topics: www.speakernetnews.com.

■ INDUSTRY ASSOCIATIONS

Association of Executive Search Consultants. AESC is a worldwide organization for executive search consulting firms and helps organizations recruit the best executive talent in the market: www.aesc.org.

Association of Management Consulting Firms. This association (formerly ACME) fosters understanding of the profession's scope and purposes, provides a forum for confronting common challenges, expands the knowledge base of member firms and their clients, and champions a code of professional conduct: www.amcf.org.

The Authors Guild. For more than 80 years, the Guild has been the authoritative voice of American writers: www.authorsguild.org.

Institute for Public Relations. IPR serves as a catalyst for creating and disseminating research that is usable by public relations senior management, agencies, clients, and everyday practitioners: www.instituteforpr.com.

Institute of Management Consultants USA. The IMC USA mission is to provide certification, education, and professional resources to management consultants: www.imcusa.org.

National Speakers Association. The leading organization for those who speak professionally, NSA provides resources and education to advance the skills, integrity, and value of its members and the speaking profession: www.nsaspeaker.org.

About the Authors

Jay Conrad Levinson is the author of the best-selling marketing series in history, *Guerrilla Marketing*, plus 28 other business books. His books appear in 37 languages and are required reading for MBA programs worldwide. More than a million copies of his *Guerrilla* books are in print. A former vice president and creative director at J. Walter Thompson and Leo Burnett Advertising, he is chairman of Guerrilla Marketing International, a consulting firm serving large and small businesses worldwide. He lives in Marin County, California. You can reach him at: www.gmarketing.com.

Michael W. McLaughlin is a principal with Deloitte Consulting. In his 20 years with Deloitte, Michael has sold hundreds of consulting projects. He was the managing director for Deloitte Consulting Chicago, where he had market responsibility for a practice of 800 consultants. He has been a frequent speaker; has been interviewed on radio, television, and for national publications; and he has written articles for newspapers, magazines, and trade journals. Michael publishes *Management Consulting News (MCNews)*, a free monthly zine for consulting professionals. He holds an MBA in corporate finance. Visit www.ManagementConsultingNews.com and www .GuerrillaConsulting.com.

Index